William Keeble

OF
BLOUNT COUNTY
TENNESSEE

Albert W. Dockter, Jr.

HERITAGE BOOKS
2007

HERITAGE BOOKS

AN IMPRINT OF HERITAGE BOOKS, INC.

Books, CDs, and more—Worldwide

For our listing of thousands of titles see our website
at
www.HeritageBooks.com

Published 2007 by
HERITAGE BOOKS, INC.
Publishing Division
65 East Main Street
Westminster, Maryland 21157-5026

International Standard Book Number: 978-0-7884-4176-9

BOOK II

WILLIAM KEEBLE OF BLOUNT COUNTY, TENNESSEE

By: ALBERT W. DOCKTER, JR.

Descendants of William Keeble

Generation No. 1

1. WILLIAM[1] KEEBLE was born May 21, 1755, and died December 30, 1834 in Blount County, Tennessee. He met (1) SARAH UNKNOWN Bef. 1799 in Unknown. He married (2) MARY KEEBLE December 17, 1799 in Fauquier County, Virginia, daughter of RICHARD KEEBLE and HANNAH STAMPS. She was born February 29, 1784, and died June 15, 1855 in Blount County, Tennessee.

More About WILLIAM KEEBLE:
Burial: Keeble Cemetery, Blount County, Tennessee

More About SARAH UNKNOWN:
1st Marriage: Unknown, Four chiodren by unknown wife

More About MARY KEEBLE:
Burial: June 1855, Keeble Cemetery, Blount County, Tennessee

Marriage Notes for WILLIAM KEEBLE and MARY KEEBLE:
Mary had written permission from her father, Richard Keeble for her marriage to William.
They were married by The Rev. John Pickett, a Minister of the Gospel in the Baptist Faith.
In attendance at the wedding was a friend of Marys'-Eleanor Harris (nee Smith) daughter of Andrew Smith who had been a soldier in the Revolutionary Army with William.

Children of WILLIAM KEEBLE and SARAH UNKNOWN are:
  i. SALLY[2] KEEBLE, b. Abt. 1780.
  ii. WILLIAM KEEBLE, b. Abt. 1782.
  iii. NANCY KEEBLE, b. Abt. 1784.
  iv. JOHN KEEBLE, b. Abt. 1786.

Children of WILLIAM KEEBLE and MARY KEEBLE are:
  2.   v.   THOMAS[2] KEEBLE, b. July 31, 1800, Blount County, Tennessee; d. August 25, 1873, Blount County, Tennessee.
        vi.   SAMUEL KEEBLE, b. March 02, 1802; d. September 1869.
  3.   vii. HANNAH STAMPS KEEBLE, b. March 12, 1805; d. January 06, 1892.
  4.   viii. MANLY KEEBLE, b. July 03, 1807, Blount County, Tennessee; d. January 01, 1882, Blount County, Tennessee.
  5.   ix.   REBECCA KEEBLE, b. January 09, 1810; d. October 14, 1881.
  6.   x.   RICHARD PORTER KEEBLE, b. May 19, 1811; d. April 23, 1894.
        xi.   HARRIOTT KEEBLE, b. February 28, 1813.
  7.   xii. WALTER HARRISON KEEBLE, b. November 14, 1815; d. April 25, 1897.
  8.   xiii. MARY BANKS KEEBLE, b. December 14, 1817.
  9.   xiv. CHARLOTTE WHITE KEEBLE, b. May 21, 1819; d. October 09, 1847.
        xv.   JANE HENRY KEEBLE, b. January 12, 1821.

Generation No. 2

2. THOMAS[2] KEEBLE *(WILLIAM[1])* was born July 31, 1800 in Blount County, Tennessee, and died August 25, 1873 in Blount County, Tennessee. He married (1) ELIZABETH SMITH October 14, 1823 in Blount County, Tennessee, daughter of JOSEPH SMITH and MARGARET MCCUTCHIN. She was born August 20, 1805, and died Unknown in Blount County, Tennessee. He married (2) NANCY ANN CANNON February 16, 1847 in Blount County, Tennessee, daughter of JOHN CANNON and NANCY. She was born 1821, and died 1896 in Blount County, Tennessee.

More About THOMAS KEEBLE:

1st Marriage: October 14, 1823, Blount County, Tennessee
Burial: Keeble Cemetery, Blount County, Tennessee

More About ELIZABETH SMITH:
Burial: Keeble Cemetery, Blount County, Tennessee

More About NANCY ANN CANNON:
Burial: Liberty Baptist Cemetery, Blount County, Tennessee

Children of THOMAS KEEBLE and ELIZABETH SMITH are:
10. i.   JAMES H.[3] KEEBLE, b. December 04, 1824, Blount County, Tennessee; d. 1886.
11. ii. WILLIAM MCCUTCHIN KEEBLE, b. March 01, 1827, Blount County, Tennessee; d. May 09, 1895, Blount County, Tennessee.
     iii. JOSEPH H. KEEBLE, b. January 04, 1829.
     iv. THOMAS J. KEEBLE, b. February 16, 1831.
12. v.   MARY KEEBLE, b. March 04, 1833; d. September 14, 1895.

Children of THOMAS KEEBLE and NANCY CANNON are:
13. vi.   ELIZA JANE[3] KEEBLE, b. February 15, 1848; d. August 11, 1931.
     vii. ROBERT MARION KEEBLE, b. September 25, 1850, Blount County, Tennessee; d. Blount County, Tennessee.
14. viii. JOHN ANDERSON KEEBLE, b. July 17, 1853, Blount County, Tennessee; d. November 21, 1922.
15. ix.   ALFRED HENRY KEEBLE, b. November 07, 1855, Blount County, Tennessee; d. March 21, 1906.

3. HANNAH STAMPS[2] KEEBLE *(WILLIAM[1])* was born March 12, 1805, and died January 06, 1892. She married JOSEPH ANDERSON DUNLAP October 14, 1824 in Blount County, Tennessee, son of ADAM DUNLAP and MARGARET PORTER. He was born February 12, 1798, and died 1857.

Children of HANNAH KEEBLE and JOSEPH DUNLAP are:
     i.   JAMES C.[3] DUNLAP, b. Abt. 1826; m. RUTHA BOLING.
     ii.   ADAM H DUNLAP, b. Abt. 1829.
     iii. JOSEPH DUNLAP, b. Abt. 1832.
     iv.   POLLY DUNLAP, b. Abt. 1835.
     v.   SAMUEL P DUNLAP, b. November 27, 1838; m. SARAH CAROLINE DAVIS.
     vi.   LORENZO DUNLAP, b. Abt. 1839.
     vii. HYRUM DUNLAP, b. Abt. 1843.
     viii. MARY DUNLAP, b. Abt. 1843.
     ix.   RHODA DUNLAP, b. Abt. 1845.
     x.   JEFFERSON DUNLAP, b. Abt. 1848; m. NANCY J. DAVIS.

4. MANLY[2] KEEBLE *(WILLIAM[1])* was born July 03, 1807 in Blount County, Tennessee, and died January 01, 1882 in Blount County, Tennessee. He married (1) REBECCA RHEA August 08, 1829 in Blount County, Tennessee, daughter of JESSE RHEA and MARGARET BLAIR. She was born December 13, 1807, and died March 04, 1864 in Blount County, Tennessee. He married (2) REBECCA JANE MURPHYE August 18, 1864 in Knox County, Tennessee, daughter of MALACHI MURPHYE and DORCAS DOBKINS. She was born October 23, 1820, and died July 15, 1876.

More About MANLY KEEBLE:
Burial: Blount County, Tennessee

Children of MANLY KEEBLE and REBECCA RHEA are:
     i.   MARGARET ANN[3] KEEBLE, b. December 30, 1830; d. April 15, 1859; m. REV.PLEASANT HUGH HENRY, March 12, 1857, Blount County, Tennessee; b. March 25, 1838; d. June 25, 1911.
     ii. WILLIAM KEEBLE, b. October 25, 1832; d. October 25, 1832.
16. iii. MARY REBECCA KEEBLE, b. May 15, 1834; d. April 25, 1916.
     iv. SALLIE M. KEEBLE, b. September 20, 1836, Blount County, Tennessee; d. February 14, 1850, Blount County, Tennessee.

17.	v.	CATHERINE WALKER KEEBLE, b. October 10, 1838; d. May 04, 1892.
	vi.	JOHN HARRISON KEEBLE, b. May 29, 1840; d. April 27, 1865.
18.	vii.	SAMUEL KEEBLE, b. December 22, 1842; d. May 30, 1908.
19.	viii.	PLEASANT MARION KEEBLE, b. September 13, 1845; d. March 04, 1931.
	ix.	ANDREW MURRIN KEEBLE, b. January 06, 1848; d. July 05, 1867.
20.	x.	RICHARD HENRY KEEBLE, b. March 05, 1852; d. December 12, 1897.

5. REBECCA² KEEBLE *(WILLIAM¹)* was born January 09, 1810, and died October 14, 1881. She married SOLOMAN FARMER July 04, 1829 in Blount County, Tennessee, son of JOHN FARMER and ELIZABETH. He was born January 05, 1807, and died January 27, 1886.

Children of REBECCA KEEBLE and SOLOMAN FARMER are:

	i.	WILLIAM³ FARMER, b. January 11, 1834; m. MARY E. LATHAM.
	ii.	JOSEPH FARMER, b. January 06, 1836; m. SARAH A. HENRY.
	iii.	HOUSTON FARMER, b. September 25, 1837.
	iv.	JAMES FARMER, b. February 28, 1840; m. R. JANE DAVIS.
	v.	MARY FARMER, b. January 10, 1842; m. JAMES DAVIS.
	vi.	JOHN FARMER, b. November 09, 1843; m. EMALINE SUMMEY.
21.	vii.	ELIZABETH FARMER, b. June 28, 1846; d. September 15, 1900.

6. RICHARD PORTER² KEEBLE *(WILLIAM¹)* was born May 19, 1811, and died April 23, 1894. He married ELIZABETH RHEA November 17, 1831 in Blount Countty, Tennessee, daughter of JESSE RHEA and MARGARET BLAIR. She was born March 1815, and died 1875.

Children of RICHARD KEEBLE and ELIZABETH RHEA are:

22.	i.	MARGARET³ KEEBLE, b. May 06, 1833; d. October 19, 1884.
23.	ii.	MARION KEEBLE, b. July 09, 1840; d. May 05, 1890.

7. WALTER HARRISON² KEEBLE *(WILLIAM¹)* was born November 14, 1815, and died April 25, 1897. He married MARY (POLLY) WHITE August 15, 1836 in Blount County, Tennessee. She was born Abt. 1819, and died 1896.

Children of WALTER KEEBLE and MARY WHITE are:

	i.	WILLIAM³ KEEBLE, b. May 20, 1837.
24.	ii.	JOHN KEEBLE, b. August 20, 1838.
25.	iii.	NANCY KEEBLE, b. August 22, 1840; d. August 11, 1913.
26.	iv.	SAMUEL KEEBLE, b. April 12, 1843; d. January 24, 1913.
	v.	MARY KEEBLE, b. October 24, 1845; d. February 14, 1915.
27.	vi.	JANE KEEBLE, b. September 05, 1853; d. August 18, 1913.
28.	vii.	RICHARD KEEBLE, b. February 14, 1849; d. December 12, 1897.

8. MARY BANKS² KEEBLE *(WILLIAM¹)* was born December 14, 1817. She married STEPHEN DAVIS April 05, 1838 in Blount Countty, Tennessee, son of THOMAS DAVIS and SARAH MIZE. He was born July 12, 1817.

Children of MARY KEEBLE and STEPHEN DAVIS are:

	i.	CHARLOTTE³ DAVIS, b. Abt. 1840.
	ii.	ELIJAH DAVIS, b. Abt. 1843; d. June 29, 1865.
	iii.	JANE DAVIS, b. Abt. 1846.
	iv.	MARY DAVIS, b. Abt. 1848.
	v.	SARAH DAVIS, b. Abt. 1850.
	vi.	WILLIAM DAVIS, b. Abt. 1854.
	vii.	REBECCA DAVIS, b. Abt. 1856.
	viii.	WALTER DAVIS, b. Abt. 1860.

9. CHARLOTTE WHITE² KEEBLE *(WILLIAM¹)* was born May 21, 1819, and died October 09, 1847. She married ANDREW JACKSON MURRIN August 27, 1844 in Blount Countty, Tennessee, son of ROBERT MURRIN and SARAH.

He was born October 12, 1815, and died January 31, 1873.

Child of CHARLOTTE KEEBLE and ANDREW MURRIN is:
  i.   MARY³ MURRIN, b. Abt. 1845; m. JACOB H. HARMON, March 10, 1875, Blount County, Tennessee.

Generation No. 3

10. JAMES H.³ KEEBLE *(THOMAS², WILLIAM¹)* was born December 04, 1824 in Blount County, Tennessee, and died 1886. He married MARY ANN SNEED February 25, 1844 in Blount County, Tennessee, daughter of TAYLOR SNEED and FRANCES (UNKNOWN). She was born May 08, 1820, and died December 04, 1884.

Notes for MARY ANN SNEED:
Her father was Taylor Sneed and her mother was Francis Alice _____
They were the parents of ten children.

Children of JAMES KEEBLE and MARY SNEED are:
29.   i.   JOHN HOUSTON⁴ KEEBLE, b. 1845; d. 1882.
30.   ii.   ELIZABETH J. KEEBLE, b. November 20, 1847; d. May 23, 1898.
31.   iii. SARAH ALICE KEEBLE, b. 1849.
32.   iv.   TAYLOR S. KEEBLE, b. December 23, 1849; d. August 04, 1917.
33.   v.   WILLIAM THOMAS KEEBLE, b. 1852; d. 1900.
34.   vi.   MAHALIA KEEBLE, b. July 04, 1857.
35.   vii. JAMES W. KEEBLE, b. Abt. 1858.
36.   viii. ATHELLA KEEBLE, b. February 13, 1861; d. December 19, 1919.
37.   ix.   ORPHELIA KEEBLE, b. February 13, 1861; d. December 19, 1919.
38.   x.   JOE MORRIS KEEBLE, b. December 11, 1862; d. April 17, 1925.

11. WILLIAM MCCUTCHIN³ KEEBLE *(THOMAS², WILLIAM¹)* was born March 01, 1827 in Blount County, Tennessee, and died May 09, 1895 in Blount County, Tennessee. He married (1) MARY TOWNSEND November 20, 1845 in Blount County, Tennessee. He married (2) NANCY JENKINS August 14, 1862 in Sevier County, Tennessee, daughter of CALEB JENKINS and JANE GIBSON. She was born April 11, 1843, and died July 22, 1921.

More About WILLIAM MCCUTCHIN KEEBLE:
Burial: Keeble Cemetery Blount County, Tennessee

Children of WILLIAM KEEBLE and MARY TOWNSEND are:
39.   i.   JAMES THOMAS⁴ KEEBLE, b. July 02, 1847; d. November 15, 1880.
40.   ii.   JOHN KEEBLE, b. 1852; d. 1879.
      iii. WILLIAM KEEBLE, b. 1854; m. TENNESSEE BOLING, Sevier County, Tennessee.
41.   iv.   SALLY KEEBLE, b. Aft. 1856.
      v.   MARIAM KEEBLE, b. Aft. 1858.

Children of WILLIAM KEEBLE and NANCY JENKINS are:
42.   vi.   MARY MARTIN (POLLY)⁴ KEEBLE, b. January 14, 1863; d. December 19, 1956, Sevier County Tennessee.
43.   vii. FANNY CAROLYN KEEBLE, b. October 10, 1865; d. July 11, 1899.
44.   viii. CALEB LAVERNE KEEBLE, SR., b. October 1867; d. July 26, 1948.
45.   ix.   ADALINE L. KEEBLE, b. November 11, 1869; d. March 15, 1917.
      x.   ISAAC KEEBLE, b. March 1872; d. October 24, 1894.
46.   xi.   SUSAN JANE KEEBLE, b. May 09, 1873; d. October 11, 1910.
47.   xii. PRUDANCE KEEBLE, b. March 30, 1877; d. November 07, 1964.
48.   xiii. LABAN KEEBLE, b. October 12, 1879, Sevier County Tennessee; d. September 20, 1953, Blount memorial Hospital Maryville, Tenn..
49.   xiv. MARINDA KEEBLE, b. January 01, 1882.

12. MARY³ KEEBLE *(THOMAS², WILLIAM¹)* was born March 04, 1833, and died September 14, 1895. She married

JOHN SIMS BOLING January 12, 1853 in Blount County, Tennessee, son of ROBERT BOLING and SALLY CLAMPETT. He was born November 29, 1833, and died December 21, 1906.

Children of MARY KEEBLE and JOHN BOLING are:

    i.   MARGARET[4] BOLING, m. A .R . HARMON.
    ii.   NANCY C . BOLING, m. W. R. HARMON.
   iii.   THOMAS L. BOLING, m. ANN DUGGAN.
   iv.   JAMES W. BOLING, m. ELIZABETH B. ANGEL.
    v.   JOHN H. BOLING, b. March 02, 1867; m. FLORENCE MCCROSKEY.
   vi.   ELIZA JANE BOLING.
  vii.   SAMUEL BOLING.
 viii.   ARTHUS C. BOLING.

13. ELIZA JANE[3] KEEBLE *(THOMAS[2], WILLIAM[1])* was born February 15, 1848, and died August 11, 1931. She married ELI FARMER August 13, 1868 in Blount County, Tessessee, son of JOSEPH FARMER and TINY. He was born December 15, 1843, and died May 30, 1912.

Children of ELIZA KEEBLE and ELI FARMER are:

50.   i.   ROBERT M.[4] FARMER, b. April 26, 1869; d. December 16, 1939.
51.   ii.   JOSEPH H. FARMER, b. March 01, 1871; d. November 13, 1953.
       iii.   NANCY JANE FARMER, b. May 12, 1873; d. February 06, 1949.
       iv.   THOMAS FARMER, b. September 03, 1875; d. June 05, 1876.
        v.   MARGARET CLEMENTINE FARMER, b. March 23, 1877; m. WILLIAM RUSSELL.
       vi.   MARY CATHERINE FARMER, b. October 11, 1879; m. SAM R. SHERRILL.
      vii.   ELLY GRACE FARMER, b. August 06, 1882; d. 1974.

14. JOHN ANDERSON[3] KEEBLE *(THOMAS[2], WILLIAM[1])* was born July 17, 1853 in Blount County, Tennessee, and died November 21, 1922. He met SARAH DAVIS December 25, 1882 in Blount County, Tennessee, daughter of JAMES DAVIS and MARY FARMER. She was born January 22, 1861, and died March 15, 1922.

Children of JOHN KEEBLE and SARAH DAVIS are:

52.   i.   BERTHA[4] KEEBLE, b. September 15, 1883; d. October 19, 1950.
      ii.   SAMUEL HUSTON KEEBLE, b. May 17, 1885; d. April 1886.

          More About SAMUEL HUSTON KEEBLE:
          Burial: Keeble Cemetery, Blount County, Tennessee

      iii.   MARGARET ANN KEEBLE, b. June 01, 1887; d. May 01, 1906; m. WILLIAM BREWER, Blount County, Tennessee; b. October 14, 1886; d. January 08, 1952.
53.   iv.   LIDA KEEBLE, b. Abt. 1889; d. August 13, 1967.
54.   v.   JAMES EDWARD KEEBLE, b. November 25, 1893; d. December 25, 1957.
      vi.   ABSHUR ANDREW KEEBLE, b. March 29, 1896; d. July 1898.

          More About ABSHUR ANDREW KEEBLE:
          Burial: Keeble Cemetery Blount County, Tennessee

15. ALFRED HENRY[3] KEEBLE *(THOMAS[2], WILLIAM[1])* was born November 07, 1855 in Blount County, Tennessee, and died March 21, 1906. He married (1) MILLIE JANE DAVIS, daughter of WILLIAM DAVIS and CASS MCCLANAHAN. He married (2) RACHEL F. DONALDSON January 19, 1886 in Blount County,, Tennessee, daughter of JAMES DONALDSON and JANE BURNETTE. She was born September 03, 1867, and died October 18, 1896.

Children of ALFRED KEEBLE and MILLIE DAVIS are:

55.   i.   WILLIAM THOMAS[4] KEEBLE.
56.   ii.   JOHN ROBERT KEEBLE, b. 1880; d. June 08, 1940.
57.   iii.   CHARLES GARFIELD KEEBLE, b. August 11, 1881; d. July 09, 1949.

Children of ALFRED KEEBLE and RACHEL DONALDSON are:

58. iv. ELIZA JANE[4] KEEBLE, b. March 26, 1886; d. December 16, 1934.
  v. JAMES EDWARD KEEBLE, b. May 13, 1888; d. July 04, 1908.
  vi. HUGH LEONARD KEEBLE, b. March 25, 1890; d. April 1912.
59. vii. DOCIE DON KEEBLE,SR., b. April 15, 1892; d. February 08, 1980.
60. viii. LUTITIA KEEBLE, b. October 17, 1894.
  ix. ELLEN KEEBLE, b. October 1896; d. October 22, 1896.

16. MARY REBECCA[3] KEEBLE *(MANLY[2], WILLIAM[1])* was born May 15, 1834, and died April 25, 1916. She married MATTHEW BOGLE GARNER May 23, 1861 in Blount County, Tennessee, son of ELI GARNER and ELIZABETH ROGERS. He was born October 30, 1841, and died June 14, 1924.

Children of MARY KEEBLE and MATTHEW GARNER are:

  i. REBECCA E.[4] GARNER, b. Abt. 1866; m. FRED BOLING.
  ii. SAMUEL GARNER, b. Abt. 1868; m. MARY DAVIS.
  iii. MARGARETTE JANE GARNER, b. January 12, 1869; m. WILLIAM MARION TIPTON.
  iv. JOHN FRANCIS GARNER, b. Abt. 1872; m. ELLA BOLING.

17. CATHERINE WALKER[3] KEEBLE *(MANLY[2], WILLIAM[1])* was born October 10, 1838, and died May 04, 1892. She married JESSE CAGLE March 06, 1862 in Blount Countty,Tennessee, son of GEORGE CAGLE and MARY LATHAM. He was born December 07, 1840, and died March 09, 1914.

Children of CATHERINE KEEBLE and JESSE CAGLE are:

  i. REBECCA[4] CAGLE, b. December 1863.
  ii. LUCILLE RHONDA CAGLE, b. 1867; m. JESSE ROGERS.
  iii. GEORGE ANDERSON CAGLE, b. May 31, 1869; m. BERTHA CORDELIA HOOD.
  iv. SARAH ELLEN CAGLE, b. 1871; m. TOM WILSON.
  v. ANGELINE MATILDA CAGLE, b. December 1874; m. JAMES DAVIS.
  vi. WILLIAM HOLBERT CAGLE, b. April 20, 1877; d. November 30, 1954; m. BETTY ANN JONES.
  vii. JAMES CAGLE, b. 1879; m. RHODA SHOEMAKER.

18. SAMUEL[3] KEEBLE *(MANLY[2], WILLIAM[1])* was born December 22, 1842, and died May 30, 1908. He married JANE GARNER November 09, 1865 in Blount County, Tennessee, daughter of ELIJAH GARNER and ELIZABETH ROGERS. She was born January 01, 1847, and died March 19, 1939.

Children of SAMUEL KEEBLE and JANE GARNER are:

61. i. NANCY ANN[4] KEEBLE, b. August 06, 1866; d. December 14, 1930.
62. ii. MARY ELIZABETH KEEBLE, b. November 25, 1867; d. January 22, 1898.
63. iii. PLEASANT KEEBLE, b. July 01, 1869; d. April 13, 1946.
64. iv. REBECCA JANE KEEBLE, b. February 27, 1871; d. January 23, 1964.
65. v. SARAH KEEBLE, b. December 31, 1873; d. May 08, 1958.
  vi. ELI KEEBLE, b. January 15, 1875; d. November 22, 1894.
66. vii. EVALINE KEEBLE, b. November 17, 1877; d. December 10, 1971.
  viii. MANLY KEEBLE, b. July 12, 1879; d. 1888.
67. ix. MARTHA CAROLINE KEEBLE, b. February 07, 1880; d. October 07, 1966.
  x. EMILY KEEBLE, b. November 24, 1882; d. 1892.
68. xi. JOHN RICHARD KEEBLE, b. August 13, 1884; d. September 02, 1963.
  xii. SAM WILEY KEEBLE, b. February 15, 1886; d. 1892.

19. PLEASANT MARION[3] KEEBLE *(MANLY[2], WILLIAM[1])* was born September 13, 1845, and died March 04, 1931. He married MARGARET ELIZABETH MCTEER September 22, 1870 in Blount Countty,Tennessee, daughter of JAMES MCTEER and LOVICA PITNER. She was born August 17, 1851, and died February 17, 1901.

Children of PLEASANT KEEBLE and MARGARET MCTEER are:

69. i. NELLIE ARIZONA[4] KEEBLE, b. October 28, 1871; d. April 03, 1954.

70.	ii.	WILLIAM HOUSTON KEEBLE, b. May 09, 1873; d. June 03, 1963.
	iii.	JAMES RICHARD KEEBLE, b. July 17, 1875; d. September 29, 1915.
71.	iv.	JOHN EDMUND KEEBLE, b. November 07, 1877; d. October 17, 1940.
	v.	SAMUEL ANDERSON KEEBLE, b. August 26, 1879; d. April 15, 1883.
72.	vi.	ANDREW ELMER KEEBLE, b. September 11, 1881; d. July 07, 1969.
73.	vii.	NORA ELIZABETH KEEBLE, b. June 20, 1884; d. June 13, 1962.
	viii.	MARY ESTELLE KEEBLE, b. June 13, 1886; d. May 26, 1895.
74.	ix.	ANNA RACHEL KEEBLE, b. October 17, 1889; d. April 26, 1952.
	x.	EDGAR RHEA KEEBLE, b. September 25, 1893; d. May 31, 1991; m. MABEL MATHIS BEAN, December 23, 1933, Knox County, Tennessee; b. June 13, 1892; d. December 28, 1972.

20. RICHARD HENRY[3] KEEBLE *(MANLY[2], WILLIAM[1])* was born March 05, 1852, and died December 12, 1897. He married MARTHA ELLEN STONE Abt. 1877, daughter of JOEL STONE and NANCY NIPPER. She was born September 07, 1855, and died September 15, 1900.

Children of RICHARD KEEBLE and MARTHA STONE are:

75.	i.	WILLIAM ARTHUR[4] KEEBLE, SR., b. April 24, 1878.
76.	ii.	SAMUEL WILEY KEEBLE, b. April 14, 1881; d. May 18, 1935.
	iii.	CHARLES W. KEEBLE, b. November 1884; m. MAGGIE JEFFRIES, February 16, 1903, Knox County, Tennessee.
	iv.	EDWARD KEEBLE, b. April 1887.
	v.	JAMES RICHARD KEEBLE, b. March 06, 1897; d. October 24, 1978.
77.	vi.	IZORA MAUDE KEEBLE, b. September 07, 1890; d. December 26, 1956.

21. ELIZABETH[3] FARMER *(REBECCA[2] KEEBLE, WILLIAM[1])* was born June 28, 1846, and died September 15, 1900. She married RICHARD KEEBLE July 02, 1873 in Blount Countty, Tennessee, son of WALTER KEEBLE and MARY WHITE. He was born February 14, 1849, and died December 12, 1897.

Children of ELIZABETH FARMER and RICHARD KEEBLE are:

	i.	MARY[4] KEEBLE, b. Abt. 1875.
	ii.	REBECCA KEEBLE, b. Abt. 1877.
	iii.	BRUCE KEEBLE, b. Abt. 1879.
	iv.	WALTER HARRISON KEEBLE, b. August 16, 1881.

22. MARGARET[3] KEEBLE *(RICHARD PORTER[2], WILLIAM[1])* was born May 06, 1833, and died October 19, 1884. She married REV. JAMES RICHARD COULTER January 22, 1852 in Blount County, Tennessee, son of ANDREW COULTER and NANCT JAMES. He was born October 10, 1830, and died July 05, 1902.

Children of MARGARET KEEBLE and REV. JAMES COULTER are:

	i.	RICHARD A[4] COULTER, b. 1852; m. (1) ELLA BROWN; m. (2) MARCIE BROWN.
	ii.	WILLIAM A. COULTER, b. November 25, 1854; m. MARY NIMAN.
	iii.	ELIZABETH COULTER, b. October 1857; m. JOHN NEUBERT.
	iv.	NANCY JANE COULTER, b. May 26, 1864; m JAMES OLIVER GODDARD; b. January 21, 1868.
	v.	JAMES M. COULTER, b. October 30, 1869; m. LORA MCTEER.

23. MARION[3] KEEBLE *(RICHARD PORTER[2], WILLIAM[1])* was born July 09, 1840, and died May 05, 1890. He married MARTHA JANE CLARK December 21, 1864 in Blount Countty, Tennessee, daughter of JOHN CLARK and MATILDA THOMPSON. She was born April 16, 1844, and died December 22, 1890.

More About MARION KEEBLE:
Burial: Keeble Cemetery Blount County, Tennessee

More About MARTHA JANE CLARK:
Burial: Keeble Cemetery Blount County, Tennessee

Children of MARION KEEBLE and MARTHA CLARK are:

	i.	NANCY ANN[4] KEEBLE, b. September 21, 1865; d. September 23, 1865.
78.	ii.	ELIZABETH JANE KEEBLE, b. September 17, 1866; d. December 23, 1919.
	iii.	RICHARD PORTER KEEBLE, b. August 06, 1868; d. December 26, 1935; m. ORA BELLE TROTTNER, October 10, 1910, Santa Clara County, California; b. Abt. 1870.
79.	iv.	JOHN ELLISON KEEBLE, b. August 11, 1869; d. April 16, 1933.
80.	v.	MARGARET CLEMENTINE KEEBLE, b. March 08, 1871; d. January 18, 1919.
81.	vi.	EDWARD GEORGE KEEBLE,SR., b. April 04, 1872; d. February 15, 1939.
82.	vii.	MATILDA CLARINDA KEEBLE, b. June 01, 1874; d. September 29, 1954.
83.	viii.	MARY LOUISA KEEBLE, b. October 28, 1875; d. June 17, 1909.
84.	ix.	MARION PRISCILLA KEEBLE, b. September 05, 1878; d. July 15, 1965.
	x.	HENRY FITCHUE KEEBLE, b. October 28, 1880; d. December 03, 1880.
85.	xi.	MARTHA ADALINE KEEBLE, b. September 21, 1882; d. September 02, 1971.
	xii.	SINA GERTRUDE KEEBLE, b. May 03, 1887; d. June 19, 1964; m. JAMES G. MCFADDEN, March 12, 1912; b. December 03, 1881; d. April 08, 1948.
	xiii.	ROSA LEE KEEBLE, b. November 30, 1890; d. November 30, 1890.

24. JOHN[3] KEEBLE *(WALTER HARRISON[2], WILLIAM[1])* was born August 20, 1838. He married NANCY A. PARKS May 08, 1868 in Blount Countty,Tennessee, daughter of JOSEPH PARKS and NANCY FROST. She was born November 07, 1851.

Children of JOHN KEEBLE and NANCY PARKS are:

	i.	HOUSTON KELLY[4] KEEBLE, b. Abt. 1868; m. LIZZIE E. SHAVER.
86.	ii.	MARY JANE KEEBLE, b. 1872.

25. NANCY[3] KEEBLE *(WALTER HARRISON[2], WILLIAM[1])* was born August 22, 1840, and died August 11, 1913.

Child of NANCY KEEBLE is:

87.	i.	STEPHEN[4] KEEBLE,SR., b. May 16, 1880; d. November 10, 1945.

26. SAMUEL[3] KEEBLE *(WALTER HARRISON[2], WILLIAM[1])* was born April 12, 1843, and died January 24, 1913. He married SARAH ELIZABETH JENKINS December 14, 1865 in Blount Countty,Tennessee, daughter of JOHN JENKINS and MARGARET. She was born November 14, 1847, and died February 29, 1916.

Child of SAMUEL KEEBLE and SARAH JENKINS is:

88.	i.	MARY CALEDONIA[4] KEEBLE, b. September 17, 1875; d. April 09, 1960.

27. JANE[3] KEEBLE *(WALTER HARRISON[2], WILLIAM[1])* was born September 05, 1853, and died August 18, 1913.

Children of JANE KEEBLE are:

89.	i.	PEARL[4] KEEBLE, d. September 1956.
90.	ii.	WILLIAM MARTIN KEEBLE, b. April 08, 1885; d. July 10, 1957.
	iii.	GEORGIA O. KEEBLE, b. October 1890.
91.	iv.	JOHN JASON KEEBLE, b. May 29, 1895; d. February 09, 1971.
	v.	JANE KEEBLE, b. March 1899.
92.	vi.	CATHERINE ALICE ARIZONA KEEBLE, b. March 10, 1904.

28. RICHARD[3] KEEBLE *(WALTER HARRISON[2], WILLIAM[1])* was born February 14, 1849, and died December 12, 1897. He married ELIZABETH FARMER July 02, 1873 in Blount Countty,Tennessee, daughter of SOLOMAN FARMER and REBECCA KEEBLE. She was born June 28, 1846, and died September 15, 1900.

Children are listed above under (21) Elizabeth Farmer.

Generation No. 4

29. JOHN HOUSTON[4] KEEBLE *(JAMES H.[3], THOMAS[2], WILLIAM[1])* was born 1845, and died 1882. He married (1) EMMA SUSAN MULDREW COOK, daughter of JOHN MULDREW and MARTHA BAKER. She was born February 07, 1843, and died January 23, 1917. He married (2) MARTHA CAROLINE MULDREW in Randolph County, Alabama, daughter of JOHN MULDREW and MARTHA BAKER. She was born February 17, 1850, and died March 23, 1875.

Notes for EMMA SUSAN MULDREW COOK:
She the daughter of John D. Muldrew and Martha C. Baker. This lady is a sister to wife # 1

Children of JOHN KEEBLE and EMMA COOK are:
      i.   SAMUEL[5] KEEBLE, b. 1881.

            Notes for SAMUEL KEEBLE:
            Samuel died in infancy

93.   ii. GEORGIA HOUSTON KEEBLE, b. September 30, 1882; d. April 23, 1911.

Children of JOHN KEEBLE and MARTHA MULDREW are:
94.   iii. JAMES TAYLOR[5] KEEBLE, b. February 12, 1867; d. May 20, 1923.
95.   iv. JOHN DAVID KEEBLE, b. July 09, 1869; d. June 14, 1897.
96.   v.   WILLIAM LAFAYETTE KEEBLE, b. June 02, 1872; d. June 20, 1946.
97.   vi. MARY CAROLINE KEEBLE, b. July 09, 1874; d. October 07, 1957.

30. ELIZABETH J.[4] KEEBLE *(JAMES H.[3], THOMAS[2], WILLIAM[1])* was born November 20, 1847, and died May 23, 1898. She married WILLIAM ALFRED MULDREW. He was born November 07, 1846, and died July 30, 1919.

Children of ELIZABETH KEEBLE and WILLIAM MULDREW are:
      i.   MARY EMMA[5] MULDREW, b. December 23, 1866; m. TOM ANGLIN.
      ii. SARAH FRANCES MULDREW, b. September 21, 1868; m. HENRY HOWELL.
     iii. MARTHA JANE MULDREW, b. December 12, 1869; m. MARION RICHARD STEVENS.
     iv. CAROLINE HOUSTON MULDREW, b. July 31, 1882; m. RUFUS BARTLETT.
      v.   WILLIE MAYBELL MULDREW, b. September 15, 1887; m. SAM SEEGAN.

31. SARAH ALICE[4] KEEBLE *(JAMES H.[3], THOMAS[2], WILLIAM[1])* was born 1849. She married (1) MILTON SHEPPARD. She married (2) DEMPSEY DAVIS.

Children of SARAH KEEBLE and MILTON SHEPPARD are:
      i.   LIZZIE[5] SHEPPARD, m. JOHN TOWLER.
      ii. WILLIAM SHEPPARD, m. LUCINDA HALL.
     iii. JOHN SHEPPARD, m. MARTHA TOWLER.
     iv. EMMA SHEPPARD, m. (1) JIM BURSON; m. (2) CHARLES MATTHEWS.

Children of SARAH KEEBLE and DEMPSEY DAVIS are:
      v.   JOSEPH[5] DAVIS, m. FANNY PITTS.
     vi. SAMUEL DAVIS, m. PEARL.

32. TAYLOR S.[4] KEEBLE *(JAMES H.[3], THOMAS[2], WILLIAM[1])* was born December 23, 1849, and died August 04, 1917. He married LUCY A. MORTON September 15, 1873. She was born February 17, 1856, and died April 17, 1920.

Children of TAYLOR KEEBLE and LUCY MORTON are:
98.   i.   JAMES THOMAS[5] KEEBLE, b. December 19, 1874; d. August 14, 1956.
99.   ii. KATE MARVILLE KEEBLE, b. November 06, 1876; d. April 1946.
100.   iii. J.D. KEEBLE, b. November 07, 1878; d. December 30, 1938.

101.   iv.   SAMUEL E. KEEBLE, b. February 13, 1880; d. October 27, 1924.
102.   v.   JOHN H. KEEBLE, b. December 20, 1881; d. February 08, 1921.
103.   vi.   JERRY MACK KEEBLE, b. February 14, 1883; d. November 02, 1956.
104. vii.   ANDREW DAVIS KEEBLE, b. February 17, 1885; d. March 06, 1938.
105. viii.   BYRD KEEBLE, b. February 13, 1886; d. March 21, 1939.
        ix.   D.T. KEEBLE, b. February 26, 1887; d. March 19, 1887.
106.   x.   HATTIE KEEBLE, b. August 21, 1891; d. January 05, 1921.
107.   xi.   ROBERT PATE KEEBLE, b. November 03, 1893; d. October 10, 1980.
108. xii.   PIERCE MACK KEEBLE,SR., b. April 11, 1896; d. February 22, 1985.

33. WILLIAM THOMAS[4] KEEBLE *(JAMES H.[3], THOMAS[2], WILLIAM[1])* was born 1852, and died 1900. He married (1) LILLA SUDDETH. He married (2) ISABELLA TRENT December 06, 1877 in Randolph County, Alabama, daughter of POWHATAN TRENT and MATILDA STEWART. She was born Abt. 1858, and died Abt. 1892.

Children of WILLIAM KEEBLE and ISABELLA TRENT are:
        i.   LESSIE BELLE[5] KEEBLE, b. April 18, 1878; d. December 28, 1894.
109.   ii.   WILLIAM EMMETT KEEBLE, b. August 20, 1880; d. September 30, 1944.
110. iii.   GLOVER TRENT KEEBLE, b. December 31, 1882; d. February 11, 1957.
111.   iv.   TRESSVANT THOMAS KEEBLE, b. November 12, 1887; d. February 23, 1965.

34. MAHALIA[4] KEEBLE *(JAMES H.[3], THOMAS[2], WILLIAM[1])* was born July 04, 1857. She married (1) JOHN W. O'NEAL in Heard County, Georgia, son of WILLIAM JASPER O'NEAL. He was born 1856, and died 1908. She married (2) PITTS.

Children of MAHALIA KEEBLE and JOHN O'NEAL are:
        i.   MARY EUGENIA[5] O'NEAL, b. July 28, 1878; m. ERASTUS ALEXANDER MCCLENDON.
       ii.   HUBERT ELMER O'NEAL.
      iii.   MYRTLE LEE O'NEAL.
       iv.   MAYZELLE O'NEAL, m. WILLIAM HENRY TEDFORD.
        v.   WILLIAM HOYT O'NEAL.
       vi.   HOWARD EUCAREY O'NEAL.
      vii.   OMAR LAMAR O'NEAL.
     viii.   DORIS WILLENE O'NEAL.

35. JAMES W.[4] KEEBLE *(JAMES H.[3], THOMAS[2], WILLIAM[1])* was born Abt. 1858. He married EUGENIA (UNKNOWN).

Child of JAMES KEEBLE and EUGENIA (UNKNOWN) is:
        i.   LOUIZA[5] KEEBLE, b. February 1880.

36. ATHELLA[4] KEEBLE *(JAMES H.[3], THOMAS[2], WILLIAM[1])* was born February 13, 1861, and died December 19, 1919. She married LEWIS HENDON.

Child of ATHELLA KEEBLE and LEWIS HENDON is:
        i.   WILL[5] HENDON, m. JOSIE BOYD.

37. ORPHELIA[4] KEEBLE *(JAMES H.[3], THOMAS[2], WILLIAM[1])* was born February 13, 1861, and died December 19, 1919. She married WILLIAM DAVID HENDON December 23, 1881 in Randolph County, Alabama. He was born February 11, 1861, and died April 28, 1920.

Children of ORPHELIA KEEBLE and WILLIAM HENDON are:
        i.   THOMAS M[5] HENDON, m. DALLAS HARDY.
       ii.   DELLA MAE HENDON, m. THOMAS SANFORD SHELNUTT.

38. JOE MORRIS[4] KEEBLE *(JAMES H.[3], THOMAS[2], WILLIAM[1])* was born December 11, 1862, and died April 17,

1925. He married REBECCA WHITAKER December 06, 1883.

Children of JOE KEEBLE and REBECCA WHITAKER are:
112.   i.   MARY LOU⁵ KEEBLE, b. September 28, 1884; d. October 24, 1969.
113.   ii. S.T. KEEBLE, b. December 16, 1890.
       iii. LOLA PEARL KEEBLE, b. October 07, 1892.
114.   iv. JESSE HOWARD KEEBLE, b. September 10, 1894.
115.   v.   HORACE FRANKLIN KEEBLE, b. July 22, 1896; d. November 19, 1966.
116.   vi. MAYNELLE CARMEN KEEBLE, b. February 21, 1898.
117.   vii. SARAH FRANCES KEEBLE, b. October 23, 1901.

39. JAMES THOMAS⁴ KEEBLE *(WILLIAM McCUTCHIN³, THOMAS², WILLIAM¹)* was born July 02, 1847, and died November 15, 1880. He married PRUDANCE CAROLINE JENKINS December 24, 1868 in Sevier County, Tennessee, daughter of LABAN JENKINS and ELIZABETH LEWELLYN. She was born January 29, 1851, and died March 23, 1923.

Children of JAMES KEEBLE and PRUDANCE JENKINS are:
118.   i.   LABAN ELIZABETH⁵ KEEBLE, b. February 16, 1869; d. March 12, 1928.
119.   ii. MARY ANN KEEBLE, b. January 23, 1872; d. November 12, 1965.
120.   iii. SALLY JANE KEEBLE, b. September 28, 1873; d. March 03, 1933.
121.   iv. SUSAN MARINDA KEEBLE, b. April 03, 1874; d. December 09, 1951.
       v.   NANCY T. KEEBLE, b. March 27, 1877; d. June 01, 1878.
122.   vi. ELIZA KEEBLE, b. December 06, 1878; d. April 18, 1910.

40. JOHN⁴ KEEBLE *(WILLIAM McCUTCHIN³, THOMAS², WILLIAM¹)* was born 1852, and died 1879. He married REBECCA JENKINS December 25, 1873 in Sevier County, Tennessee, daughter of LABAN JENKINS and ELIZABETH LEWELLYN. She was born February 23, 1857, and died June 30, 1903.

Children of JOHN KEEBLE and REBECCA JENKINS are:
123.   i.   WILLIAM DOCKERY⁵ KEEBLE, b. October 04, 1870; d. March 30, 1948.
124.   ii. MARTHA ALICE KEEBLE, b. November 18, 1875; d. July 26, 1946.
       iii. LUTUTIA ELIZABETH KEEBLE, b. September 18, 1878; d. January 02, 1905; m. MATTHEW EVANS, January 31, 1901, Sevier County, Tennessee; b. June 24, 1876; d. October 04, 1916.

41. SALLY⁴ KEEBLE *(WILLIAM McCUTCHIN³, THOMAS², WILLIAM¹)* was born Aft. 1856. She married JOHN BOLING April 12, 1838 in Blount County, Tennessee.

Children of SALLY KEEBLE and JOHN BOLING are:
       i.   MARY⁵ BOLING, m. CHARLES BOLING.
       ii. CECELIA BOLING, m. (1) JACK HENDRIX; m. (2) FRANK BAKER.
       iii. SAMUEL BOLING, m. MARY HOUSER.
       iv. ALVA BOLING.

42. MARY MARTIN (POLLY)⁴ KEEBLE *(WILLIAM McCUTCHIN³, THOMAS², WILLIAM¹)* was born January 14, 1863, and died December 19, 1956 in Sevier County Tennessee. She married HARRISON HELTON July 18, 1883 in Sevier County, Tennessee, son of ALEXANDER HELTON and NANCY JEFFERIES. He was born March 15, 1863, and died October 12, 1927.

Children of MARY KEEBLE and HARRISON HELTON are:
       i.   MARGARET⁵ HELTON, b. March 18, 1884; m. LAFAYETTE CHRISTOPHER.
       ii.   WILLIAM ALEXANDER HELTON, b. August 25, 1885; m. CORDELIA LEWELLYN.
       iii. JAMES CALEB HELTON, b. July 04, 1887; m. (1) RACHEL SHELLEY; m. (2) ROSALIE (UNKNOWN).
       iv.   JOHN HOUK HELTON, b. September 04, 1890; m. NETTIE HODGE.
       v.   JOSEPH HARRISON HELTON, b. May 27, 1893; m. ELLA RUPE.
       vi.   THOMAS GRADON HELTON, b. May 19, 1900; m. JOHNNIE RUSSELL.
       vii. JEPTHA LAFAYETTE HELTON, b. July 03, 1904; m. LELA CLARK.

43. FANNY CAROLYN[4] KEEBLE *(WILLIAM MCCUTCHIN[3], THOMAS[2], WILLIAM[1])* was born October 10, 1865, and died July 11, 1899. She married JOSEPH MCCLELLAN GORMAN January 22, 1888 in Sevier County, Tennessee, son of JAKE GORMAN and MARGARET COLE. He was born August 1863, and died May 24, 1905.

Children of FANNY KEEBLE and JOSEPH GORMAN are:

- i. JAMES GASTON[5] GORMAN, b. January 11, 1889.
- ii. ROBERT WILLIAM GORMAN, b. April 16, 1891; m. (1) RUBY FOGLESONG; m. (2) HATTIE LEWELLYN.
- iii. MARY EDNA GORMAN, b. September 16, 1894; d. October 20, 1898.
- iv. GEORGIA BELL GORMAN, b. October 09, 1895; m. WILLIAM DOUGLAS HOUSER.
- v. JOHN CATLETT GORMAN, b. May 23, 1898; m. JANIE BROOKS.

44. CALEB LAVERNE[4] KEEBLE, SR. *(WILLIAM MCCUTCHIN[3], THOMAS[2], WILLIAM[1])* was born October 1867, and died July 26, 1948. He married (1) MARTHA E. JOHNSON April 26, 1893 in Sevier County, Tennessee. She died March 1899. He married (2) NANCY ELIZABETH SHARP September 21, 1901 in Sevier County, Tennessee, daughter of JOHN SHARP and LUCY CATLETT. She was born December 28, 1872, and died May 20, 1948.

Child of CALEB KEEBLE and MARTHA JOHNSON is:

| 125. | i. | MELVIN[5] KEEBLE, b. April 10, 1896; d. October 01, 1977. |

Children of CALEB KEEBLE and NANCY SHARP are:

126.	ii.	REBA[5] KEEBLE, b. 1902.
127.	iii.	HUBERT KEEBLE, b. 1904, Anthony Kansas; d. 1972.
128.	iv.	CLYDE PETE KEEBLE, b. 1907, Santa Rosa, California.
	v.	CALEB LAVERNE KEEBLE, JR., b. March 02, 1910; d. 1955.

45. ADALINE L.[4] KEEBLE *(WILLIAM MCCUTCHIN[3], THOMAS[2], WILLIAM[1])* was born November 11, 1869, and died March 15, 1917. She married RICHARD BURDETT FLOYD April 02, 1892 in Sevier County, Tennessee, son of ELI FLOYD and HETTIE KING. He was born February 26, 1870, and died November 07, 1948.

Children of ADALINE KEEBLE and RICHARD FLOYD are:

- i. NANCY ELLEN[5] FLOYD, b. December 03, 1894; m. MILLARD EDMOND TARWATER.
- ii. ANNA MARINDA FLOYD, b. February 17, 1905; m. LON PARROTT.

46. SUSAN JANE[4] KEEBLE *(WILLIAM MCCUTCHIN[3], THOMAS[2], WILLIAM[1])* was born May 09, 1873, and died October 11, 1910. She married DOUGLAS HEADRICK January 23, 1890 in Sevier County, Tennessee, son of WILLIAM HEADRICK and MARTHA GORMAN. He was born July 16, 1870, and died December 29, 1947.

Children of SUSAN KEEBLE and DOUGLAS HEADRICK are:

- i. WILLIAM W.[5] HEADRICK, b. October 10, 1891; d. June 20, 1943.
- ii. NANCY ANN HEADRICK, b. July 08, 1894; m. JOHN FIELDER.
- iii. DANIEL HOLSTON HEADRICK, b. July 19, 1896; d. 1926.
- iv. LOLA MARINDA HEADRICK, b. May 22, 1898; m. RAY NELSON JONES.
- v. MATTIE VICTORIA HEADRICK, b. August 23, 1900; d. 1915.
- vi. LOTTIE FAYE HEADRICK, b. July 21, 1904; m. SAM COWDEN.
- vii. LETIE MAE HEADRICK, b. July 21, 1904; m. JOHN CARETTO.

47. PRUDANCE[4] KEEBLE *(WILLIAM MCCUTCHIN[3], THOMAS[2], WILLIAM[1])* was born March 30, 1877, and died November 07, 1964. She married (1) CALEB E. FLOYD May 21, 1895 in Sevier County, Tennessee, son of ELI FLOYD and HETTIE KING. He was born March 15, 1876, and died July 04, 1946. She married (2) SAMUEL SCHMIDKE, JR. October 30, 1948 in Pomona California, son of SAMUEL SCHMIDKE and ANNA HOUSER. He was born November 14, 1881.

Children of PRUDANCE KEEBLE and CALEB FLOYD are:
   i.   ELI[5] MCCUTCHIN.FLOYD, b. December 03, 1895; m. CORRINE.
   ii. HETTIE BIRD FLOYD, b. November 06, 1900; d. April 12, 1912.
   iii. RICHARD B . FLOYD, b. April 14, 1902.

48. LABAN[4] KEEBLE *(WILLIAM MCCUTCHIN[3], THOMAS[2], WILLIAM[1])* was born October 12, 1879 in Sevier County Tennessee, and died September 20, 1953 in Blount memorial Hospital Maryville,Tenn.. He married (1) ALICE GRAHAM January 15, 1899 in Sevier County,Tennessee, daughter of GEORGE GRAHAM and ELIZA DIXON. She was born May 27, 1877, and died February 23, 1901 in Sevier County,Tennessee. He married (2) CATHERINE GARNER September 21, 1901 in Blount County,Tennessee, daughter of FRANCIS GARNER and SARAH DAVIS. She was born February 04, 1882, and died January 29, 1960 in Blount County,Tennessee.

More About LABAN KEEBLE:
Burial: Grandview Cemetery,Maryville,Tenn.

More About CATHERINE GARNER:
Burial: Grandview Cemetery,Maryville,Blount County,Tennessee

Child of LABAN KEEBLE and ALICE GRAHAM is:
   i.   JENNIE MAE[5] KEEBLE, b. May 15, 1900, Sevier County,Tennessee; d. January 30, 1997, Maryville,Tennessee; m. WILLIAM LEONARD GREDIG, July 08, 1920, Blount County,Tennessee; b. August 02, 1897; d. June 30, 1974.

Children of LABAN KEEBLE and CATHERINE GARNER are:
129.   ii.   SARAH ALICE[5] KEEBLE, b. October 09, 1902; d. April 06, 1957, Blount County,Tennessee.
130.   iii. WILLIAM KENNETH KEEBLE,SR., b. August 20, 1905; d. March 26, 1960, Blount County,Tennessee.
131.   iv.   CALEB ANDERSON KEEBLE, b. June 03, 1907, Blount County,Tennessee; d. February 12, 1972, Texas.
132.   v.   GEORGE LEONARD KEEBLE, b. February 07, 1909; d. July 10, 1974.
133.   vi.   CLYDE ECKLES KEEBLE, b. December 10, 1910; d. October 24, 1990.
134.   vii. CHARLES HOWARD KEEBLE, b. March 09, 1913; d. January 31, 1985.
135.   viii. NITA JANE KEEBLE, b. February 11, 1915.
136.   ix.   JOSEPH THOMAS KEEBLE, b. February 11, 1918; d. August 11, 2005.
137.   x.   JAMES LABAN KEEBLE,SR., b. April 04, 1921.
138.   xi.   ELLA MARIE KEEBLE, b. August 11, 1923.

49. MARINDA[4] KEEBLE *(WILLIAM MCCUTCHIN[3], THOMAS[2], WILLIAM[1])* was born January 01, 1882. She married JOHN CLINTON October 23, 1898, son of CALVIN CLINTON and MARY JENKINS. He was born March 09, 1876, and died January 04, 1935.

Children of MARINDA KEEBLE and JOHN CLINTON are:
   i.   ELECTA[5] CLINTON, b. 1900; m. UNKNOWN WARD.
   ii. LEONA CLINTON, m. JOHN MILLER.
   iii. WILLIAM CLINTON, b. 1901.
   iv. NANCY CLINTON, b. 1903.

50. ROBERT M.[4] FARMER *(ELIZA JANE[3] KEEBLE, THOMAS[2], WILLIAM[1])* was born April 26, 1869, and died December 16, 1939. He married ELIZABETH JANE KEEBLE May 29, 1890 in Blount Countty,Tennessee, daughter of MARION KEEBLE and MARTHA CLARK. She was born September 17, 1866, and died December 23, 1919.

Children of ROBERT FARMER and ELIZABETH KEEBLE are:
   i.   SAMUEL JOSEPH[5] FARMER.
   ii. NOLA MAE FARMER, m. RALEIGH NOE.
   iii. MARTHA CLARINDA FARMER, b. Abt. 1894; m. NOAH EVERETT.
   iv. CORA JANE FARMER, b. April 12, 1896; m. BENJAMIN H. WATERS.
   v.   WILLIAM HARVEY FARMER, b. Abt. 1899; m. GLADYS BRUBAKER.

     vi.   BENJAMIN FRANKLIN FARMER, b. Abt. 1900; m. ANNIE LAFTER.

    vii.   LEVI HENRY FARMER, b. Abt. 1902; m. EULA GRANGER.

   viii.   JAMES ROBERT FARMER, b. Abt. 1904; m. VOLA CURTIS.

    ix.   MICHAEL MARION FARMER, b. Abt. 1906; m. HAZEL BUTLER.

     x.   ARTHUR ALVIN FARMER, b. April 12, 1907; m. MARY BELLE PEDIGO.

    xi.   GRACE GERTRUDE FARMER, b. Abt. 1909; m. WALTER.

    xii.   JOHN MARTIN FARMER, m. MARGIE WELLS.

51. JOSEPH H.[4] FARMER *(ELIZA JANE[3] KEEBLE, THOMAS[2], WILLIAM[1])* was born March 01, 1871, and died November 13, 1953. He married MARY LOUISA KEEBLE July 18, 1894 in Blount Countty, Tennessee, daughter of MARION KEEBLE and MARTHA CLARK. She was born October 28, 1875, and died June 17, 1909.

Children of JOSEPH FARMER and MARY KEEBLE are:

     i.   WILEY H.[5] FARMER, b. July 26, 1895.

    ii.   ELLA G. FARMER, b. January 30, 1898; m. HOUSTON DUNLAP.

   iii.   CLEMMIE PRISCILLA.FARMER, b. August 31, 1900; m. CHARLES ANDERSON DUNLAP.

   iv.   LUCY L. FARMER, b. September 28, 1903; m. HOBART CAGLE.

    v.   LEONARD FARMER, m. (1) ETHELEEN; m. (2) SILVA; m. (3) MARGARET MITCHELL.

52. BERTHA[4] KEEBLE *(JOHN ANDERSON[3], THOMAS[2], WILLIAM[1])* was born September 15, 1883, and died October 19, 1950. She married WILLIAM THOMAS JACKSON December 02, 1910 in Blount County, Tennessee, son of GEORGE JACKSON and FRANKIE GARDNER. He was born October 25, 1891, and died February 14, 1954.

Children of BERTHA KEEBLE and WILLIAM JACKSON are:

     i.   EDNA[5] JACKSON, b. July 19, 1912; m. (1) GLEN ENDMAN; m. (2) JOHN O . MARTIN.

    ii.   MARIE JACKSON, b. July 12, 1914; m. JESS TIPTON.

53. LIDA[4] KEEBLE *(JOHN ANDERSON[3], THOMAS[2], WILLIAM[1])* was born Abt. 1889, and died August 13, 1967. She married CHARLIE HENRY September 17, 1921 in Blount County, Tennessee, son of JAMES HENRY and GENELA SLOAN. He was born October 14, 1895, and died November 05, 1968.

Children of LIDA KEEBLE and CHARLIE HENRY are:

     i.   STANLEY[5] HENRY, b. August 28, 1922; m. BEATRICE JANE HARRIS.

    ii.   IMODENE HENRY.

   iii.   MAX HENRY.

   iv.   GIRL HENRY.

54. JAMES EDWARD[4] KEEBLE *(JOHN ANDERSON[3], THOMAS[2], WILLIAM[1])* was born November 25, 1893, and died December 25, 1957. He married JESSIE SIMERLY in Hamilton County, Ohio, daughter of NATHANIEL SIMERLY and MARY STEELE. She was born November 1900, and died November 1970.

Child of JAMES KEEBLE and JESSIE SIMERLY is:

139.   i.   ROBERT GERALD[5] KEEBLE, b. September 16, 1937.

55. WILLIAM THOMAS[4] KEEBLE *(ALFRED HENRY[3], THOMAS[2], WILLIAM[1])* He married NORA WHISNANT.

Children of WILLIAM KEEBLE and NORA WHISNANT are:

     i.   FRED[5] KEEBLE, m. WATERHOUSE.

    ii.   CLARENCE HOUSTON KEEBLE, d. August 29, 1964, Johnson City, Tennessee; m. (1) UNKNOWN ROPER; m. (2) ELLA MARIE HAWK; m. (3) ELOISE CLAY.

   iii.   MYRTLE KEEBLE.

   iv.   HAZEL KEEBLE.

    v.   GLADYS KEEBLE.

56. JOHN ROBERT[4] KEEBLE *(ALFRED HENRY[3], THOMAS[2], WILLIAM[1])* was born 1880, and died June 08, 1940. He married LUCY LATHAM in McMinn County, Tennessee, daughter of ANDREW LATHAM and MATTIE HILL. She was born September 1886, and died May 23, 1976.

Children of JOHN KEEBLE and LUCY LATHAM are:

       i.   BEATRICE[5] KEEBLE, m. CARL K . BENNETT.
140.   ii. PAUL E. KEEBLE,SR., b. January 04, 1904; d. December 24, 1946.
      iii. THERMAN KEEBLE.
      iv. DEAN KEEBLE.
      v. ELIZABETH KEEBLE, m. EARL J. LAMB, November 17, 1923, Knox County, Tennessee.
      vi. IRENE KEEBLE.

57. CHARLES GARFIELD[4] KEEBLE *(ALFRED HENRY[3], THOMAS[2], WILLIAM[1])* was born August 11, 1881, and died July 09, 1949. He married (1) CALLIE L. HATCHER, daughter of VESTER HATCHER and LIZA PAINE. She was born August 18, 1918, and died September 07, 2005. He married (2) MARY MALINDA MAPLES July 22, 1902 in Blount County, Tennessee, daughter of REMOND MAPLES and NANCY JONES. She was born November 07, 1885, and died August 20, 1932. He married (3) ALICE HATCHER February 27, 1933 in Blount Countty, Tennessee, daughter of VESTER HATCHER and LIZA PAINE. She was born April 23, 1918, and died 1970.

Children of CHARLES KEEBLE and CALLIE HATCHER are:

141.   i. MILDRED[5] KEEBLE, b. June 05, 1936.
142.   ii. LEONARD KEEBLE, b. August 26, 1941.
143.   iii. DON KEEBLE.

Children of CHARLES KEEBLE and MARY MAPLES are:

144.   iv. MAUD[5] KEEBLE, b. May 05, 1903; d. November 08, 1977.
145.   v. LUNA LILLIAN KEEBLE, b. March 15, 1908; d. June 07, 1997.
146.   vi. ANNA ISABELLE KEEBLE, b. November 24, 1910.
147.   vii. HAZEL MAE KEEBLE, b. July 19, 1913.
148.   viii. WILLIAM ALFRED KEEBLE, b. May 05, 1917; d. November 02, 1983.
149.   ix. CHARLES ERNEST KEEBLE, b. December 26, 1920.
150.   x. JAMES ANDERSON KEEBLE, b. August 20, 1922.

Children of CHARLES KEEBLE and ALICE HATCHER are:

151.   xi. BETTY SUE[5] KEEBLE, b. April 21, 1934; d. March 10, 1994.
152.   xii. MARY MALINDA KEEBLE, b. April 24, 1936.
153.   xiii. POLLY ANN KEEBLE, b. August 24, 1939.
      xiv. BEN KEEBLE, b. October 01, 1941; d. November 10, 1992.

58. ELIZA JANE[4] KEEBLE *(ALFRED HENRY[3], THOMAS[2], WILLIAM[1])* was born March 26, 1886, and died December 16, 1934. She married MARSHALL GARNER October 14, 1903 in Loudon County, Tennessee, son of LEVI GARNER and LYDIA BARBRA. He was born December 27, 1884, and died 1972.

Children of ELIZA KEEBLE and MARSHALL GARNER are:

      i. MARTIN[5] GARNER, b. February 06, 1905.
      ii. ZORA GARNER, b. July 31, 1907; m. MOSS STOUT.
      iii. THEODORE VIRGIL GARNER, b. May 30, 1909; m. GERTRUDE KEENER.
      iv. LEON CHESTER GARNER, b. April 06, 1912; m. LUCILLE MAGILL.
      v. CALLIE VERSIE GARNER, b. July 02, 1914; m. GILBERT JOHNSTON.
      vi. MAGGIE MAE GARNER, b. September 15, 1917; m. THEODORE MARTIN.
      vii. HATTIE LEORE GARNER, b. January 24, 1921; m. W. B. CHAMBERLAIN.
      viii. HERBERT GLEN GARNER, b. March 05, 1924; d. February 07, 1926.

59. DOCIE DON[4] KEEBLE,SR. *(ALFRED HENRY[3], THOMAS[2], WILLIAM[1])* was born April 15, 1892, and died February 08, 1980. He married HAZEL MARIE MILLER December 26, 1914 in Blount Countty, Tennessee, daughter of JOHN

MILLER and BRENA EVERETT. She was born June 09, 1892, and died September 09, 1979.

Children of DOCIE KEEBLE and HAZEL MILLER are:
154.	i.	ALLISON HILDRED⁵ KEEBLE,SR., b. March 15, 1915; d. March 28, 2003.
	ii.	WILLIAM FRANK KEEBLE, b. January 25, 1917; d. February 22, 1917.
	iii.	DOCIE DON KEEBLE,JR., b. January 26, 1918; d. April 01, 1922.
155.	iv.	HAROLD VINCENT KEEBLE, b. November 30, 1920.
	v.	LLOYD MILLER KEEBLE, b. June 16, 1923; d. June 27, 1932.
156.	vi.	HELEN RUTH KEEBLE, b. September 07, 1925.
157.	vii.	JOHN CURTIS KEEBLE,SR., b. December 13, 1927.
158.	viii.	DOROTHY JEAN KEEBLE, b. January 31, 1930.

60. LUTITIA⁴ KEEBLE *(ALFRED HENRY³, THOMAS², WILLIAM¹)* was born October 17, 1894. She married JAMES HENSLEY KERLEY August 20, 1910, son of JACKSON KERLEY and MARGARET DRINNEN. He was born October 30, 1882.

Children of LUTITIA KEEBLE and JAMES KERLEY are:
- i. NELLIE MAY⁵ KERLEY, b. June 03, 1915; m. OREN DENNIS CARR.
- ii. MILDRED IRENE KERLEY, b. September 29, 1919; m. DONALD LUCINS PAYNE.
- iii. WILLIAM W. KERLEY, b. September 19, 1922; m. MARY CLANCY.
- iv. BIRL KERLEY, b. March 20, 1924; m. ERNESTINE BROWN.
- v. CHARLOTTE ANN KERLEY, b. September 01, 1926; m. EUGENE RYALL.

61. NANCY ANN⁴ KEEBLE *(SAMUEL³, MANLY², WILLIAM¹)* was born August 06, 1866, and died December 14, 1930. She married JORDAN ANDREW HAYNES May 07, 1896 in Blount Countty,Tennessee, son of HENRY HAYNES and ELIZA RULE. He was born April 05, 1849, and died August 14, 1917.

Children of NANCY KEEBLE and JORDAN HAYNES are:
159.	i.	CHARLES EGBERT⁵ KEEBLE, b. March 28, 1893; d. October 09, 1927.
	ii.	SARAH HAYNES.
	iii.	EARL HAYNES.
	iv.	ELI HAYNES.

62. MARY ELIZABETH⁴ KEEBLE *(SAMUEL³, MANLY², WILLIAM¹)* was born November 25, 1867, and died January 22, 1898. She married TILFORD JOHN REAGAN October 17, 1889 in Blount Countty,Tennessee, son of JAMES REAGAN and LAVINA ROGERS. He was born November 13, 1865, and died July 19, 1956.

Children of MARY KEEBLE and TILFORD REAGAN are:
- i. DOLLY BELLE⁵ REAGAN, b. August 15, 1890; d. 1890.
- ii. EDWARD REAGAN, b. May 30, 1892; d. 1892.
- iii. OMER REAGAN, b. August 16, 1893.
- iv. NORA ESTER REAGAN, b. June 04, 1895; d. 1895.

63. PLEASANT⁴ KEEBLE *(SAMUEL³, MANLY², WILLIAM¹)* was born July 01, 1869, and died April 13, 1946. He married MARGARET ANN BARBRA November 26, 1893 in Blount Countty,Tennessee, daughter of WILLIAM BARBRA and SARAH BAKER. She was born February 01, 1872, and died December 07, 1956.

Children of PLEASANT KEEBLE and MARGARET BARBRA are:
160.	i.	EDGAR LAWSON⁵ KEEBLE, b. August 23, 1894.
	ii.	GERTRUE ESTEL KEEBLE, b. August 11, 1895; m. WILLIAM RUSSELL HOLLIINGSWORTH, August 21, 1922, Blount Countty,Tennessee; b. June 22, 1877; d. October 06, 1957.
161.	iii.	ANDY RICHARD KEEBLE, b. February 21, 1897; d. August 01, 1985.
162.	iv.	SAMUELL WILLIAM KEEBLE, b. November 29, 1900.
163.	v.	ROY ELMER KEEBLE, b. June 01, 1903.
164.	vi.	OTIS VIRGIL KEEBLE, b. October 29, 1908; d. February 28, 1968.

64. REBECCA JANE[4] KEEBLE *(SAMUEL[3], MANLY[2], WILLIAM[1])* was born February 27, 1871, and died January 23, 1964. She married LOUIS ANDERSON BARBRA August 04, 1892 in Blount Countty, Tennessee, son of WILLIAM BARBRA and SARAH BAKER. He was born May 15, 1867, and died October 30, 1951.

Children of REBECCA KEEBLE and LOUIS BARBRA are:
- i. INA[5] BARBRA, b. June 16, 1893; m. SAM HENRY.
- ii. IRA BARBRA, b. January 11, 1896; m. (1) MARY GREDIG; m. (2) ESSIE PARKER.
- iii. LUCY BARBRA, b. November 18, 1899; m. DALE (DOLE) WHITEHEAD.
- iv. SADIE BARBRA, b. September 15, 1902; m. OTHA MCGILL.
- v. OTHA BARBRA, b. January 13, 1907; m. STELLA RASAR.
- vi. VIRGIL BARBRA, b. July 20, 1909; m. HAZEL HAUN.
- vii. EULA BARBRA, b. September 10, 1915; m. MILLARD CAYLOR.

65. SARAH[4] KEEBLE *(SAMUEL[3], MANLY[2], WILLIAM[1])* was born December 31, 1873, and died May 08, 1958. She married ALBERT WILLIAM BARBRA December 14, 1910 in Blount County, Tennessee, son of WILLIAM BARBRA and SARAH BAKER. He was born December 31, 1875, and died August 30, 1961.

Child of SARAH KEEBLE and ALBERT BARBRA is:
- i. MANERVA[5] BARBRA, b. July 26, 1912; m. A.CONLEY TARWATER.

66. EVALINE[4] KEEBLE *(SAMUEL[3], MANLY[2], WILLIAM[1])* was born November 17, 1877, and died December 10, 1971. She married ELIJAH ANDREW DUNLAP December 15, 1895 in Blount Countty, Tennessee, son of ANDREW DUNLAP and MARY HATCHER. He was born March 03, 1873, and died February 17, 1958.

Children of EVALINE KEEBLE and ELIJAH DUNLAP are:
- i. JENNIE[5] DUNLAP, b. 1897; m. ALBERT WILLIAMS.
- ii. JOHN DUNLAP, b. 1901; m. BESS BLEVINS.
- iii. DORA DUNLAP, b. 1905; m. HOUSTON WILLIAMS.
- iv. ROBERT A. DUNLAP, b. July 08, 1917; m. MARIAN RAY.

67. MARTHA CAROLINE[4] KEEBLE *(SAMUEL[3], MANLY[2], WILLIAM[1])* was born February 07, 1880, and died October 07, 1966. She married SAMUEL W. HUMPHREYS June 13, 1909 in Blount Countty, Tennessee, son of JOSEPH HUMPHREYS and MARY CARROLL. He was born April 10, 1885, and died March 01, 1968.

Child of MARTHA KEEBLE and SAMUEL HUMPHREYS is:
- i. JANE ANN[5] HUMPHREYS, b. April 23, 1910; d. April 17, 1994.

68. JOHN RICHARD[4] KEEBLE *(SAMUEL[3], MANLY[2], WILLIAM[1])* was born August 13, 1884, and died September 02, 1963. He married MARY CLEMENTINE LATHAM October 11, 1906 in McMinn County, Tennessee, daughter of JOHN LATHAM and MILLIE HOLLYFIELD. She was born October 02, 1883, and died January 13, 1961.

Children of JOHN KEEBLE and MARY LATHAM are:
165.	i.	MILLIE JANE[5] KEEBLE, b. July 18, 1907; d. May 01, 1981.
166.	ii.	BURL ROBERT KEEBLE, b. January 10, 1909; d. January 16, 1973.
	iii.	SAMUEL EGBERT KEEBLE, b. September 07, 1910; d. December 01, 1969; m. WILLIE STERLING.
167.	iv.	RAY ELIJAH KEEBLE, SR., b. April 16, 1912; d. November 27, 1965.
	v.	BEULAH MAE KEEBLE, b. January 17, 1915; d. June 06, 1915.
	vi.	JOHNNY ELMER KEEBLE, b. May 11, 1916; d. February 01, 1917.
168.	vii.	PAUL ANDREWS KEEBLE, b. April 04, 1918; d. January 15, 2003.
169.	viii.	MYRTLE ANNIE ELLER KEEBLE, b. February 02, 1922.

69. NELLIE ARIZONA[4] KEEBLE *(PLEASANT MARION[3], MANLY[2], WILLIAM[1])* was born October 28, 1871, and died April 03, 1954. She married (1) HIRAM P. DUNLAP September 14, 1892, son of CAROLINE DUNLAP. He was born April 22, 1868, and died July 16, 1895. She married (2) WILLIAM THOMAS VINEYARD June 02, 1907, son of JORDAN VINEYARD and S.LAVINA FLANAGIN. He was born August 07, 1878.

Children of NELLIE KEEBLE and HIRAM DUNLAP are:
    i.   ELIZABETH CAROLINE[5] DUNLAP, b. October 01, 1893; m. JAMES WILEY DAVIS.
    ii.   MAUD ESTELLE DUNLAP, b. September 21, 1895; d. September 28, 1896.

70. WILLIAM HOUSTON[4] KEEBLE *(PLEASANT MARION[3], MANLY[2], WILLIAM[1])* was born May 09, 1873, and died June 03, 1963. He married NELLE MCSPADDEN August 20, 1907. She was born January 20, 1876, and died November 15, 1975.

Child of WILLIAM KEEBLE and NELLE MCSPADDEN is:
    i.   HELEN ELIZABETH[5] KEEBLE, b. March 10, 1910; m. ROBERT LESLIE SCRIBNER, June 09, 1956, Hanover County,Virginia; b. May 13, 1912; d. September 26, 1981.

71. JOHN EDMUND[4] KEEBLE *(PLEASANT MARION[3], MANLY[2], WILLIAM[1])* was born November 07, 1877, and died October 17, 1940. He married EFFIE CRAYTON AMBRISTER March 12, 1908 in Blount Countty,Tennessee, daughter of JOHN AMBRISTER and JANE MCTEER. She was born March 28, 1881, and died May 06, 1966.

Children of JOHN KEEBLE and EFFIE AMBRISTER are:
    i.   KATHLEEN KEITH[5] KEEBLE, b. August 28, 1909; d. February 03, 1985.
    ii.   DELSIA HAZEL KEEBLE, b. July 17, 1912; d. February 23, 1926.
170.   iii.   HAZEN KEEBLE, b. July 17, 1912.
171.   iv.   EARL ELGERT KEEBLE, b. January 18, 1916.
    v.   MARGARET ELAINE KEEBLE, b. September 02, 1923; d. January 01, 1924.

72. ANDREW ELMER[4] KEEBLE *(PLEASANT MARION[3], MANLY[2], WILLIAM[1])* was born September 11, 1881, and died July 07, 1969. He married ROVA WHITE April 30, 1918 in Knox County,Tennessee, daughter of JAMES WHITE and REBECCA IDOL. She was born December 07, 1885, and died July 04, 1973.

Child of ANDREW KEEBLE and ROVA WHITE is:
    i.   ELEANOR LOUISE[5] KEEBLE, b. September 15, 1922; d. October 15, 2005; m. JOSEPH MCCAMMON GUESS, August 07, 1948, Knox County,Tennessee; b. January 19, 1926; d. March 27, 1980.

73. NORA ELIZABETH[4] KEEBLE *(PLEASANT MARION[3], MANLY[2], WILLIAM[1])* was born June 20, 1884, and died June 13, 1962. She married J.WALTER WHITE August 03, 1918, son of JOSEPH WHITE and CLARINDA MONDAY. He was born July 08, 1883, and died April 07, 1963.

Children of NORA KEEBLE and J.WALTER WHITE are:
    i.   RUTH ESTELLE[5] WHITE, b. September 16, 1919.
    ii.   BURL KEEBLE WHITE, b. July 10, 1921; m. CLEO TREECE.

74. ANNA RACHEL[4] KEEBLE *(PLEASANT MARION[3], MANLY[2], WILLIAM[1])* was born October 17, 1889, and died April 26, 1952. She married WILLIAM GUSS DAVIS September 23, 1913 in Knox County,Tennessee, son of ANTHONY DAVIS and SALLY KENNEDY. He was born November 06, 1885, and died May 07, 1955.

Children of ANNA KEEBLE and WILLIAM DAVIS are:
    i.   LOIS ELIZABETH[5] DAVIS, b. March 03, 1915; m. BIDDLE HUTCHINS.
    ii.   DOROTHY KENNEDY DAVIS, b. December 26, 1919; m. PAUL TUCK.

75. WILLIAM ARTHUR[4] KEEBLE,SR. *(RICHARD HENRY[3], MANLY[2], WILLIAM[1])* was born April 24, 1878. He married (1) LUCY WHITE. She was born April 15, 1885. He married (2) MARTHA CLEMONS WILLIAMS KEEBLE July 05, 1942 in Blount Countty,Tennessee, daughter of MOSE WILLIAMS and TENNESSEE BROADY. She was born

December 17, 1884, and died May 25, 1952.

Children of WILLIAM KEEBLE and LUCY WHITE are:
- i. MAUDE ELAINE[5] KEEBLE, b. April 15, 1906; m. BEDFORD, Norman Oklahoma.
- ii. HELEN KEEBLE, b. March 17, 1908.
- iii. WILLIAM ARTHUR KEEBLE, JR., b. December 20, 1911.
- iv. ELMA KEEBLE, b. October 11, 1914.
- v. HAROLD KEEBLE, b. July 06, 1916.
- vi. FLORENCE MARIE KEEBLE, b. March 20, 1919.
- vii. VIRGINIA ELIZABETH KEEBLE, b. July 17, 1924.
- viii. EDYTHA ELLEN KEEBLE, b. June 25, 1927.

76. SAMUEL WILEY[4] KEEBLE *(RICHARD HENRY[3], MANLY[2], WILLIAM[1])* was born April 14, 1881, and died May 18, 1935. He married MARTHA CLEMONS WILLIAMS September 10, 1901 in Blount Countty, Tennessee, daughter of MOSE WILLIAMS and TENNESSEE BROADY. She was born December 17, 1884, and died May 25, 1952.

Children of SAMUEL KEEBLE and MARTHA WILLIAMS are:
172.	i.	ELLEN TENNESSEE[5] KEEBLE, b. July 28, 1902; d. March 10, 1991.
173.	ii.	NORA FLORENCE KEEBLE, b. August 08, 1904; d. August 07, 1976.
174.	iii.	MAE BELLE KEEBLE, b. October 05, 1906; d. March 23, 1999.
175.	iv.	FLORA ELIZABETH KEEBLE, b. September 02, 1908; d. April 14, 1994.
176.	v.	SARAH MAUDE KEEBLE, b. October 02, 1910; d. September 25, 2002.
177.	vi.	WILLIAM THOMAS KEEBLE, b. December 02, 1912.
178.	vii.	EDGAR KEEBLE, b. November 20, 1915.
179.	viii.	EDNA KEEBLE, b. November 20, 1915; d. May 18, 1985.
180.	ix.	LLOYD CATLETT KEEBLE, b. December 24, 1918; d. January 01, 1983.
181.	x.	ROBERT PAUL KEEBLE, b. January 15, 1921.
182.	xi.	SAMUEL CARL KEEBLE, b. November 24, 1923.
183.	xii.	BERNICE KEEBLE, b. January 18, 1927.

77. IZORA MAUDE[4] KEEBLE *(RICHARD HENRY[3], MANLY[2], WILLIAM[1])* was born September 07, 1890, and died December 26, 1956. She married SIMEON BRADLEY December 24, 1909 in Flint, Michigan, son of NELSON BRADLEY and EUCEBIA OSTRANDER. He was born January 17, 1885, and died October 26, 1941.

Children of IZORA KEEBLE and SIMEON BRADLEY are:
- i. HELEN[5] BRADLEY, m. TERMINI.
- ii. OPAL MAUDE BRADLEY, m. ARNOLD GROOMS.
- iii. LAUDRA BRADLEY, m. HAMILTON.

78. ELIZABETH JANE[4] KEEBLE *(MARION[3], RICHARD PORTER[2], WILLIAM[1])* was born September 17, 1866, and died December 23, 1919. She married ROBERT M. FARMER May 29, 1890 in Blount Countty, Tennessee, son of ELI FARMER and ELIZA KEEBLE. He was born April 26, 1869, and died December 16, 1939.

Children are listed above under (50) Robert M. Farmer.

79. JOHN ELLISON[4] KEEBLE *(MARION[3], RICHARD PORTER[2], WILLIAM[1])* was born August 11, 1869, and died April 16, 1933. He married CATHERINE JANE HEADRICK September 06, 1889 in Blount Countty, Tennessee, daughter of WILLIAM HEADFRICK and SARAH WILLIAMS. She was born September 06, 1873, and died July 18, 1957.

Children of JOHN KEEBLE and CATHERINE HEADRICK are:
184.	i.	MARTHA JANE[5] KEEBLE, b. July 03, 1891; d. February 25, 1963.
	ii.	WRIGHT KEEBLE, b. November 20, 1893; d. August 22, 1946; m. FLORENCE, Abt. 1920.
	iii.	SARAH ANN KEEBLE, b. November 04, 1895; d. August 01, 1973; m. J.PAUL LEAMAN, March 06, 1950; b. May 16, 1900.
185.	iv.	JOHN MARION KEEBLE, b. July 22, 1898; d. May 19, 1960.

80. MARGARET CLEMENTINE⁴ KEEBLE *(MARION³, RICHARD PORTER², WILLIAM¹)* was born March 08, 1871, and died January 18, 1919. She married SAMUEL JACKSON GAMBLE June 15, 1890 in Blount Countty,Tennessee, son of JOHN GAMBLE and MALVINA WILLIAMS. He was born June 20, 1868, and died June 26, 1920.

Children of MARGARET KEEBLE and SAMUEL GAMBLE are:
- i. LILLIE JANE⁵ GAMBLE, b. April 05, 1891; m. ASHLEY THOMAS BRADLEY.
- ii. WILLIAM HOUSTON GAMBLE, b. September 15, 1893.
- iii. MALVINA MAE GAMBLE, b. February 06, 1896; m. BOYD E. LAYTON.
- iv. JOHN EDWARD GAMBLE, b. August 11, 1898; m. ETHEL BROWNING.
- v. MARY GEORGIA GAMBLE, b. January 20, 1901; m. CARL HOMER DUNN.
- vi. CARRIE VICTORIA GAMBLE, b. January 20, 1901; m. SAM MITCHELL.
- vii. MARTHA GERTRUDE GAMBLE, b. March 20, 1904; m. WADE MOFFETT.
- viii. LENNIE LEE GAMBLE, b. July 31, 1906; m. RAY BENNETT.
- ix. RENE ARELLE GAMBLE, b. May 12, 1910; m. LOUIS JONES.

81. EDWARD GEORGE⁴ KEEBLE,SR. *(MARION³, RICHARD PORTER², WILLIAM¹)* was born April 04, 1872, and died February 15, 1939. He married (1) MARY CATHERINE HATCHER September 09, 1894 in Blount Countty,Tennessee, daughter of JOSEPH HATCHER and REBECCA WALKER. She was born April 10, 1874, and died January 17, 1934. He married (2) ELLA WHITE ROYSE KLEWISH September 24, 1919 in Redwood City,California, daughter of JOHN ROYCE and REBECCA STEVENS. She died June 20, 1942.

Children of EDWARD KEEBLE and MARY HATCHER are:
- 186.   i. ANNA PEARL⁵ KEEBLE, b. August 07, 1895; d. June 02, 1963.
- 187.   ii. REBECCA JANE KEEBLE, b. August 08, 1897; d. May 14, 1961.
-         iii. WILLIE KEEBLE, b. April 21, 1901; d. April 24, 1901.
-         iv. CHARLIE KEEBLE, b. June 01, 1902; d. June 01, 1902.
- 188.   v. EDWARD GEORGE KEEBLE,JR., b. May 08, 1903; d. July 15, 1962.
- 189.   vi. FLORENCE JOSEPHINE KEEBLE, b. February 25, 1906; d. December 07, 1983.
-         vii. MARTIN JESSIE KEEBLE, b. January 05, 1908; d. March 09, 1986; m. ASTRID VICTORIA SWANSON, November 24, 1936; b. November 05, 1908.

82. MATILDA CLARINDA⁴ KEEBLE *(MARION³, RICHARD PORTER², WILLIAM¹)* was born June 01, 1874, and died September 29, 1954. She married WILLIAM JACK HATCHER October 13, 1894 in Blount County, Tennessee, son of JOSEPH HATCHER and REBECCA WALKER. He was born February 06, 1872, and died July 15, 1942.

Children of MATILDA KEEBLE and WILLIAM HATCHER are:
- i. LENNIE⁵ HATCHER, b. December 15, 1892; m. LINK SULLIVAN.
- ii. ROSE HATCHER, b. December 12, 1896; m. MATTHEW GARNER.
- iii. ALEX HATCHER, b. May 12, 1901; m. (1) BEULAH COLLINS; m. (2) ANNA GREEN.
- iv. MARTHA HATCHER, b. October 05, 1903; m. JAMES HEADRICK.
- v. CHARLES HATCHER, b. May 12, 1906; m. SARAH MCNIELLY.
- vi. HOMER HATCHER, b. December 30, 1908; m. IVA HATCHER.
- vii. EDNA GERTRUDE HATCHER, b. May 05, 1911; m. CHESTER BURNS.
- viii. FRED MARTIN HATCHER, b. July 26, 1914; m. ANNA MAE BIVENS.
- ix. WADE HOUSTON HATCHER, b. May 03, 1916; m. (1) RUTH GAINER; m. (2) JO ANN HENDERSON.

83. MARY LOUISA⁴ KEEBLE *(MARION³, RICHARD PORTER², WILLIAM¹)* was born October 28, 1875, and died June 17, 1909. She married JOSEPH H. FARMER July 18, 1894 in Blount Countty,Tennessee, son of ELI FARMER and ELIZA KEEBLE. He was born March 01, 1871, and died November 13, 1953.

Children are listed above under (51) Joseph H. Farmer.

84. MARION PRISCILLA⁴ KEEBLE *(MARION³, RICHARD PORTER², WILLIAM¹)* was born September 05, 1878, and died July 15, 1965. She married RILEY A. GRAVES March 29, 1895 in Blount Countty,Tennessee, son of RILEY GRAVES and ELIZABETH WILSON. He was born August 30, 1866, and died January 21, 1955.

Children of MARION KEEBLE and RILEY GRAVES are:
- i.   MARTIN EDWARD[5] GRAVES, b. September 22, 1908; m. MAE NUCHOLS.
- ii. SINA EDNA GRAVES, b. September 22, 1908; m. WILLIAM TOYE SHIELDS.

85. MARTHA ADALINE[4] KEEBLE *(MARION[3], RICHARD PORTER[2], WILLIAM[1])* was born September 21, 1882, and died September 02, 1971. She married WARREN STANFORD PERKINS July 04, 1911, son of ISAAC PERKINS and CAROLINE COLEMAN. He was born March 11, 1866, and died May 31, 1959.

Children of MARTHA KEEBLE and WARREN PERKINS are:
- i.   CHARLES ALVIN[5] PERKINS, b. May 27, 1912; d. June 26, 1997; m. (1) ALICE LAWSON; m. (2) THELMA BEAVER.
- ii. MARION STANFORD PERKINS, b. February 20, 1914; m. PHYLLIS MARIE JENSEN.

86. MARY JANE[4] KEEBLE *(JOHN[3], WALTER HARRISON[2], WILLIAM[1])* was born 1872. She married OMER HENSLEY.

Child of MARY KEEBLE and OMER HENSLEY is:
- i.   MAUDE[5] HENSLEY, m. STEPHENSON.

87. STEPHEN[4] KEEBLE, SR. *(NANCY[3], WALTER HARRISON[2], WILLIAM[1])* was born May 16, 1880, and died November 10, 1945. He married LOYE ANNIS DYER December 08, 1901 in Blount Countty, Tennessee, daughter of JAMES DYER and PHOEBE WILLOCKS. She was born May 05, 1884, and died September 15, 1937.

Children of STEPHEN KEEBLE and LOYE DYER are:
	i.	ANNAS[5] KEEBLE, b. November 13, 1902; d. December 22, 1902.
190.	ii.	VOLA KEEBLE, b. January 28, 1905; d. November 19, 1976.
191.	iii.	CECIL KEEBLE, b. December 25, 1907; d. May 19, 1975.
192.	iv.	CARA LONNIE KEEBLE, b. April 23, 1911; d. July 23, 1992.
193.	v.	ISA MAE KEEBLE, b. January 13, 1914; d. September 02, 2002.
	vi.	HAZEL BEATRICE KEEBLE, b. October 14, 1917; d. January 02, 1918.
194.	vii.	ROY VIRGIL KEEBLE, b. June 21, 1919; d. September 05, 1996.
	viii.	STEPHEN KEEBLE, JR., b. May 27, 1924; d. November 18, 1942.

88. MARY CALEDONIA[4] KEEBLE *(SAMUEL[3], WALTER HARRISON[2], WILLIAM[1])* was born September 17, 1875, and died April 09, 1960. She married SAMUEL HAMILTON.

Child of MARY KEEBLE and SAMUEL HAMILTON is:
- i.   PAUL[5] HAMILTON, d. February 14, 1969.

89. PEARL[4] KEEBLE *(JANE[3], WALTER HARRISON[2], WILLIAM[1])* died September 1956. She married WILLIAM FERGUSON in Knox County, Tennessee. He died 1956.

Children of PEARL KEEBLE and WILLIAM FERGUSON are:
- i.   CHARLES[5] FERGUSON, m. PURKEY.
- ii. HAZEL FERGUSON, m. CLABOUGH.
- iii. JUANITA FERGUSON, m. JAMES PAYNE.
- iv. MARY HELEN FERGUSON.

90. WILLIAM MARTIN[4] KEEBLE *(JANE[3], WALTER HARRISON[2], WILLIAM[1])* was born April 08, 1885, and died July 10, 1957. He married MARTHA FLORENCE SUMMEY July 18, 1907 in Blount County, Tennessee, daughter of GEORGE SUMMEY and MAE RAMSEY. She was born December 02, 1893.

Children of WILLIAM KEEBLE and MARTHA SUMMEY are:
- i.   MANDA LYNN[5] KEEBLE.

195. ii.   VELVA OELA KEEBLE, b. August 05, 1912.
      iii. JAMES RAY KEEBLE, b. March 02, 1914.
196. iv.   HULA VIRGINIA KEEBLE, b. March 13, 1919.
197. v.   GEORGE WASHINGTON KEEBLE, b. November 07, 1920.
198. vi.   HELEN RUTH KEEBLE, b. December 28, 1922.
      vii. FRANKLIN BYRON KEEBLE, b. February 10, 1927; d. September 23, 1964; m. CHARLOTTE, Cullman
            County, Alabama.

91. JOHN JASON[4] KEEBLE *(JANE[3], WALTER HARRISON[2], WILLIAM[1])* was born May 29, 1895, and died February 09, 1971. He married (1) HETTIE GIBSON December 24, 1913 in Knox County, Tennessee. He married (2) DELLA RABY CASE July 17, 1936 in Atlanta Georgia, daughter of WILLIAM CASE and WILLIAMS. She was born 1896, and died March 03, 1962. He married (3) LINNIE POE SHULAR July 19, 1966 in Knox County, Tennessee, daughter of WILLIAM POE and MARY BARGER. She was born March 23, 1888.

Child of JOHN KEEBLE and HETTIE GIBSON is:
      i.   CATHERINE ALICE[5] KEEBLE.

92. CATHERINE ALICE ARIZONA[4] KEEBLE *(JANE[3], WALTER HARRISON[2], WILLIAM[1])* was born March 10, 1904. She married (1) HERMAN THOMPSON April 17, 1915 in Blount County, Tennessee, son of JAMES THOMPSON and SUSAN. She married (2) WILLIAM MARTIN WELLS March 23, 1925 in Knox County, Tennessee, son of RAYMOND WELLS and ADA SHOMAN. He was born December 25, 1900.

Children of CATHERINE KEEBLE and WILLIAM WELLS are:
      i.   IDA ELOISE[5] WELLS, b. May 05, 1922.
      ii.   WILLIAM EDWARD WELLS, b. October 04, 1924.
      iii. JEWEL EVELYN WELLS, b. March 11, 1926.
      iv.   MARY LEE WELLS, b. February 14, 1928.
      v.   DIXIE IRETA WELLS, b. October 14, 1930.
      vi.   DARREL ALFRED WELLS, b. September 11, 1932.
      vii. ALLEN CARROLL WELLS, b. September 11, 1932.
      viii. THOMAS FARRELL WELLS, b. September 01, 1934.
      ix.   JAMES LARRY WELLS, b. February 20, 1936.
      x.   PATRICIA NORMA WELLS, b. February 28, 1938.

Generation No. 5

93. GEORGIA HOUSTON[5] KEEBLE *(JOHN HOUSTON[4], JAMES H.[3], THOMAS[2], WILLIAM[1])* was born September 30, 1882, and died April 23, 1911. She married DAVID J. MEREDITH November 24, 1898.

Children of GEORGIA KEEBLE and DAVID MEREDITH are:
      i.   THELMA[6] MEREDITH.
      ii.   WILLIAM MEREDITH.
      iii. ODETTA MEREDITH.
      iv.   KEEBLE C. MEREDITH.
      v.   ROYAL MEREDITH.

94. JAMES TAYLOR[5] KEEBLE *(JOHN HOUSTON[4], JAMES H.[3], THOMAS[2], WILLIAM[1])* was born February 12, 1867, and died May 20, 1923. He married LOU EMMA WARNER December 27, 1894 in Henderson County, Texas, daughter of JOHN WARNER and LOUISA SMITH. She was born March 28, 1880, and died December 22, 1941.

Children of JAMES KEEBLE and LOU WARNER are:
      i.   JESSIE MAE[6] KEEBLE, b. January 21, 1895; d. June 13, 1972; m. HENRY L. SANDERS, February 02, 1913.
      ii.   JOHN TAYLOR KEEBLE, b. August 18, 1896; d. July 25, 1953; m. (1) VELMA COOK; m. (2) EDNA
            MCDONALD, September 07, 1918.

            Notes for JOHN TAYLOR KEEBLE:

John Taylor Keeble had two wives. #1 Edna McDonald
#2 Velma Cook

    iii. ALFORD DAVID KEEBLE, b. August 14, 1899; d. October 31, 1945.

    Notes for ALFORD DAVID KEEBLE:
    Alford David Keeble didnot marry.

    iv. JAMES JEROME KEEBLE, b. September 14, 1901.

    Notes for JAMES JEROME KEEBLE:
    Never married

    v. MARY LORENE KEEBLE, b. June 01, 1903; d. 1972; m. JESSE A. RECER, August 16, 1919.
    vi. MATTIE VERA KEEBLE, b. July 13, 1905; m. COMMODORE PEERY GLOVER.
    vii. VERGIE LOUISA KEEBLE, b. December 12, 1907; m. JOSEPH LEONARD GLOVER, February 18, 1923.
199. viii. LOUISA NEOMA KEEBLE, b. January 12, 1910.
    ix. JOSEPH SAMUEL KEEBLE, b. April 10, 1912; d. 1914.
    x. IDA LILLIAN KEEBLE, b. May 17, 1914; m. SAMUEL Q. SPINKS, September 27, 1930.
    xi. ALTA MARIE KEEBLE, b. April 18, 1917; d. 1917.
    xii. EUGENE DAUFUL KEEBLE, b. April 05, 1918; m. VICKY (UNKNOWN).
    xiii. WILLIAM PERRY KEEBLE, b. November 09, 1921.

95. JOHN DAVID[5] KEEBLE *(JOHN HOUSTON[4], JAMES H.[3], THOMAS[2], WILLIAM[1])* was born July 09, 1869, and died June 14, 1897. He married SARAH ADDIE HOBBS August 13, 1893.

Children of JOHN KEEBLE and SARAH HOBBS are:
    i. JESSIE JEWEL[6] KEEBLE, b. June 20, 1894.
    ii. JOHN KEEBLE.
    iii. DAVID M. KEEBLE, b. December 03, 1897; d. February 06, 1899.

96. WILLIAM LAFAYETTE[5] KEEBLE *(JOHN HOUSTON[4], JAMES H.[3], THOMAS[2], WILLIAM[1])* was born June 02, 1872, and died June 20, 1946. He married PERMELIA ANN WARNER June 22, 1894, daughter of JOHN WARNER and LOUISA SMITH. She was born September 11, 1877, and died January 1971.

Notes for PERMELIA ANN WARNER:
She was the daughter of John Calhoun Warner and Louisa Matilda Smith

Children of WILLIAM KEEBLE and PERMELIA WARNER are:
    i. SAM HOUSTON[6] KEEBLE, b. June 06, 1896; d. February 21, 1944; m. JESSIE MAHONE, May 30, 1915.
200. ii. HOMER PRESTON KEEBLE, b. August 10, 1898; d. June 12, 1963.
201. iii. WILLIE FAE KEEBLE, b. December 25, 1900; d. January 1988.
202. iv. JOSEPH KEEBLE, b. April 07, 1903; d. March 13, 1963.

97. MARY CAROLINE[5] KEEBLE *(JOHN HOUSTON[4], JAMES H.[3], THOMAS[2], WILLIAM[1])* was born July 09, 1874, and died October 07, 1957. She married JAMES F. MEREDITH December 18, 1895. He was born September 19, 1867, and died July 06, 1944.

Children of MARY KEEBLE and JAMES MEREDITH are:
    i. JAMES VURTON[6] MEREDITH, b. March 10, 1897.
    ii. LOCKIE ARENTHA MEREDITH, b. August 10, 1903.
    iii. ALFA MARY MAY MEREDITH, b. June 02, 1908.

98. JAMES THOMAS[5] KEEBLE *(TAYLOR S.[4], JAMES H.[3], THOMAS[2], WILLIAM[1])* was born December 19, 1874, and died August 14, 1956. He married EMMA (SIS) KNIGHT.

Children of JAMES KEEBLE and EMMA KNIGHT are:
203. i. SALLY LOU⁶ KEEBLE, b. April 15, 1903.
204. ii. ANNIE MAUDE, KEEBLE, b. July 28, 1907.
      iii. BILLY KEEBLE.
      iv. CURTIS KEEBLE.
      v. JIMMY KEEBLE.

99. KATE MARVILLE⁵ KEEBLE *(TAYLOR S.⁴, JAMES H.³, THOMAS², WILLIAM¹)* was born November 06, 1876, and died April 1946. She married JOHN WILLIAM SWANN May 10, 1903 in Randolph County, Alabama.

Children of KATE KEEBLE and JOHN SWANN are:
      i. MYRTIE LEE⁶ SWANN, b. December 25, 1903.
      ii. GERTRUDE SWANN, b. April 10, 1905; m. PETE WORKMAN.
      iii. ARTHUR SWANN, b. December 25, 1906.
      iv. S.T. SWANN, b. August 28, 1908; m. ANNIE LEE EARLES.
      v. JESSE SWANN, b. February 15, 1910; m. THELMA ELIZABETH STILL.
      vi. ORA M. SWANN, b. September 19, 1911; m. (1) ROY LESTER; m. (2) ROY MOODY.
      vii. JOHN D. SWANN, b. June 02, 1913; m. JESSIE MAE TREDWELL.
      viii. KATIE SWANN, b. April 11, 1916; m. JAMES DENSON KENT.
      ix. SADIE SWANN, b. January 27, 1919; m. WYATT LEE POTTS.

100. J.D.⁵ KEEBLE *(TAYLOR S.⁴, JAMES H.³, THOMAS², WILLIAM¹)* was born November 07, 1878, and died December 30, 1938. He married CORA SEXTON 1894.

Children of J.D. KEEBLE and CORA SEXTON are:
205. i. LULA MAE⁶ KEEBLE, b. October 30, 1896.
206. ii. EUNICE INEZ KEEBLE, b. April 10, 1898.
207. iii. REUBEN TAYLOR KEEBLE.
208. iv. BARNEY TRESSFORD KEEBLE, b. January 03, 1904.
209. v. ROSA BELLE KEEBLE, b. February 28, 1907.

101. SAMUEL E.⁵ KEEBLE *(TAYLOR S.⁴, JAMES H.³, THOMAS², WILLIAM¹)* was born February 13, 1880, and died October 27, 1924. He married (1) PEARL VESTA SEXTON December 02, 1902 in Randolph County, Alabama. She was born March 10, 1883, and died June 08, 1920. He married (2) MARGIE MARSHALL August 01, 1923. She was born March 17, 1904, and died August 10, 1989.

Children of SAMUEL KEEBLE and PEARL SEXTON are:
210. i. WILLIAM GLOVER⁶ KEEBLE, b. January 20, 1904; d. September 12, 1978.
211. ii. CLEO KEEBLE, b. April 16, 1905; d. December 14, 1980.
      iii. LULA BELL KEEBLE, b. January 17, 1907; d. January 20, 1907.
212. iv. ALLEN TAYLOR KEEBLE, b. December 22, 1907; d. February 19, 1976.
213. v. DILLIE MAE KEEBLE, b. February 06, 1910; d. March 31, 1979.
214. vi. JANEY IRENE KEEBLE, b. May 14, 1912.
215. vii. IDA LOU KEEBLE, b. June 28, 1914; d. December 24, 1934.
      viii. CHARLIE KEEBLE, b. August 11, 1917; d. March 01, 1929.
216. ix. MARY KEEBLE, b. February 23, 1920.

Child of SAMUEL KEEBLE and MARGIE MARSHALL is:
217. x. FRANCES⁶ KEEBLE, b. May 28, 1924.

102. JOHN H.⁵ KEEBLE *(TAYLOR S.⁴, JAMES H.³, THOMAS², WILLIAM¹)* was born December 20, 1881, and died February 08, 1921. He married PEARL SWANN May 24, 1903 in Randolph County, Alabama.

Children of JOHN KEEBLE and PEARL SWANN are:
218. i. OWEN⁶ KEEBLE.

219.	ii.	FLOYD KEEBLE.
220.	iii.	JAMES TAYLOR KEEBLE, b. April 17, 1903; d. July 25, 1974.
221.	iv.	ANNIE RAE KEEBLE.
222.	v.	LURLEEN KEEBLE.
223.	vi.	INEZ KEEBLE.
	vii.	SARAH KEEBLE.
224.	viii.	MELBA KEEBLE.

103. JERRY MACK[5] KEEBLE *(TAYLOR S.[4], JAMES H.[3], THOMAS[2], WILLIAM[1])* was born February 14, 1883, and died November 02, 1956. He married IVA (SWEET) OSBORNE January 21, 1906 in Randolph County, Alabama. She was born July 04, 1887, and died December 29, 1952.

Children of JERRY KEEBLE and IVA OSBORNE are:

225.	i.	MARY LOU[6] KEEBLE, b. December 16, 1906.
226.	ii.	WILLIAM TAYLOR KEEBLE, b. June 09, 1911; d. 1977.
227.	iii.	JERRY LILES KEEBLE, b. October 14, 1916.
	iv.	JAMES ANDREW KEEBLE.

104. ANDREW DAVIS[5] KEEBLE *(TAYLOR S.[4], JAMES H.[3], THOMAS[2], WILLIAM[1])* was born February 17, 1885, and died March 06, 1938. He married SADIE SARAH CARGAL October 22, 1907.

Children of ANDREW KEEBLE and SADIE CARGAL are:

	i.	JAMES TAYLOR[6] KEEBLE, b. November 15, 1908; d. March 10, 1970; m. EDNA BOONE SLAVIN, February 13, 1932; b. December 03, 1907.
228.	ii.	TRESFORD KEEBLE, b. June 18, 1913; d. October 18, 1988.
229.	iii.	(ANDREW DAVIS KEEBLE (A.D.), b. September 26, 1916.

105. BYRD[5] KEEBLE *(TAYLOR S.[4], JAMES H.[3], THOMAS[2], WILLIAM[1])* was born February 13, 1886, and died March 21, 1939. He married DORA COTTLE March 1909. She was born November 20, 1889.

Children of BYRD KEEBLE and DORA COTTLE are:

230.	i.	VERNA LAMERLE[6] KEEBLE, b. February 28, 1911.
231.	ii.	CURTIS TAYLOR KEEBLE, b. October 02, 1912.
232.	iii.	EARL CORTEZ KEEBLE, b. November 05, 1914.

106. HATTIE[5] KEEBLE *(TAYLOR S.[4], JAMES H.[3], THOMAS[2], WILLIAM[1])* was born August 21, 1891, and died January 05, 1921. She married WILLIS J REDMOND October 03, 1909. He was born December 27, 1885, and died February 29, 1956.

Children of HATTIE KEEBLE and WILLIS REDMOND are:

| | i. | MILDRED[6] REDMOND, b. September 19, 1910; m. ROY REEVES. |
| | ii. | WALTER B. REDMOND, b. March 03, 1913; m. CORDELL SUDDUTH. |

107. ROBERT PATE[5] KEEBLE *(TAYLOR S.[4], JAMES H.[3], THOMAS[2], WILLIAM[1])* was born November 03, 1893, and died October 10, 1980. He married SALLIE DOLLAR August 31, 1914, daughter of C DOLLAR and ELIZABETH GASTON. She was born November 22, 1896, and died April 06, 1987.

Children of ROBERT KEEBLE and SALLIE DOLLAR are:

233.	i.	LUCY WILLENE[6] KEEBLE, b. May 25, 1915.
	ii.	LILLIAN ELIZABETH KEEBLE, b. October 14, 1916; d. June 16, 1917.
234.	iii.	MAZELLE KEEBLE, b. May 21, 1918.
235.	iv.	JESSE EDWIN KEEBLE, b. January 04, 1924.
236.	v.	ROBERT FRANK KEEBLE, b. September 21, 1926.
237.	vi.	JULIA MAE KEEBLE, b. May 19, 1929.
	vii.	BILLY ALEXANDER KEEBLE, b. February 03, 1933; d. March 13, 1934.

108. PIERCE MACK[5] KEEBLE,SR. *(TAYLOR S.[4], JAMES H.[3], THOMAS[2], WILLIAM[1])* was born April 11, 1896, and died February 22, 1985. He married WILLIE GLADYS HODGES May 06, 1916 in Randolph County, Alabama, daughter of THOMAS HODGES and MATTIE PINKARD. She was born September 01, 1900, and died November 11, 1977.

Children of PIERCE KEEBLE and WILLIE HODGES are:
238.   i.   THOMAS EARNEST[6] KEEBLE, b. September 16, 1917.
239.   ii.   PIERCE MACK KEEBLE,JR., b. August 13, 1921; d. June 30, 1995.
        iii. MILFORD TAYLOR KEEBLE.

109. WILLIAM EMMETT[5] KEEBLE *(WILLIAM THOMAS[4], JAMES H.[3], THOMAS[2], WILLIAM[1])* was born August 20, 1880, and died September 30, 1944. He married KATIE BELLE OWENS March 29, 1903 in Randolph County,Alabama. She was born August 15, 1887, and died 1962.

Children of WILLIAM KEEBLE and KATIE OWENS are:
240.   i.   HENRY WILLIAM ERASTUS[6] KEEBLE, b. April 05, 1903; d. February 09, 1981.
241.   ii.   GLOVER GREEN KEEBLE, b. February 20, 1905.
242.   iii. MATTIE BELLE KEEBLE, b. November 10, 1907.
243.   iv.   ESTA RAE KEEBLE, b. October 10, 1909.
        v.   ALICE KEEBLE, b. June 15, 1915; m. DEWEY ROBARD.
244.   vi.   DORIS KEEBLE, b. October 04, 1918.
245.   vii. LEROY KEEBLE, b. July 10, 1919; d. 1996.
246.   viii. KATIE MAE KEEBLE, b. January 12, 1921.
247.   ix.   WILLIAM ALLEN WILSON KEEBLE.

110. GLOVER TRENT[5] KEEBLE *(WILLIAM THOMAS[4], JAMES H.[3], THOMAS[2], WILLIAM[1])* was born December 31, 1882, and died February 11, 1957. He married CORA LEE CROUCH August 06, 1907 in Randolph County,Alabama, daughter of VACHEL CROUCH and MARY LEE. She was born May 08, 1887, and died February 16, 1982.

Children of GLOVER KEEBLE and CORA CROUCH are:
        i.   MARY EDNA[6] KEEBLE, b. May 05, 1908; d. December 23, 1989; m. CLAUDE E. CARR.
248.   ii.   VACHEL LEE KEEBLE, b. December 26, 1909; d. June 13, 1985.
249.   iii. WILLIAM ARTHUR KEEBLE, b. May 03, 1912.
        iv.   ISABEL KATHERINE KEEBLE, b. August 06, 1916; d. January 22, 1990; m. MILTON C. JACKSON, Columbus,Georgia.

111. TRESSVANT THOMAS[5] KEEBLE *(WILLIAM THOMAS[4], JAMES H.[3], THOMAS[2], WILLIAM[1])* was born November 12, 1887, and died February 23, 1965. He married EFFIE BELLE BROWN December 12, 1912 in Hopkins County,Texas, daughter of GEORGE BROWN and PERMILIA ODOM. She was born December 24, 1895, and died August 31, 1987.

Children of TRESSVANT KEEBLE and EFFIE BROWN are:
        i.   IRENE BELLE[6] KEEBLE, b. September 15, 1913; d. July 23, 1914.
250.   ii.   CORA LEE KEEBLE, b. May 22, 1915.
        iii. GEORGIA MAE KEEBLE, b. July 05, 1918; m. (1) ANCLE ARRETUS RAGAN, February 17, 1940, Houston Texas; d. December 10, 1962; m. (2) JAMES WILBURN MCILROY, March 13, 1964, Houston ,Texas; b. December 18, 1918; d. May 27, 1982; m. (3) ERNEST H. THOMAS,JR., March 16, 1989, San Marcam,Texas; d. July 04, 1993.
251.   iv.   KATHERINE KEEBLE, b. October 01, 1921.
252.   v.   WILLIAM THOMAS KEEBLE, b. October 10, 1926.
253.   vi.   MAX RAY KEEBLE,SR., b. November 22, 1937; d. May 27, 1997.

112. MARY LOU[5] KEEBLE *(JOE MORRIS[4], JAMES H.[3], THOMAS[2], WILLIAM[1])* was born September 28, 1884, and died October 24, 1969. She married ADE L. ALBRIGHT.

Children of MARY KEEBLE and ADE ALBRIGHT are:
  i. DORIS MAE[6] ALBRIGHT, m. GUY W. LAYTON.
  ii. WILLIAM L. ALBRIGHT.
  iii. NEAL ALBRIGHT.
  iv. JOE M. ALBRIGHT.
  v. JERRY DON ALBRIGHT.

113. S.T.[5] KEEBLE *(JOE MORRIS[4], JAMES H.[3], THOMAS[2], WILLIAM[1])* was born December 16, 1890. He married NETTIE ALENE KIRBY.

Children of S.T. KEEBLE and NETTIE KIRBY are:
254.   i. MARY REBECCA[6] KEEBLE.
         ii. KATHLEEN KEEBLE.
         iii. NETTIE KEEBLE.
         iv. MERLE KEEBLE.

114. JESSE HOWARD[5] KEEBLE *(JOE MORRIS[4], JAMES H.[3], THOMAS[2], WILLIAM[1])* was born September 10, 1894. He married MAGGIE KIRBY.

Children of JESSE KEEBLE and MAGGIE KIRBY are:
  i. LAWRENCE[6] KEEBLE.
  ii. WILFORD KEEBLE.

115. HORACE FRANKLIN[5] KEEBLE *(JOE MORRIS[4], JAMES H.[3], THOMAS[2], WILLIAM[1])* was born July 22, 1896, and died November 19, 1966. He married VELMA CHAPPELL.

Children of HORACE KEEBLE and VELMA CHAPPELL are:
255.   i. HORACECHRISTINE[6] KEEBLE, b. July 17, 1917.
         ii. FRANK O'NEAL KEEBLE, b. 1920.
         iii. WILMER LAUNA KEEBLE, b. 1920; m. WATSON BUSKINS.
256.   iv. JAMES HAROLD KEEBLE, SR., b. 1929.

116. MAYNELLE CARMEN[5] KEEBLE *(JOE MORRIS[4], JAMES H.[3], THOMAS[2], WILLIAM[1])* was born February 21, 1898. She married EVAN COOPER.

Children of MAYNELLE KEEBLE and EVAN COOPER are:
  i. WILLIE JOE[6] COOPER.
  ii. ESTELLE COOPER.
  iii. WAYNE COOPER.

117. SARAH FRANCES[5] KEEBLE *(JOE MORRIS[4], JAMES H.[3], THOMAS[2], WILLIAM[1])* was born October 23, 1901. She married DEWEE KNIGHT.

Children of SARAH KEEBLE and DEWEE KNIGHT are:
  i. FRED[6] KNIGHT.
  ii. MAURICE KNIGHT.
  iii. LEATRICE KNIGHT.
  iv. FRANCIS KNIGHT.

118. LABAN ELIZABETH[5] KEEBLE *(JAMES THOMAS[4], WILLIAM McCUTCHIN[3], THOMAS[2], WILLIAM[1])* was born February 16, 1869, and died March 12, 1928. She married ZACHARIAH HARRISON WALKER February 10, 1889 in Sevier County, Tennessee, son of WILLIAM WALKER and SARAH MURPHY. He was born December 03, 1866.

Children of LABAN KEEBLE and ZACHARIAH WALKER are:

i. MAUD ETTA[6] WALKER, b. November 26, 1889; m. H. R. TARWATER.
ii. LEVATORELSBURY WALKER, b. April 16, 1891; m. ARLIE BAKER.
iii. NINA BELLE WALKER, b. March 21, 1893.
iv. JAMES WILLIAM WALKER, b. September 23, 1895; m. ELMA PATTERSON.
v. GRACE DOVEY WALKER, b. January 25, 1898; m. WILLIAM TARWATER.
vi. DIXIE LOUISE WALKER, b. May 30, 1902; m. VERLIN LATHAM.
vii. JOHN BURNSIDE WALKER, b. August 14, 1903; m. MAUDE RULE.
viii. VOLA ESTELLE WALKER, b. October 13, 1907; m. WILEY RULE.

119. MARY ANN[5] KEEBLE *(JAMES THOMAS[4], WILLIAM MCCUTCHIN[3], THOMAS[2], WILLIAM[1])* was born January 23, 1872, and died November 12, 1965. She married SAM WILEY GIBSON March 19, 1892 in Sevier County, Tennessee, son of JASPER GIBSON and NANCY LEWELLYN. He was born June 14, 1871, and died February 15, 1941.

Children of MARY KEEBLE and SAM GIBSON are:

i. TINA GERTRUDE[6] GIBSON, b. June 05, 1893; m. IRA RULE.
ii. JAMES CALLAWAY GIBSON, b. April 29, 1895; m. GERTRUDE ANDREWS.
iii. FLORA JANE GIBSON, b. December 22, 1897; m. ALBERT ROSE.
iv. DOYLE LAFAYETTE GIBSON, b. October 20, 1911; m. DEE THOMAS.
v. MARY HAZEL GIBSON, b. October 28, 1915; m. WOODROW REED.

120. SALLY JANE[5] KEEBLE *(JAMES THOMAS[4], WILLIAM MCCUTCHIN[3], THOMAS[2], WILLIAM[1])* was born September 28, 1873, and died March 03, 1933. She married JAMES WILLIAM LATHAN December 24, 1898 in Sevier County, Tennessee, son of VINSANT LATHAM and MARY BADGETT. He was born September 22, 1874, and died April 07, 1944.

Children of SALLY KEEBLE and JAMES LATHAN are:

i. CLARENCE MAYNARD[6] LATHAN, b. October 11, 1899; m. FLORA SAULTZ.
ii. MAYFORD CHRISTIAN LATHAN, b. September 28, 1901; m. (1) MILDRED HOUK; m. (2) JANE HURST.
iii. LOLA BELLE LATHAN, b. May 29, 1904; m. CARL LEWELLING.
iv. BESSIE LOUISE LATHAN, b. November 01, 1906; m. LEE DOUGLAS.
v. JAMES VINSANT OTIS LATHAN, b. January 03, 1909; m. MAMIE BAKER.
vi. WILLIAM FRED LATHAN, b. November 21, 1914.
vii. MARY PRUDANCE IRENE LATHAN, b. August 1916; m. CHARLES MARSH.

121. SUSAN MARINDA[5] KEEBLE *(JAMES THOMAS[4], WILLIAM MCCUTCHIN[3], THOMAS[2], WILLIAM[1])* was born April 03, 1874, and died December 09, 1951. She married MARION ROBERT RULE January 06, 1895 in Sevier County, Tennessee, son of CALEB RULE and LYDIA PIERCE. He was born November 13, 1871, and died January 24, 1956.

Children of SUSAN KEEBLE and MARION RULE are:

i. WALTER STUART[6] RULE, b. October 13, 1895; m. ANN M TARWATER.
ii. ADAM SYLVESTER RULE, b. Abt. 1897.
iii. LENNIS RULE, b. February 20, 1899; m. G. D. MONROE.
iv. JAMES CLIFFORD RULE, b. October 08, 1901; m. VIRGINIA DOSS.
v. VICTOR CALEB RULE, b. April 15, 1904; m. MILDRED OLDHAM.
vi. FRED OLIVER RULE, b. September 30, 1906; m. MABEL HEADRICK.
vii. VERNA INEZ RULE, b. December 29, 1907; m. GILBERT E. PROCTOR.
viii. GEORGE CHARLETON RULE, b. March 16, 1916; m. (1) GRACE COPE; m. (2) JOHNNIE DOCKERY.
ix. WILLIAM ROBERT RULE, b. July 17, 1918; m. MILDRED FAIRBETTER.
x. ROGER DEWITT RULE, b. October 10, 1919; m. BETTY TULLOCH.

122. ELIZA[5] KEEBLE *(JAMES THOMAS[4], WILLIAM MCCUTCHIN[3], THOMAS[2], WILLIAM[1])* was born December 06, 1878, and died April 18, 1910. She married CHRISTOPHER COLUMBUS BALL November 21, 1898 in Sevier

County, Tennessee, son of ROBERT BALL and MARTHA SHULTZ?. He was born November 30, 1876, and died April 01, 1951.

Children of ELIZA KEEBLE and CHRISTOPHER BALL are:
 i. BIRD VIOLET[6] BALL, b. May 18, 1902; m. JOHN HOUSTON TAYLOR.
 ii. STANLEY OQU BALL, b. October 20, 1904.
 iii. DELLA JANE BALL, b. January 01, 1907; m. JAMES AMBROSE DITTO.
 iv. WILLIE STUART BALL, b. August 01, 1909.

123. WILLIAM DOCKERY[5] KEEBLE *(JOHN[4], WILLIAM McCUTCHIN[3], THOMAS[2], WILLIAM[1])* was born October 04, 1870, and died March 30, 1948. He married MARGARET J. LEWELLING November 09, 1893 in Sevier County, Tennessee, daughter of MALVINUS LEWELLING and SARAH HEATH. She died April 08, 1947.

Children of WILLIAM KEEBLE and MARGARET LEWELLING are:
257. i. VIOLA[6] KEEBLE, b. February 24, 1895.
258. ii. JOHN DECATER KEEBLE, b. January 09, 1897; d. September 28, 1964.
 iii. HOMER T. KEEBLE, b. March 18, 1899; d. March 28, 1922.
 iv. THOMAS BUFORD KEEBLE, b. March 04, 1901; d. March 02, 1969.
 v. JAMES KEEBLE, b. September 21, 1902; d. October 06, 1902.
 vi. WILLIAM ERNEST KEEBLE, b. August 09, 1905; d. July 12, 1951.

124. MARTHA ALICE[5] KEEBLE *(JOHN[4], WILLIAM McCUTCHIN[3], THOMAS[2], WILLIAM[1])* was born November 18, 1875, and died July 26, 1946. She married WILLIAM BENJAMIN BURNETTE September 02, 1894 in Sevier County, Tennessee, son of JOHN BURNETTE and MARTHA PIERCE. He was born October 27, 1869, and died February 25, 1941.

Children of MARTHA KEEBLE and WILLIAM BURNETTE are:
 i. LELA[6] BURNETTE, b. September 10, 1895; m. CLARENCE H. WEBB.
 ii. VERNA BURNETTE, b. July 23, 1897; m. DONALD TEAGUE.
 iii. IVA (ELVA) BURNETTE, b. July 10, 1899; m. WILLIAM L. JENKINS.
 iv. VILLARD BURNETTE, b. November 04, 1904; m. VELMA DEAN JENKINS.
 v. WENDELL EUGENE BURNETTE, b. December 06, 1917; m. (1) GERRY GILES; m. (2) JOANN HUFFAKER.

125. MELVIN[5] KEEBLE *(CALEB LAVERNE[4], WILLIAM McCUTCHIN[3], THOMAS[2], WILLIAM[1])* was born April 10, 1896, and died October 01, 1977. He married SIDONA BELLE WELLS August 05, 1917. She was born February 22, 1895, and died July 25, 1962.

Children of MELVIN KEEBLE and SIDONA WELLS are:
259. i. VERNA LOUISE[6] KEEBLE, b. June 21, 1918; d. February 21, 1987.
260. ii. BURTON CHASTINE KEEBLE, b. September 24, 1919.
 iii. VERA MAE KEEBLE, b. May 1927.

126. REBA[5] KEEBLE *(CALEB LAVERNE[4], WILLIAM McCUTCHIN[3], THOMAS[2], WILLIAM[1])* was born 1902. She married DAUGHERTY.

Child of REBA KEEBLE and DAUGHERTY is:
 i. VIRGINIA[6] DAUGHERTY, d. 1964.

127. HUBERT[5] KEEBLE *(CALEB LAVERNE[4], WILLIAM McCUTCHIN[3], THOMAS[2], WILLIAM[1])* was born 1904 in Anthony Kansas, and died 1972. He married NOT MARRIED.

Children of HUBERT KEEBLE and NOT MARRIED are:
 i. BURL[6] KEEBLE.
 ii. CHILD KEEBLE.

       iii. CHILD KEEBLE.
       iv. EDDIE KEEBLE.

128. CLYDE PETE[5] KEEBLE *(CALEB LAVERNE[4], WILLIAM MCCUTCHIN[3], THOMAS[2], WILLIAM[1])* was born 1907 in Santa Rosa,California.

Notes for CLYDE PETE KEEBLE:
One of Clyde Keeble's sons fell off an oil derrick and was killed. Word has it that the other son was killed in a racing accident. Clyde Sr. was reported to have been a "bootlegger".

Children of CLYDE PETE KEEBLE are:
       i. CLYDE[6] KEEBLE,JR..
       ii. BOBBY KEEBLE.
       iii. BETTY KEEBLE.

129. SARAH ALICE[5] KEEBLE *(LABAN[4], WILLIAM MCCUTCHIN[3], THOMAS[2], WILLIAM[1])* was born October 09, 1902, and died April 06, 1957 in Blount County,Tennessee. She married JAKE WHITEHEAD July 09, 1920 in Blount County,Tennessee, son of SAMUEL WHITEHEAD and NANCY DONALDSON. He was born September 19, 1901, and died June 22, 1962 in Knox County,Tennessee.

More About SARAH ALICE KEEBLE:
Burial: Grandview Cemetery Maryville,Blount County,Tennessee

More About JAKE WHITEHEAD:
Burial: Grandview Cemetery,Maryville,Blount County,Tenn.

Children of SARAH KEEBLE and JAKE WHITEHEAD are:
       i. ELSIE MAE[6] WHITEHEAD, b. November 22, 1921; m. HAROLD GROW.
261.   ii. DOROTHY KATHLEEN WHITEHEAD, b. May 15, 1923, Blount County Tennessee; d. September 30, 1982, Alcoa,Blount County,Tennessee.
       iii. WILMA IMOGENE WHITEHEAD, b. November 18, 1924; m. (1) FRANK HUSKEY; m. (2) OLLIE CHAMBERS.
       iv. JAKE CLYDE WHITEHEAD, b. August 04, 1928; m. OVA LARGEN.
       v. BILLIE JUNE WHITEHEAD, b. February 28, 1932; m. MARVIN WILDE.

130. WILLIAM KENNETH[5] KEEBLE,SR. *(LABAN[4], WILLIAM MCCUTCHIN[3], THOMAS[2], WILLIAM[1])* was born August 20, 1905, and died March 26, 1960 in Blount County,Tennessee. He married ONNIE LUCILLE KIRBY January 29, 1931 in Blount County,Tennessee, daughter of THE KIRBY and MALINDA HUFFAKER. She was born January 29, 1907, and died March 12, 1998 in Blount County,Tennessee.

More About WILLIAM KENNETH KEEBLE,SR.:
Burial: Grandview Cemetery,Maryville,Blount County,Tenn.

More About ONNIE LUCILLE KIRBY:
Burial: Grandview Cemetery,Maryville,Blount County,Tenn.

Children of WILLIAM KEEBLE and ONNIE KIRBY are:
262.   i. WILLIAM KENNETH[6] KEEBLE,JR., b. January 22, 1934.
       ii. HELEN RUTH KEEBLE, b. October 14, 1935; m. THE REV.CLARENCE GUNN DURHAM, February 04, 1961, Ware County,Georgia; b. July 27, 1932.
263.   iii. CARL LOREN KEEBLE, b. October 27, 1936.
       iv. CLARA JEAN KEEBLE, b. April 23, 1949.

131. CALEB ANDERSON[5] KEEBLE *(LABAN[4], WILLIAM MCCUTCHIN[3], THOMAS[2], WILLIAM[1])* was born June 03, 1907 in Blount County,Tennessee, and died February 12, 1972 in Texas. He married MYRL BALLARD April 29, 1934 in Knox County,Tennessee, daughter of ELIJAH BALLARD and MARTHA BOLING. She was born November 08, 1908, and died October 27, 1997 in Texas.

Children of CALEB KEEBLE and MYRL BALLARD are:
264.   i.   HAROLD ANDERSON[6] KEEBLE, b. February 02, 1935.
265.   ii.   BETTY MARIE KEEBLE, b. June 22, 1936.

132. GEORGE LEONARD[5] KEEBLE *(LABAN[4], WILLIAM MCCUTCHIN[3], THOMAS[2], WILLIAM[1])* was born February 07, 1909, and died July 10, 1974. He married VIOLA PICKENS April 22, 1934 in Blount County, Tennessee, daughter of OLIVER PICKENS and CORNELIA MCCROSKEY. She was born April 23, 1908, and died June 05, 1992 in Blount County, Tennessee.

Children of GEORGE KEEBLE and VIOLA PICKENS are:
266.   i.   MARILYN CORNELIA[6] KEEBLE, b. April 03, 1936.
267.   ii.   TERRY PICKENS KEEBLE, b. January 26, 1939.
268.   iii. JULIA ELIZABETH KEEBLE, b. June 29, 1944.
269.   iv. JANET TERESA KEEBLE, b. December 28, 1950.

133. CLYDE ECKLES[5] KEEBLE *(LABAN[4], WILLIAM MCCUTCHIN[3], THOMAS[2], WILLIAM[1])* was born December 10, 1910, and died October 24, 1990. He married LOIS MALINDA LONG October 06, 1935 in Blount County, Tennessee, daughter of ARTHUR LONG and KATE WALKER. She was born January 20, 1910, and died December 25, 2000.

Children of CLYDE KEEBLE and LOIS LONG are:
270.   i.   MARY KATE[6] KEEBLE, b. December 07, 1938.
        ii.   ARTHUR LABAN KEEBLE, b. March 16, 1943.

134. CHARLES HOWARD[5] KEEBLE *(LABAN[4], WILLIAM MCCUTCHIN[3], THOMAS[2], WILLIAM[1])* was born March 09, 1913, and died January 31, 1985. He married LAURA ETTA SPENCER January 01, 1935 in Blount County, Tennessee, daughter of MELVIN SPENCER and ETTA STUART. She was born October 07, 1913, and died August 08, 2001.

Children of CHARLES KEEBLE and LAURA SPENCER are:
271.   i.   ETTA KAY[6] KEEBLE, b. February 09, 1941.
        ii.   DONALD SPENCER KEEBLE, b. May 06, 1947; m. (1) DEBORAH SHAWN BUDD, June 18, 1983, Washington County, Tennessee; b. November 16, 1955; m. (2) SARA ANN STEMPFLY, October 05, 1996, Hamilton County, Ohio; b. January 29, 1966.

135. NITA JANE[5] KEEBLE *(LABAN[4], WILLIAM MCCUTCHIN[3], THOMAS[2], WILLIAM[1])* was born February 11, 1915. She married ROBERT J. MARTIN February 01, 1936 in Monroe County, Tennessee, son of JAMES MARTIN and MAGGIE WALKER. He was born August 07, 1913, and died December 24, 2000.

Children of NITA KEEBLE and ROBERT MARTIN are:
        i.   BOBBIE JEAN[6] MARTIN, b. August 19, 1937; m. JAKE WARREN HOWELL.
        ii.   JAMES LABAN MARTIN, b. May 22, 1940; m. SARAH PAULINE COOK.
        iii. FREDERICK HOUSTON MARTIN, b. September 17, 1945; m. CAROLE DIANE SMITH.

136. JOSEPH THOMAS[5] KEEBLE *(LABAN[4], WILLIAM MCCUTCHIN[3], THOMAS[2], WILLIAM[1])* was born February 11, 1918, and died August 11, 2005. He married WILMA JUNE MCNIELLY July 20, 1939 in Swain County, North Carolina, daughter of JOHN MCNIELLY and RHODA WEBB. She was born February 18, 1920.

Children of JOSEPH KEEBLE and WILMA MCNIELLY are:
        i.   CAROLE JEAN[6] KEEBLE, b. August 03, 1940; m. DUANE EDWIN OXLEY, March 26, 1972, Wythe County, Virginia; b. November 18, 1934.
272.   ii.   CYNTHIA FAYE KEEBLE, b. May 05, 1946.

137. JAMES LABAN[5] KEEBLE, SR. *(LABAN[4], WILLIAM MCCUTCHIN[3], THOMAS[2], WILLIAM[1])* was born April 04, 1921. He married DORA BELLE HARGIS June 21, 1946 in Blount County, Tennessee, daughter of DAVE HARGIS and MARGARET STEPHENS. She was born January 07, 1921, and died May 12, 2004.

Children of JAMES KEEBLE and DORA HARGIS are:

273.	i.	LINDA DORIS[6] KEEBLE, b. May 11, 1947.
	ii.	SUSAN MARIE KEEBLE, b. January 01, 1950.
274.	iii.	KATHRYN ANN KEEBLE, b. January 21, 1954.
275.	iv.	JAMES LABAN KEEBLE, JR., b. July 13, 1958.

138. ELLA MARIE[5] KEEBLE *(LABAN[4], WILLIAM MCCUTCHIN[3], THOMAS[2], WILLIAM[1])* was born August 11, 1923. She married CHARLES VINCENT HALE March 07, 1947 in Blount County, Tennessee, son of EDWARD HALE and DAISY HORTON. He was born October 10, 1919, and died June 06, 1992.

Child of ELLA KEEBLE and CHARLES HALE is:

	i.	KATHRYN DENISE[6] HALE, b. February 01, 1959; m. STEVE BROOKS, September 25, 1982.

139. ROBERT GERALD[5] KEEBLE *(JAMES EDWARD[4], JOHN ANDERSON[3], THOMAS[2], WILLIAM[1])* was born September 16, 1937. He married SYVIA GONZALES August 15, 1960 in Bexar County, Texas, daughter of RAYMOND GONZALES and CONSUELO BENAVIDES. She was born December 26, 1935.

Children of ROBERT KEEBLE and SYVIA GONZALES are:

276.	i.	MICHAEL ROBERT[6] KEEBLE, b. July 30, 1961.
277.	ii.	CAROL DIANE KEEBLE, b. October 17, 1965.

140. PAUL E.[5] KEEBLE, SR. *(JOHN ROBERT[4], ALFRED HENRY[3], THOMAS[2], WILLIAM[1])* was born January 04, 1904, and died December 24, 1946. He married IRENE JONES December 04, 1924 in Blount County, Tennessee, daughter of JACK JONES and PEARL COULTER. She was born November 01, 1906, and died July 11, 1992.

Children of PAUL KEEBLE and IRENE JONES are:

	i.	WANDA[6] KEEBLE, b. January 08, 1926; m. JOHN EGGERS, December 19, 1946, Blount Countty, Tennessee; b. September 09, 1924.
	ii.	PAUL E. KEEBLE, JR., b. April 12, 1927; d. June 03, 1975; m. JO ANN MAYS.
278.	iii.	MARY SUE KEEBLE, b. April 01, 1930.
279.	iv.	PATRICIA ANN KEEBLE, b. July 21, 1931.

141. MILDRED[5] KEEBLE *(CHARLES GARFIELD[4], ALFRED HENRY[3], THOMAS[2], WILLIAM[1])* was born June 05, 1936. She married CLELL COULTER April 18, 1952 in Blount Countty, Tennessee, son of ARTHUR COULTER and SARAH WILLIAMS. He was born June 29, 1919, and died July 04, 1984.

Children of MILDRED KEEBLE and CLELL COULTER are:

	i.	RAY[6] COULTER, b. November 29, 1952; m. AUDREY BROOKS.
	ii.	MARGARET ANN COULTER, b. July 28, 1956; m. JOHN CLAYTON GARNER.
	iii.	WANDA FAYE COULTER, b. May 10, 1959; m. ROGER MYERS.

142. LEONARD[5] KEEBLE *(CHARLES GARFIELD[4], ALFRED HENRY[3], THOMAS[2], WILLIAM[1])* was born August 26, 1941. He married JEWELL ROSALENA JENNINGS May 06, 1961 in Blount Countty, Tennessee, daughter of FRED JENNINGS and HAZEL LAMB. She was born April 06, 1946.

Children of LEONARD KEEBLE and JEWELL JENNINGS are:

280.	i.	SANDRA ROSALENA[6] KEEBLE, b. January 18, 1963.
	ii.	MICHAEL LEONARD KEEBLE, b. August 29, 1966; m. (1) MELISSA DIANE EVERETT, Blount

Countty,Tennessee; m. (2) DONNA RAYETTE VANCE PICKENS.
281.   iii.   ERIC GARFIELD KEEBLE, b. February 01, 1978.

143. DON[5] KEEBLE *(CHARLES GARFIELD[4], ALFRED HENRY[3], THOMAS[2], WILLIAM[1])* He married WANDA BLAIR, daughter of EARL BLAIR.

Children of DON KEEBLE and WANDA BLAIR are:
    i.   RANDY[6] KEEBLE.
    ii.   SAMMY KEEBLE.

144. MAUD[5] KEEBLE *(CHARLES GARFIELD[4], ALFRED HENRY[3], THOMAS[2], WILLIAM[1])* was born May 05, 1903, and died November 08, 1977. She married JAMES E. LAMB,SR. in Knox County,Tennessee.

Children of MAUD KEEBLE and JAMES LAMB are:
    i.   JAMES E.[6] LAMB,JR.
    ii.   DONALD LAMB.
    iii.   DOROTHY JEAN LAMB, m. VANNIE YATES.
    iv.   CHARLES B. LAMB.
    v.   LONNIE LAMB.
    vi.   SHIRLEY LAMB, m. IRWIN GOGGIN.

145. LUNA LILLIAN[5] KEEBLE *(CHARLES GARFIELD[4], ALFRED HENRY[3], THOMAS[2], WILLIAM[1])* was born March 15, 1908, and died June 07, 1997. She married GRANVILLE DAVID FARR February 14, 1925 in Blount Countty,Tennessee, son of GEORGE FARR and SOPHRONIA LANE. He was born June 10, 1905, and died April 09, 1987.

Children of LUNA KEEBLE and GRANVILLE FARR are:
    i.   WILMA JUNE[6] FARR, b. October 04, 1925; d. July 14, 1998; m. DAVID L. HAMMER.
    ii.   GRANVILLE DAVID FARR, b. February 12, 1928; d. December 02, 1943.
    iii.   MAX GARFIELD FARR, b. August 07, 1931; d. June 24, 1933.
    iv.   MARY ANN FARR, b. February 17, 1934; m. CLAUDE EUGENE GARDENER.
    v.   CHARLES EDWARD FARR, b. August 10, 1938; d. January 11, 1952.

146. ANNA ISABELLE[5] KEEBLE *(CHARLES GARFIELD[4], ALFRED HENRY[3], THOMAS[2], WILLIAM[1])* was born November 24, 1910. She married (1) FERDINAND ALLEN in Los Angeles,California.   She married (2) WOODROW NICHOLS in Cakifornia.   She married (3) ROY CHARLES WILLIAMS March 14, 1927 in Knox County,Tennessee, son of WILLIAM WILLIAMS and OLLIE THOMAS. He was born Abt. 1903.

Child of ANNA KEEBLE and ROY WILLIAMS is:
    i.   WILLIAM FRANCIS[6] WILLIAMS, b. February 09, 1935; m. BETTY CHASE.

147. HAZEL MAE[5] KEEBLE *(CHARLES GARFIELD[4], ALFRED HENRY[3], THOMAS[2], WILLIAM[1])* was born July 19, 1913. She married (1) JACK GORDON in Silanis, California.   She married (2) PAUL B. HALE September 06, 1930 in Blount Countty,Tennessee.

Child of HAZEL KEEBLE and PAUL HALE is:
    i.   MOLLIE[6] HALE, m. DAVID OCHE, Cakifornia.

148. WILLIAM ALFRED[5] KEEBLE *(CHARLES GARFIELD[4], ALFRED HENRY[3], THOMAS[2], WILLIAM[1])* was born May 05, 1917, and died November 02, 1983. He married (1) FLORINE KINGSTON August 03, 1940 in Knox County,Tennessee.   He married (2) THELMA LENORE ROBERTS February 05, 1964 in Fontana, California, daughter of WORTH ROBERTS and MYRTLE MEEKS. She was born May 18, 1918.

Children of WILLIAM KEEBLE and FLORINE KINGSTON are:
282.   i.   WILLIAM GARFIELD[6] KEEBLE, b. December 29, 1940.
283.   ii.   DONALD EDWARD KEEBLE, d. April 11, 1998.

149. CHARLES ERNEST[5] KEEBLE (*CHARLES GARFIELD[4], ALFRED HENRY[3], THOMAS[2], WILLIAM[1]*) was born December 26, 1920. He married PRITZIE UNKNOWN in Panama.

Child of CHARLES KEEBLE and PRITZIE UNKNOWN is:
       i.   GORDON[6] KEEBLE.

150. JAMES ANDERSON[5] KEEBLE (*CHARLES GARFIELD[4], ALFRED HENRY[3], THOMAS[2], WILLIAM[1]*) was born August 20, 1922. He married (1) OPAL MAE MINOR March 23, 1945 in Rossville, Georgia, daughter of GEORGE MINOR and MARTHA COLE. She was born January 25, 1927. He married (2) OPAL MAE MINOR THOMPSON 1952, daughter of JOHN MINOR and MARTHA COLE. She was born January 25, 1927.

Children of JAMES KEEBLE and OPAL MINOR are:
284.   i.   JAMES STEVEN[6] KEEBLE,SR., b. April 14, 1946; d. June 03, 1976.
285.   ii.   TERRY ALLAN KEEBLE, b. October 12, 1949.
286.   iii.   VALERIE ANN KEEBLE, b. November 16, 1950.

Children of JAMES KEEBLE and OPAL THOMPSON are:
287.   iv.   MARY ANN KEEBLE WAS BORN A[6] THOMPSON, b. February 01, 1954.
      v.   TINA GAIL KEEBLE, b. April 12, 1961; m. DENNIS GREEN, San Diego Co.,California.

151. BETTY SUE[5] KEEBLE (*CHARLES GARFIELD[4], ALFRED HENRY[3], THOMAS[2], WILLIAM[1]*) was born April 21, 1934, and died March 10, 1994. She married ERNEST EUGENE BUTLER October 23, 1954 in Blount County, Tennessee, son of DAVID BUTLER and ESTA RUTHERFORD. He was born August 02, 1931, and died August 22, 2005.

Children of BETTY KEEBLE and ERNEST BUTLER are:
       i.   RICKY EUGENE[6] BUTLER, b. November 06, 1959; m. SANDRA MYERS.
      ii.   GARY LYNN BUTLER, b. June 14, 1961; m. LOIS MOORE.
    iii.   LINDA GAIL BUTLER, b. November 02, 1965; m. PAUL BREWER.

152. MARY MALINDA[5] KEEBLE (*CHARLES GARFIELD[4], ALFRED HENRY[3], THOMAS[2], WILLIAM[1]*) was born April 24, 1936. She married WILLIAM KENNETH MYERS July 31, 1952 in Blount Countty,Tennessee, son of LEE MYERS and BEULAH UNKNOWN.

Children of MARY KEEBLE and WILLIAM MYERS are:
       i.   WILLARD RAY[6] MYERS, b. September 14, 1952.
      ii.   LINDA DARLENE MYERS, b. April 28, 1954; m. DAVID LEDFORD.
    iii.   LARRY GLEN MYERS, b. August 02, 1956; m. BRENDA EVERETT.
    iv.   LLOYD ALVIN MYERS, b. January 01, 1962; m. GERALDINE GIBSON.
     v.   BRENDA GAIL MYERS, b. May 16, 1964; m. RICKY CROMWELL.
    vi.   MICHAEL LYNN MYERS, b. November 04, 1965; m. MELISSA HICKS.
   vii.   ROGER DALE MYERS, b. February 14, 1971.
  viii.   TERESA KAY MYERS, b. January 26, 1972.

153. POLLY ANN[5] KEEBLE (*CHARLES GARFIELD[4], ALFRED HENRY[3], THOMAS[2], WILLIAM[1]*) was born August 24, 1939. She married HAROLD ROBERT HEADRICK April 26, 1955 in Blount Countty,Tennessee, son of JAMES HEADRICK and MARTHA HATCHER. He was born July 06, 1930, and died 1999.

Children of POLLY KEEBLE and HAROLD HEADRICK are:
       i.   JAMES HAROLD[6] HEADRICK, b. March 16, 1957.

    ii.   MARTHA ANN HEADRICK, b. January 21, 1960.
   iii.   CHARLES LEON HEADRICK, b. August 14, 1961.
   iv.   CAROLYN SUE HEADRICK, b. July 05, 1963; m. GARY VANCE.
    v.   ROSE MARIE HEADRICK, b. February 02, 1965.
   vi.   DONNA JEAN HEADRICK, b. July 02, 1967.
  vii.   JUDY CHARLENE HEADRICK, b. October 31, 1970; m. BOBBY POPLIN.

154. ALLISON HILDRED[5] KEEBLE,SR. *(DOCIE DON[4], ALFRED HENRY[3], THOMAS[2], WILLIAM[1])* was born March 15, 1915, and died March 28, 2003. He married ETHEL ALICE WHITEHEAD June 25, 1936 in Blount Countty,Tennessee, daughter of HARVEY WHITEHEAD and LAURA ANDERSON. She was born April 03, 1914.

Children of ALLISON KEEBLE and ETHEL WHITEHEAD are:
288.   i.   ALLISON HILDRED[6] KEEBLE,JR., b. September 14, 1939.
       ii.   PHILLIP MICHAEL KEEBLE, b. November 06, 1949.

155. HAROLD VINCENT[5] KEEBLE *(DOCIE DON[4], ALFRED HENRY[3], THOMAS[2], WILLIAM[1])* was born November 30, 1920. He married MELBA OPAL LITTLETON March 04, 1943 in Rossville,Georgia, daughter of MARTIN LITTLETON and SUSAN JOHNSTON. She was born December 31, 1920, and died January 24, 1990.

Children of HAROLD KEEBLE and MELBA LITTLETON are:
       i.   DON EVERETT[6] KEEBLE, b. December 17, 1943; m. JOAN ANN HARRELL; b. October 28, 1939.
289.   ii.   VIVIAN JANE KEEBLE, b. November 15, 1946.

156. HELEN RUTH[5] KEEBLE *(DOCIE DON[4], ALFRED HENRY[3], THOMAS[2], WILLIAM[1])* was born September 07, 1925. She married JOHNNY CONARD EVERHART May 22, 1946 in Blount Countty,Tennessee, son of GEORGE EVERHART and JANE HUSKEY. He was born October 14, 1924.

Children of HELEN KEEBLE and JOHNNY EVERHART are:
       i.   LINDA JOYCE[6] EVERHART, b. August 15, 1952; m. KENNETH BEAN.
      ii.   CAROLYN JANE EVERHART, b. March 28, 1955; m. JACK EWIG.
    iii.   PAMELA MARIE EVERHART, b. October 25, 1959; m. RONNALD JAMES.

157. JOHN CURTIS[5] KEEBLE,SR. *(DOCIE DON[4], ALFRED HENRY[3], THOMAS[2], WILLIAM[1])* was born December 13, 1927. He married BELVA MERLE MAULDIN February 18, 1950 in San Antonio,Texas, daughter of DAIID MAULDIN and FLOY STODGHILL. She was born December 29, 1925.

Children of JOHN KEEBLE and BELVA MAULDIN are:
290.   i.   JOHNCURTIS[6] KEEBLE,JR., b. January 29, 1953.
      ii.   MATTHEW JOHNSON KEEBLE, b. May 14, 1955; m. CELESTE SARVIS.
291.   iii.   MARK MAULDIN KEEBLE, b. May 21, 1958.
    iv.   STEPHEN MILLER KEEBLE, b. June 21, 1959.
292.   v.   NATHAN WILSON KEEBLE, b. November 01, 1962.

158. DOROTHY JEAN[5] KEEBLE *(DOCIE DON[4], ALFRED HENRY[3], THOMAS[2], WILLIAM[1])* was born January 31, 1930. She married HIRAM ABBBITT SCOTT,JR. August 01, 1952 in Blount County,Tennessee, son of HIRAM SCOTT and LENA ABBOTT. He was born May 30, 1932.

Child of DOROTHY KEEBLE and HIRAM SCOTT is:
       i.   REGINA CHERYL[6] SCOTT, b. April 02, 1955; m. KENNETH OSTER, 1978.

159. CHARLES EGBERT[5] KEEBLE *(NANCY ANN[4], SAMUEL[3], MANLY[2], WILLIAM[1])* was born March 28, 1893, and died October 09, 1927. He married BELLE GARNER January 03, 1915 in Blount Countty,Tennessee, daughter of WILLIAM GARNER and MARGARET TIPTON. She was born March 04, 1889, and died June 09, 1927.

Children of CHARLES KEEBLE and BELLE GARNER are:
      i.   PAULEDA[6] KEEBLE, b. April 13, 1916; d. April 26, 1916.
293.   ii. MYRTIS KEEBLE, b. January 28, 1917; d. 1999.
294.   iii. MARGARETTE KEEBLE, b. August 30, 1920; d. September 24, 1994.

160. EDGAR LAWSON[5] KEEBLE *(PLEASANT[4], SAMUEL[3], MANLY[2], WILLIAM[1])* was born August 23, 1894. He married (1) LUCY SIMERLY June 30, 1917 in Blount Countty, Tennessee, daughter of NATHANIEL SIMERLY and MARY STEELE. She was born July 15, 1895. He married (2) ANNA MAE REBMAN November 17, 1956, daughter of CARL JONES and CORDIA SILYERS. She was born November 24, 1912.

Children of EDGAR KEEBLE and LUCY SIMERLY are:
295.   i.   EDNA[6] KEEBLE.
296.   ii. MARIE KEEBLE.
297.   iii. CHARLOTTE KEEBLE.
298.   iv. HELEN KEEBLE.

161. ANDY RICHARD[5] KEEBLE *(PLEASANT[4], SAMUEL[3], MANLY[2], WILLIAM[1])* was born February 21, 1897, and died August 01, 1985. He married HATTIE ALICE FARR October 20, 1917 in Blount Countty, Tennessee, daughter of WILLIAM FARR and EMMALINE WHITE. She was born January 15, 1901, and died March 06, 1989.

Children of ANDY KEEBLE and HATTIE FARR are:
299.   i.   CHARLES EDGAR[6] KEEBLE, b. October 17, 1918.
300.   ii. JAMES ELMER KEEBLE, b. April 26, 1921; d. March 21, 1984.
301.   iii. RUBY KEEBLE, b. April 19, 1924; d. 1984.
302.   iv. DOROTHY LAVERNE KEEBLE, b. November 12, 1926; d. October 13, 2004.
303.   v. JOHNNIE KEEBLE, b. June 09, 1929.

162. SAMUELL WILLIAM[5] KEEBLE *(PLEASANT[4], SAMUEL[3], MANLY[2], WILLIAM[1])* was born November 29, 1900. He married (1) LILLIAN BUCHANAN February 19, 1924 in Knox County, Tennessee. He married (2) RUTH HAINES August 16, 1936, daughter of ISAAC HAINES and LILLIAN CUSTIS. She was born April 15, 1906.

Child of SAMUELL KEEBLE and RUTH HAINES is:
      i.   LINDA[6] KEEBLE, b. April 20, 1937.

163. ROY ELMER[5] KEEBLE *(PLEASANT[4], SAMUEL[3], MANLY[2], WILLIAM[1])* was born June 01, 1903. He married LENNIS JOHNSON May 03, 1929 in Blount Countty, Tennessee, daughter of JOSEPH JOHNSON and MARY SHERWOOD. She was born December 13, 1907.

Children of ROY KEEBLE and LENNIS JOHNSON are:
      i.   MARVIN EUGENE[6] KEEBLE, b. July 22, 1930.
      ii. CHARLES MITCHELL KEEBLE, b. February 03, 1933; m. CLAUDETTE CHAPMAN, July 22, 1956.
      iii. EULA MAE KEEBLE, b. August 13, 1936.
      iv. WANDA CAROLYN KEEBLE, b. April 13, 1939.
      v. SINDA LORENE KEEBLE, b. June 26, 1941.
      vi. MARGARET ANN KEEBLE, b. June 10, 1945.
      vii. REBA SUE KEEBLE, b. May 29, 1946.

164. OTIS VIRGIL[5] KEEBLE *(PLEASANT[4], SAMUEL[3], MANLY[2], WILLIAM[1])* was born October 29, 1908, and died February 28, 1968. He married IDA COLEY October 06, 1934 in Loudon County, Tennessee, daughter of RULE COLEY and EVA LEE. She was born April 24, 1916.

Children of OTIS KEEBLE and IDA COLEY are:
      i.   RUTH JANE[6] KEEBLE, b. June 01, 1935; d. November 1935.

ii. ANITA GERTRUDE KEEBLE, b. July 29, 1938; d. December 13, 1940.
iii. BEVERLY JUNE KEEBLE, b. February 1941; d. December 13, 1941.

165. MILLIE JANE[5] KEEBLE *(JOHN RICHARD[4], SAMUEL[3], MANLY[2], WILLIAM[1])* was born July 18, 1907, and died May 01, 1981. She married ROBERT CHRISTOPHER DUCKETT, son of WILLIAM DUCKETT and SAFINA BURKE. He was born November 30, 1904, and died June 01, 1980.

Children of MILLIE KEEBLE and ROBERT DUCKETT are:
i. WILLIAM RICHARD VINCENT[6] DUCKETT, b. October 31, 1920; m. HELEN ELONA SCHWEITZA.
ii. ELMER LEE DUCKETT, b. September 06, 1929; m. MYRA JUNE ST JOHN.
iii. ARNOLD EUGENE DUCKETT, b. July 07, 1933.
iv. LILLIAN MARIE DUCKETT, b. June 01, 1935; m. BUDDY THOMAS LAMBERT.
v. EVELYN BERNICE DUCKETT, b. September 06, 1937; m. JAMES ARTHUR CHARLTON.
vi. HAROLD VERNON DUCKETT, b. October 1938; d. May 04, 1939.
vii. MILDRED CAROLYN DUCKETT, b. June 29, 1941; m. BILL JOEL THOMAS,SR..

166. BURL ROBERT[5] KEEBLE *(JOHN RICHARD[4], SAMUEL[3], MANLY[2], WILLIAM[1])* was born January 10, 1909, and died January 16, 1973. He married HESTER MARIE TEFFETELLER April 03, 1930 in Middlesboro,Kentucky, daughter of HARRISON TEFFETELLER and MARGARET SIMERLY. She was born September 06, 1914, and died February 19, 2000.

Children of BURL KEEBLE and HESTER TEFFETELLER are:
304.   i. WINIFRED OLIN[6] KEEBLE, b. August 16, 1931; d. November 06, 1983.
305.   ii. WILMA INEZ KEEBLE, b. April 01, 1933; d. February 10, 1990.
306.   iii. LOIS MARIE KEEBLE, b. April 13, 1935.
     iv. BARBARA SUE KEEBLE, m. WAYNE FLANAGAN.
     v. LORETTA KEEBLE, m. DOUGHER.
307.   vi. JANICE ARLEEN KEEBLE.
     vii. LESTER KEEBLE.
     viii. THELMA KEEBLE, m. THURL CRADDOCK.

167. RAY ELIJAH[5] KEEBLE,SR. *(JOHN RICHARD[4], SAMUEL[3], MANLY[2], WILLIAM[1])* was born April 16, 1912, and died November 27, 1965. He married OMA LEE EAKINS September 16, 1933 in Blount Countty,Tennessee, daughter of JAMES EAKINS and GOLDA HURST. She was born May 11, 1913, and died November 10, 1977.

Children of RAY KEEBLE and OMA EAKINS are:
308.   i. EMMA JEAN[6] KEEBLE, b. July 11, 1934.
     ii. BETTY JANE KEEBLE, b. May 24, 1936; m. JAMES DWIGHT GRAY, June 21, 1952, Blount Countty,Tennessee; b. April 21, 1934.
309.   iii. NORMA RAY KEEBLE, b. November 24, 1938.
310.   iv. RUBY LEE KEEBLE, b. January 18, 1941; d. May 31, 1993.
311.   v. JOYCE ANN KEEBLE, b. April 28, 1948.
312.   vi. RAY ELIJAH KEEBLE,JR., b. April 22, 1952.
313.   vii. JAMES RICHARD KEEBLE, b. May 01, 1953.

168. PAUL ANDREWS[5] KEEBLE *(JOHN RICHARD[4], SAMUEL[3], MANLY[2], WILLIAM[1])* was born April 04, 1918, and died January 15, 2003. He married HAZEL AGNES HALL September 05, 1936 in Monroe County,Tennessee, daughter of JAMES HALL and ANN SMITH. She was born January 17, 1918, and died May 11, 2000.

Children of PAUL KEEBLE and HAZEL HALL are:
314.   i. JACK LEE[6] KEEBLE, b. January 24, 1937.
315.   ii. BOBBY JEARLD KEEBLE, b. June 02, 1938; d. February 02, 1989.
     iii. DEWANDA LYNN KEEBLE, b. February 03, 1941; m. BILL ODOM.
316.   iv. TRENDLE JAY KEEBLE, b. October 11, 1942.
     v. THOMAS ANDREW KEEBLE, b. September 22, 1944.
     vi. JOHN RICHARD KEEBLE, b. March 15, 1947; m. ADDIE ELIZABETH GRAVES, June 11, 1966, Blount

Countty, Tennessee; b. May 31, 1949.

169. MYRTLE ANNIE ELLER[5] KEEBLE *(JOHN RICHARD[4], SAMUEL[3], MANLY[2], WILLIAM[1])* was born February 02, 1922. She married GEORGE ZEZULAK September 27, 1947 in Cleveland, Ohio.

Children of MYRTLE KEEBLE and GEORGE ZEZULAK are:
    i.   MARY JANE[6] ZEZULAK, b. February 02, 1952.
   ii.   JOSEPH HAMILTON ZEZULAK, b. April 23, 1956.

170. HAZEN[5] KEEBLE *(JOHN EDMUND[4], PLEASANT MARION[3], MANLY[2], WILLIAM[1])* was born July 17, 1912. She married CARL ELBERT PATTY February 13, 1936 in Knox County, Tennessee, son of ISAAC PATTY and MARTHA FANCHER. He was born December 30, 1911, and died April 09, 1965.

Child of HAZEN KEEBLE and CARL PATTY is:
    i.   DON EDMUND[6] PATTY, b. January 23, 1947.

171. EARL ELGERT[5] KEEBLE *(JOHN EDMUND[4], PLEASANT MARION[3], MANLY[2], WILLIAM[1])* was born January 18, 1916. He married WILLA RHEA CUTSHAW July 18, 1936 in Knox County, Tennessee, daughter of SAM CUTSHAW and VINA WILLIAMS. She was born August 02, 1917.

Children of EARL KEEBLE and WILLA CUTSHAW are:
    i.   BARBARA JEAN[6] KEEBLE, b. August 06, 1937; m. JOHN OWNBY.
   ii.   BRENDA CAROL KEEBLE, b. September 23, 1946; m. LARRY PARHAM.
  iii.   JAMES EARL KEEBLE, b. February 02, 1950.

172. ELLEN TENNESSEE[5] KEEBLE *(SAMUEL WILEY[4], RICHARD HENRY[3], MANLY[2], WILLIAM[1])* was born July 28, 1902, and died March 10, 1991. She married DONAVAN LEE MILLER June 04, 1922 in Blount County, Tennessee, son of SAMUEL C. MILLER. He was born December 18, 1898.

Children of ELLEN KEEBLE and DONAVAN MILLER are:
    i.   JAMES W.[6] MILLER.
   ii.   ALMA MILLER, m. ROBERT D. LIVESAY.
  iii.   KATHERINE MILLER, m. GEORGE BREZLER.
  iv.   NORMA MILLER, m. CAPPIELLO.

173. NORA FLORENCE[5] KEEBLE *(SAMUEL WILEY[4], RICHARD HENRY[3], MANLY[2], WILLIAM[1])* was born August 08, 1904, and died August 07, 1976. She married IRA NORTON December 25, 1923, son of GEORGE NORTON and MARY MCNARY. He was born February 12, 1897, and died August 22, 1946.

Child of NORA KEEBLE and IRA NORTON is:
    i.   YVOWNA[6] NORTON, b. May 29, 1933; m. CLARENCE OVID DICKENSON.

174. MAE BELLE[5] KEEBLE *(SAMUEL WILEY[4], RICHARD HENRY[3], MANLY[2], WILLIAM[1])* was born October 05, 1906, and died March 23, 1999. She married (1) PACKE. She married (2) WILLIAM HAROLD WOOD, SR. April 15, 1925 in Detroit Michigan. She married (3) WILLIAM F. RAHE July 28, 1930 in Detroit Michigan, son of KARL RAHE and ANNA HASPELMAN. He was born December 10, 1906, and died July 13, 1976.

Children of MAE KEEBLE and WILLIAM WOOD are:
    i.   WILLIAM HAROLD[6] WOOD, JR., b. March 09, 1926; m. EVELYN RAMSEY.
   ii.   MARGARET LOIS WOOD, b. April 24, 1928; m. DONALD H. STEWART.

Children of MAE KEEBLE and WILLIAM RAHE are:

iii.   YVONNE⁶ RAHE, b. May 29, 1931; m. JAMES E. BUNCH.
iv.   CARL LEON RAHE, b. September 01, 1935; m. JEWEL MILLS.

175. FLORA ELIZABETH⁵ KEEBLE *(SAMUEL WILEY⁴, RICHARD HENRY³, MANLY², WILLIAM¹)* was born September 02, 1908, and died April 14, 1994. She married ISAAC HERMAN RUSSELL July 04, 1925 in Blount Countty,Tennessee, son of HENRY RUSSELL and NANCY LAW. He was born September 21, 1907, and died June 10, 1998.

Children of FLORA KEEBLE and ISAAC RUSSELL are:
i.   LEONARD HOWARD⁶ RUSSELL, b. November 14, 1926; d. December 14, 1926.
ii.   ELEANOR RUSSELL, b. February 06, 1929; m. HOWARD WILBURN.
iii.   WILLIAM ARTHUR RUSSELL, b. February 25, 1931; m. STELLA CURSHAW.
iv.   RUBY LYNEITA RUSSELL, b. September 22, 1933; m. (1) LEROY STINNETT; m. (2) ALVIN ROGERS.
v.   SHIRLEY LAVERNE RUSSELL, b. March 27, 1939; m. JAMES WILBURN.
vi.   BELVA SUE RUSSELL, b. April 24, 1941; m. DONALD DUNCAN.
vii.   HENRY HARRISON RUSSELL, b. July 24, 1945; m. BRENDA SUE HOLDER.

176. SARAH MAUDE⁵ KEEBLE *(SAMUEL WILEY⁴, RICHARD HENRY³, MANLY², WILLIAM¹)* was born October 02, 1910, and died September 25, 2002. She married WILLIAM BURLEY HOWELL May 23, 1931 in Blount Countty,Tennessee, son of DAVID HOWELL and ELIZABETH PARKER. He was born October 28, 1908.

Children of SARAH KEEBLE and WILLIAM HOWELL are:
i.   MILDRED RUTH⁶ HOWELL, b. September 16, 1932; m. WINFRED MEDLIN.
ii.   BARBARA LOIS HOWELL, b. November 28, 1939; m. (1) KYLE CONWAY; m. (2) LOU ALONSO.
iii.   ARLENE JOYCE HOWELL, b. August 16, 1940; m. (1) FRANKLIN TUNNELL; m. (2) LOU ALONSO.
iv.   WILLIAM ROBERT HOWELL, b. January 18, 1943; m. (1) JANICE PAYNE; m. (2) CONNIE.
v.   JUANITA GAIL HOWELL, b. January 03, 1947; m. (1) HOWARD FLYNN; m. (2) BILL ROBERTSON.

177. WILLIAM THOMAS⁵ KEEBLE *(SAMUEL WILEY⁴, RICHARD HENRY³, MANLY², WILLIAM¹)* was born December 02, 1912. He married WILLIE MAE TEAGUE August 18, 1937 in Blount Countty,Tennessee, daughter of WILLIAM TEAGUE and MARY CLARK. She was born April 12, 1913, and died January 30, 1996.

Children of WILLIAM KEEBLE and WILLIE TEAGUE are:
317.   i.   DONNA LYNN⁶ KEEBLE, b. October 20, 1938.
318.   ii.   THOMAS ARTHUR KEEBLE, b. November 26, 1942.
319.   iii.   BETTY SUE KEEBLE, b. November 26, 1942.

178. EDGAR⁵ KEEBLE *(SAMUEL WILEY⁴, RICHARD HENRY³, MANLY², WILLIAM¹)* was born November 20, 1915. He married (1) ARIZONA RIGGS December 23, 1939 in Blount Countty,Tennessee, daughter of GEORGE RIGGS and FLORA MCNEILEY. She was born March 29, 1918, and died June 27, 1963. He married (2) JEAN SAWYER May 08, 1965 in Blount Countty,Tennessee, daughter of JOHN SAWYER and OPAL TITTSWORTH. She was born May 10, 1929.

Children of EDGAR KEEBLE and ARIZONA RIGGS are:
320.   i.   CHARLOTTE JANE⁶ KEEBLE, b. September 05, 1941.
321.   ii.   GLENDA KAY KEEBLE, b. February 21, 1946.

179. EDNA⁵ KEEBLE *(SAMUEL WILEY⁴, RICHARD HENRY³, MANLY², WILLIAM¹)* was born November 20, 1915, and died May 18, 1985. She married (1) FLOYD PATTY, son of ARTHUR PATTY and ALICE. She married (2) CECIL F. LOWRY,SR. February 14, 1943 in Kentucky, son of HENRY LOWRY and CALLIE GLENN. He was born April 08, 1908.

Child of EDNA KEEBLE and FLOYD PATTY is:
i.   FLOYD LAMAR⁶ PATTY, b. June 13, 1936.

Child of EDNA KEEBLE and CECIL LOWRY is:
    ii.   CECIL F.[6] LOWRY,JR., b. June 08, 1944.

180. LLOYD CATLETT[5] KEEBLE *(SAMUEL WILEY[4], RICHARD HENRY[3], MANLY[2], WILLIAM[1])* was born December 24, 1918, and died January 01, 1983. He married DOROTHY SERENA BOWERS July 26, 1941 in Blount Countty,Tennessee, daughter of WILLIAM BOWERS and FLORA HOUK. She was born September 06, 1921.

Children of LLOYD KEEBLE and DOROTHY BOWERS are:
322.   i.   RONALD LYNN[6] KEEBLE, b. July 08, 1942.
323.   ii.   JOHN THOMAS KEEBLE,SR., b. October 29, 1944.
324.   iii.   DAVID EUGENE KEEBLE, b. October 08, 1947.

181. ROBERT PAUL[5] KEEBLE *(SAMUEL WILEY[4], RICHARD HENRY[3], MANLY[2], WILLIAM[1])* was born January 15, 1921. He married SARAH RUTH OWNBY March 25, 1940 in Blount Countty,Tennessee, daughter of AMOS OWNBY and CHRISTINA CAMPBELL. She was born July 09, 1921, and died March 02, 2002.

Children of ROBERT KEEBLE and SARAH OWNBY are:
325.   i.   GERALDINE[6] KEEBLE, b. November 10, 1940.
326.   ii.   RANDALL PAUL KEEBLE, b. October 03, 1942.
327.   iii.   SHEILA GAIL KEEBLE, b. April 04, 1948.
328.   iv.   DANA HUGH KEEBLE, b. January 21, 1950.

182. SAMUEL CARL[5] KEEBLE *(SAMUEL WILEY[4], RICHARD HENRY[3], MANLY[2], WILLIAM[1])* was born November 24, 1923. He married LUCILLE BLAZIER September 11, 1943, daughter of CHARLES BLAZIER and JOSEPHINE WHITE. She was born January 11, 1925.

Children of SAMUEL KEEBLE and LUCILLE BLAZIER are:
329.   i.   MARTHA ANN[6] KEEBLE, b. October 02, 1945.
330.   ii.   JOSEPH HOWARD KEEBLE, b. January 10, 1952.

183. BERNICE[5] KEEBLE *(SAMUEL WILEY[4], RICHARD HENRY[3], MANLY[2], WILLIAM[1])* was born January 18, 1927. She married JOHN ELDER BLAZIER,JR. December 13, 1945 in Blount Countty,Tennessee, son of JOHN BLAZIER and TRULA JULIAN. He was born June 30, 1923, and died June 14, 1964.

Children of BERNICE KEEBLE and JOHN BLAZIER are:
    i.   DIANE KAY[6] BLAZIER, b. February 06, 1949; m. JAMES BREWER,JR..
    ii.   CAROLYN JEAN BLAZIER, b. August 10, 1955; m. (1) BOBBY MORGAN; m. (2) STEVE SUTTLES.

184. MARTHA JANE[5] KEEBLE *(JOHN ELLISON[4], MARION[3], RICHARD PORTER[2], WILLIAM[1])* was born July 03, 1891, and died February 25, 1963. She married JAMES WALTER BOGLE March 28, 1909 in Blount Countty,Tennessee, son of JAMES BOGLE and NANCY RIDDLE. He was born September 02, 1887, and died August 1982.

Children of MARTHA KEEBLE and JAMES BOGLE are:
    i.   CHARLES EDWIN[6] BOGLE, b. September 29, 1913; m. IRENE DEMORY.
    ii.   JAMES ELLIS BOGLE, b. June 14, 1915; m. NELDA LORENE COX.

185. JOHN MARION[5] KEEBLE *(JOHN ELLISON[4], MARION[3], RICHARD PORTER[2], WILLIAM[1])* was born July 22, 1898, and died May 19, 1960. He married NELDA HUFFSTETLER April 02, 1919 in Bloumt County,Tennessee, daughter of JAMES HUFFSTETLER and HATTIE WILCOX. She was born February 26, 1897.

Children of JOHN KEEBLE and NELDA HUFFSTETLER are:

331.   i.   FLOYD MARION⁶ KEEBLE, b. May 14, 1920.
332.   ii. KATHRYN ELIZABETH KEEBLE, b. October 18, 1921.
333.   iii. CHARLES RICHARD KEEBLE, b. July 25, 1929; d. November 28, 1998.

186. ANNA PEARL⁵ KEEBLE *(EDWARD GEORGE⁴, MARION³, RICHARD PORTER², WILLIAM¹)* was born August 07, 1895, and died June 02, 1963. She married JOHN OLIVER LANNIN, JR. May 05, 1920 in Santa Clara County, California, son of JOHN LANNIN and AGNES WIETHOFF. He was born August 08, 1893, and died February 21, 1943.

Children of ANNA KEEBLE and JOHN LANNIN are:
        i.   DOROTHY JANE⁶ LANNIN, b. April 18, 1921; m. RAYMOND DOUDELL.
        ii. AUDRIE MAE LANNIN, b. May 07, 1924; m. (1) GEORGE FRANCIS ELLIFF; m. (2) HENRY WEHRMAN.
        iii. MAXINE JUNE LANNIN, b. June 29, 1925; m. MILTON SINGER COHEN.

187. REBECCA JANE⁵ KEEBLE *(EDWARD GEORGE⁴, MARION³, RICHARD PORTER², WILLIAM¹)* was born August 08, 1897, and died May 14, 1961. She married (1) HERBERT MILTON SUSONG November 24, 1915 in San Jose, California, son of SAM SUSONG and FLORENCE. She married (2) RUFUS ISAAC WILLIAMS June 14, 1922 in Santa Clara County, California, son of HIRAM WILLIAMS and MARY JENKINS. He was born June 11, 1889, and died November 25, 1968.

Child of REBECCA KEEBLE and RUFUS WILLIAMS is:
        i.   MARY JANE⁶ WILLIAMS, b. December 17, 1922; d. Abt. 1968.

188. EDWARD GEORGE⁵ KEEBLE, JR. *(EDWARD GEORGE⁴, MARION³, RICHARD PORTER², WILLIAM¹)* was born May 08, 1903, and died July 15, 1962. He married CLARA MALONE October 09, 1925 in Santa Clara County, California, daughter of WILLIAM MALONE and ROMAINE HULSEY. She was born February 12, 1908, and died November 10, 1983.

Child of EDWARD KEEBLE and CLARA MALONE is:
334.   i.   EUNICE BONNIE⁶ KEEBLE, b. December 27, 1926; d. February 20, 1998.

189. FLORENCE JOSEPHINE⁵ KEEBLE *(EDWARD GEORGE⁴, MARION³, RICHARD PORTER², WILLIAM¹)* was born February 25, 1906, and died December 07, 1983. She married HARVEY LEE SIMONS August 14, 1926 in Santa Clara County, California, son of ELMER SIMONS and SUSAN BENNETT. He was born May 06, 1907, and died December 17, 1978.

Child of FLORENCE KEEBLE and HARVEY SIMONS is:
        i.   EDWARD LEE⁶ SIMONS, b. January 11, 1929; m. BONNIE JEANETTE PERRY, December 17, 1950.

190. VOLA⁵ KEEBLE *(STEPHEN⁴, NANCY³, WALTER HARRISON², WILLIAM¹)* was born January 28, 1905, and died November 19, 1976. She married HARVIE BAKER HATCHER February 09, 1928 in Knox County Tennessee, son of GEORGE HATCHER and MINNIE RHYNE. He was born September 17, 1898, and died January 21, 1971.

Children of VOLA KEEBLE and HARVIE HATCHER are:
        i.   KYLE⁶ HATCHER, b. November 01, 1928.
        ii. RAY HATCHER, b. August 07, 1942; m. KUNCHA KANG.

191. CECIL⁵ KEEBLE *(STEPHEN⁴, NANCY³, WALTER HARRISON², WILLIAM¹)* was born December 25, 1907, and died May 19, 1975. He married (1) PAULINE CRISP September 26, 1931 in Loudon County, Tennessee, daughter of ROBERT CRISP and LUCY PASS. He married (2) EDITH MARIE LIVELY May 25, 1940 in Knox County, Tennessee, daughter of GEORGE LIVELY and NELLIE CARTER. She was born July 17, 1919, and died December 07, 2000.

Children of CECIL KEEBLE and EDITH LIVELY are:
335.   i.   LAURENCE CECIL[6] KEEBLE,SR., b. December 19, 1940.
336.   ii.   KENNETH VANCE KEEBLE, b. July 21, 1942.
337.   iii.   DALLAS LEON KEEBLE, b. August 07, 1945.

192. CARA LONNIE[5] KEEBLE *(STEPHEN[4], NANCY[3], WALTER HARRISON[2], WILLIAM[1])* was born April 23, 1911, and died July 23, 1992. He married WILLA BELLE JOHNSON April 05, 1940 in Monroe County, Tennessee, daughter of ARTHUR JOHNSON and VIOLET AKINS. She was born July 04, 1919, and died December 01, 1994.

Children of CARA KEEBLE and WILLA JOHNSON are:
338.   i.   JUDITH FAYE[6] KEEBLE, b. April 25, 1948.
        ii.   DONNIE EUGENE KEEBLE, b. October 10, 1957; m. (1) JENA REBECCA WITT, February 06, 1982, Monroe County, Tennessee; b. September 19, 1956; m. (2) JANIOCE BROWN, 2004, Monroe County, Tennessee.

193. ISA MAE[5] KEEBLE *(STEPHEN[4], NANCY[3], WALTER HARRISON[2], WILLIAM[1])* was born January 13, 1914, and died September 02, 2002. She married BEN REGAN ALEXANDER July 04, 1930, son of LON ALEXANDER and MARY ARNOLD. He was born August 30, 1908, and died May 16, 1980.

Child of ISA KEEBLE and BEN ALEXANDER is:
        i.   BARBARA T[6] ALEXANDER, b. May 16, 1931; m. (1) KYLE MILLIGAN; m. (2) CURTIS GREER MILLER.

194. ROY VIRGIL[5] KEEBLE *(STEPHEN[4], NANCY[3], WALTER HARRISON[2], WILLIAM[1])* was born June 21, 1919, and died September 05, 1996. He married MARGARET LOUISE LINGENFELTER May 06, 1940, daughter of COLEMAN LINGENFELTER and LOIS CROWDER. She was born April 07, 1921, and died November 30, 1972.

Children of ROY KEEBLE and MARGARET LINGENFELTER are:
        i.   ROY LYNN[6] KEEBLE, b. September 27, 1940; d. September 27, 1940.
        ii.   BILLY RAY KEEBLE, b. December 11, 1941; d. March 09, 1942.
339.   iii.   WYVETTA DELORES KEEBLE, b. August 24, 1943.
340.   iv.   VERNON DEWAYNE KEEBLE, b. December 17, 1945.
341.   v.   WANDA SUE KEEBLE, b. December 19, 1946.
342.   vi.   LARRY STEPHEN KEEBLE, b. August 28, 1949.

195. VELVA OELA[5] KEEBLE *(WILLIAM MARTIN[4], JANE[3], WALTER HARRISON[2], WILLIAM[1])* was born August 05, 1912. She married (1) DONALD EDMONDSON, son of AL EDMONDSON and JENETT. She married (2) ROBERT GRIFFIN. She married (3) HILDRITH CLARKE STANSELL September 27, 1930 in Cullman County, Alabama, son of WILLIAM STANSELL.

Children of VELVA KEEBLE and DONALD EDMONDSON are:
        i.   STEPHEN DALE[6] EDMONDSON, b. November 1950.
        ii.   SUSAN DEAN EDMONDSON, b. March 01, 1952.

Children of VELVA KEEBLE and HILDRITH STANSELL are:
        iii.   AUDREY JOYCE[6] STANSELL, b. January 13, 1933; m. JAMES NEWCOMER.
        iv.   BETTY WYL STANSELL, b. January 14, 1935.
        v.   LINDA LOU STANSELL, b. March 05, 1937.

196. HULA VIRGINIA[5] KEEBLE *(WILLIAM MARTIN[4], JANE[3], WALTER HARRISON[2], WILLIAM[1])* was born March 13, 1919. She married LEROY WILLIAMS November 27, 1937 in Cullman County, Alabama, son of THOMAS WILLIAMS and MAUD SWAN. He was born October 18, 1918.

Children of HULA KEEBLE and LEROY WILLIAMS are:

i.   HOWARD LEONARD[6] WILLIAMS, b. April 13, 1939; m. JOY SANDLIN.
ii. GEORGE BYRON WILLIAMS, b. February 07, 1945; m. (1) PEGGY BEALL; m. (2) BRENDA TERRY.

197. GEORGE WASHINGTON[5] KEEBLE *(WILLIAM MARTIN[4], JANE[3], WALTER HARRISON[2], WILLIAM[1])* was born November 07, 1920. He married MAYBELLE WHISENANT October 1947 in Georgia, daughter of JOHN WHISENANT and BEBE BRANCH. She was born September 18, 1925.

Children of GEORGE KEEBLE and MAYBELLE WHISENANT are:
i.   WILLIAM GEORGE[6] KEEBLE, b. April 16, 1950.
ii.   MARTHA VIRGINIA KEEBLE, b. April 30, 1952.
iii. PHILLIP RAY KEEBLE.
iv.   JIMMY CARROLL KEEBLE, b. September 22, 1954.
v.   MARIE GNELIE KEEBLE.
vi.   RUTH OELA KEEBLE, b. December 1956.

198. HELEN RUTH[5] KEEBLE *(WILLIAM MARTIN[4], JANE[3], WALTER HARRISON[2], WILLIAM[1])* was born December 28, 1922. She married (1) ALVIN CAMPBELL in Georgia. She married (2) OTWELL WATERS December 24, 1939 in Cullman County, Alabama, son of OLLIE WATERS and LILLAS PATTERSON.

Child of HELEN KEEBLE and ALVIN CAMPBELL is:
i.   JOLEAN[6] CAMPBELL, b. September 05, 1955.

Children of HELEN KEEBLE and OTWELL WATERS are:
ii.   WELDON RAY[6] WATERS, b. October 10, 1941.
iii. SHERON ALETA WATERS, b. August 08, 1945.
iv.   BENNIE LYNN WATERS, b. June 05, 1949.

Generation No. 6

199. LOUISA NEOMA[6] KEEBLE *(JAMES TAYLOR[5], JOHN HOUSTON[4], JAMES H.[3], THOMAS[2], WILLIAM[1])* was born January 12, 1910. She married ROBERT WILLIAM BIRDWELL March 13, 1924 in Murray Co.Okla..

Children of LOUISA KEEBLE and ROBERT BIRDWELL are:
i.   MILDRED VALERA[7] BIRDWELL, b. December 25, 1925; m. WILLIAM BURL FARRAR.
ii.   BOBBIE JEANNE BIRDWELL, b. October 25, 1927; m. FRANK SANCHEZ.
iii. WANDA RUTH BIRDWELL, b. August 20, 1930; m. (1) JACK BURDETTE; m. (2) PAUL RINGELMAN; m. (3) STANLEY G . BRANSGROVE.

Notes for WANDA RUTH BIRDWELL:
Wanda Ruth has been married three times 1st to Jack Burdette   2nd to Paul Ringelman
and 3rd.to Stanley G.Bransgrove

200. HOMER PRESTON[6] KEEBLE *(WILLIAM LAFAYETTE[5], JOHN HOUSTON[4], JAMES H.[3], THOMAS[2], WILLIAM[1])* was born August 10, 1898, and died June 12, 1963. He married GLADYS BATES March 18, 1922.

Children of HOMER KEEBLE and GLADYS BATES are:
i.   DOROTHY NELL[7] KEEBLE, b. April 29, 1927.
ii.   BILLY GENE KEEBLE, b. July 01, 1930.
iii. PRESTON BATES KEEBLE, b. January 18, 1933.
iv.   JIMMY RAE KEEBLE, b. November 02, 1935.
343. v.   BOBBY LEE KEEBLE, b. November 04, 1940.

201. WILLIE FAE[6] KEEBLE *(WILLIAM LAFAYETTE[5], JOHN HOUSTON[4], JAMES H.[3], THOMAS[2], WILLIAM[1])* was born December 25, 1900, and died January 1988. She married THOMAS PERKINS.

Children of WILLIE KEEBLE and THOMAS PERKINS are:
  i. BOBBY JACK[7] PERKINS.
  ii. THOMAS KEEBLE PERKINS, b. January 31, 1932.

202. JOSEPH[6] KEEBLE *(WILLIAM LAFAYETTE[5], JOHN HOUSTON[4], JAMES H.[3], THOMAS[2], WILLIAM[1])* was born April 07, 1903, and died March 13, 1963. He married MARY ELIZABETH HEIDLE October 22, 1929 in VanZandt Co.Texas, daughter of JOHN HEIDLE and EMMA COUCH. She was born September 09, 1905.

Children of JOSEPH KEEBLE and MARY HEIDLE are:
344. i. JOE WAYNE[7] KEEBLE, b. August 31, 1927.
345. ii. PATSY RUTH KEEBLE, b. November 23, 1930; d. May 1991.
346. iii. DORIS JEANNENE KEEBLE, b. September 05, 1933.
347. iv. KENNETH JERRY KEEBLE, b. June 26, 1937.

203. SALLY LOU[6] KEEBLE *(JAMES THOMAS[5], TAYLOR S.[4], JAMES H.[3], THOMAS[2], WILLIAM[1])* was born April 15, 1903. She married ELBERT JOHNSON August 25, 1917. He died 1959.

Children of SALLY KEEBLE and ELBERT JOHNSON are:
  i. FLORA[7] JOHNSON.
  ii. BUD JOHNSON.
  iii. ELOISE JOHNSON.
  iv. JEAN JOHNSON.

204. ANNIE[6] MAUDE, KEEBLE *(JAMES THOMAS[5] KEEBLE, TAYLOR S.[4], JAMES H.[3], THOMAS[2], WILLIAM[1])* was born July 28, 1907. She married TOM JOHNSON. He died September 18, 1940.

Children of ANNIE MAUDE and TOM JOHNSON are:
  i. IVY DELL[7] JOHNSON.
  ii. J.W. JOHNSON.
  iii. WILMA JEAN JOHNSON.
  iv. BILLY RAE JOHNSON.

205. LULA MAE[6] KEEBLE *(J.D.[5], TAYLOR S.[4], JAMES H.[3], THOMAS[2], WILLIAM[1])* was born October 30, 1896. She married (1) BEN BEARD. She married (2) H.T.(HOOT) THROWER August 1916.

Children of LULA KEEBLE and H.T.(HOOT) THROWER are:
  i. VERA[7] THROWER.
  ii. EARL THROWER.
  iii. CARLTON THROWER.
  iv. BOBBY THROWER.

206. EUNICE INEZ[6] KEEBLE *(J.D.[5], TAYLOR S.[4], JAMES H.[3], THOMAS[2], WILLIAM[1])* was born April 10, 1898. She married (1) ROB HART. She married (2) LONNIE MURPHY.

Children of EUNICE KEEBLE and LONNIE MURPHY are:
  i. HAROLD[7] MURPHY.
  ii. BILLY MURPHY.
  iii. DONNA MURPHY.

207. REUBEN TAYLOR[6] KEEBLE *(J.D.[5], TAYLOR S.[4], JAMES H.[3], THOMAS[2], WILLIAM[1])* He married (1) WINNIE MAE SPRADLIN. He married (2) BESSIE SUTHERLIN. He married (3) RUBY INEZ ALLEN.

Children of REUBEN KEEBLE and BESSIE SUTHERLIN are:
- i.   REUBIN TRAVIS[7] KEEBLE.
- ii. DOROTHY MAE KEEBLE.
- iii. STANLEY RUDOLPH KEEBLE.

Children of REUBEN KEEBLE and RUBY ALLEN are:
- iv.   CLYDE JACKSON[7] KEEBLE.
- v.   JESSE D. KEEBLE.
- vi.   ANNIE BELL KEEBLE, m. GLENN STATON.
- vii. PEGGY JEAN KEEBLE, m. CHARLES W. PHILLIPS.
- viii. KENNETH DON KEEBLE, m. DEBORAH PAYNE.

208. BARNEY TRESSFORD[6] KEEBLE *(J.D.[5], TAYLOR S.[4], JAMES H.[3], THOMAS[2], WILLIAM[1])* was born January 03, 1904. He married TILLIE TARVIN.

Children of BARNEY KEEBLE and TILLIE TARVIN are:
- i.   KIRK[7] KEEBLE.
- ii.   JEWEL KEEBLE.
- iii. LEROY KEEBLE.
- iv.   JESSE KEEBLE.
- v.   JEROME KEEBLE.
- vi.   BETTY KEEBLE.
- vii. DOROTHY KEEBLE.
- viii. LILLIAN KEEBLE.
- ix.   MARY HELEN KEEBLE.

209. ROSA BELLE[6] KEEBLE *(J.D.[5], TAYLOR S.[4], JAMES H.[3], THOMAS[2], WILLIAM[1])* was born February 28, 1907. She married JOHNNY TIPPETT.

Children of ROSA KEEBLE and JOHNNY TIPPETT are:
- i.   HELEN[7] TIPPETT.
- ii. HUGH TIPPETT.
- iii. JOHN TIPPETT.

210. WILLIAM GLOVER[6] KEEBLE *(SAMUEL E.[5], TAYLOR S.[4], JAMES H.[3], THOMAS[2], WILLIAM[1])* was born January 20, 1904, and died September 12, 1978. He married LOIS ELECTOR BENEFIELD April 20, 1935 in Randolph Co. Alabama, daughter of WILLIAM BENEFIELD and MARTHA WILSON. She was born November 01, 1904, and died February 16, 1995.

Notes for LOIS ELECTOR BENEFIELD:
She the daughter of William Lemyard Benefield and Martha Elizabeth Wilson

Child of WILLIAM KEEBLE and LOIS BENEFIELD is:
- 348.   i.   MYRA DELORA[7] KEEBLE, b. February 03, 1940.

211. CLEO[6] KEEBLE *(SAMUEL E.[5], TAYLOR S.[4], JAMES H.[3], THOMAS[2], WILLIAM[1])* was born April 16, 1905, and died December 14, 1980. She married ALVIN IRWIN 1922.

Children of CLEO KEEBLE and ALVIN IRWIN are:
- i.   VERNA[7] IRWIN, b. May 02, 1923; m. JACOB DOYLE.
- ii. LOUIS IRWIN, b. October 16, 1925; d. December 24, 1944.
- iii. JAMES IRWIN, b. February 14, 1928; m. MACHEL BRAZEL.
- iv. BILLY IRWIN, b. July 20, 1933; m. LOTHELL PIKE.
- v.   LOIS V. IRWIN, b. October 02, 1935; m. ANDY RAHR II.
- vi. MARY ANN IRWIN, b. November 24, 1938; m. (1) PETE KEEBLE; m. (2) EVAN DEFRIEN; m. (3) A. G.

UPCHURCH.

212. ALLEN TAYLOR⁶ KEEBLE *(SAMUEL E.⁵, TAYLOR S.⁴, JAMES H.³, THOMAS², WILLIAM¹)* was born December 22, 1907, and died February 19, 1976. He married (1) ERA SMEDLEY. She was born April 12, 1908, and died October 15, 1940. He married (2) DOROTHY BARBER September 18, 1942 in Troup County,Georgia, daughter of RENDER BARBER and RUTH WHATLEY. She was born November 13, 1917, and died May 10, 1981.

Children of ALLEN KEEBLE and DOROTHY BARBER are:
349.   i.   ALLEN BARBER⁷ KEEBLE, b. June 11, 1941.
350.   ii.   DAVID MICHAEL KEEBLE, b. December 20, 1957.

213. DILLIE MAE⁶ KEEBLE *(SAMUEL E.⁵, TAYLOR S.⁴, JAMES H.³, THOMAS², WILLIAM¹)* was born February 06, 1910, and died March 31, 1979. She married WILLIAM R. NEWMAN March 01, 1923, son of URAL RUFUS NEWMAN. He was born January 26, 1905, and died August 1968.

Children of DILLIE KEEBLE and WILLIAM NEWMAN are:
       i.   JANIE BERNICE⁷ NEWMAN, b. March 27, 1928; m. PRESTON MATTUX.
       ii.   VERBIE C. NEWMAN, b. December 13, 1931; m. HAROLD BROOKS.
       iii. WILLIAM LEROY NEWMAN, b. January 06, 1933; m. MZRY JEANETTE NOBLEY.
       iv.   GERALD KENNETH NEWMAN, b. November 27, 1939; m. DORIS PAYTON.
       v.   GLADYS NEWMAN.

214. JANEY IRENE⁶ KEEBLE *(SAMUEL E.⁵, TAYLOR S.⁴, JAMES H.³, THOMAS², WILLIAM¹)* was born May 14, 1912. She married H. U. SHEETS March 25, 1934.

Children of JANEY KEEBLE and H. SHEETS are:
       i.   JOANN KEEBLE⁷ SHEETS, b. September 1935.
       ii.   HERMAN LAMAR SHEETS, b. November 19, 1942; m. DEWANNA FAE WHITEHEAD.
       iii. GARY LEE SHEETS, b. August 07, 1947; m. BRENDA DIANE FOSTER.

215. IDA LOU⁶ KEEBLE *(SAMUEL E.⁵, TAYLOR S.⁴, JAMES H.³, THOMAS², WILLIAM¹)* was born June 28, 1914, and died December 24, 1934. She married EDWIN HOPE KEEL.

Children of IDA KEEBLE and EDWIN KEEL are:
       i.   THOMAS EUGENE⁷ KEEL, m. JUNE HOLLOWAY.
       ii.   BETTY ROTH KEEL.

216. MARY⁶ KEEBLE *(SAMUEL E.⁵, TAYLOR S.⁴, JAMES H.³, THOMAS², WILLIAM¹)* was born February 23, 1920. She married (1) CALVIN DENNIS August 29, 1941. She married (2) HAZEL NORRED June 29, 1964.

Children of MARY KEEBLE and CALVIN DENNIS are:
       i.   LARRY CALVIN⁷ DENNIS, b. December 26, 1945; m. POLLY SPRADLIN.
       ii.   DEBORAH ANN DENNIS, b. February 06, 1952; m. SPEER BERDETTE III.

217. FRANCES⁶ KEEBLE *(SAMUEL E.⁵, TAYLOR S.⁴, JAMES H.³, THOMAS², WILLIAM¹)* was born May 28, 1924. She married CHARLES DUNLAP.

Child of FRANCES KEEBLE and CHARLES DUNLAP is:
       i.   JUDY⁷ DUNLAP, m. LARRY SHEETS.

218. OWEN⁶ KEEBLE *(JOHN H.⁵, TAYLOR S.⁴, JAMES H.³, THOMAS², WILLIAM¹)* He married (1) IMA GEORGE. He married (2) VELMA RICHARDS.

Child of OWEN KEEBLE and IMA GEORGE is:
     i.   RUDINE[7] KEEBLE.

Children of OWEN KEEBLE and VELMA RICHARDS are:
     ii.   OWEN[7] KEEBLE, JR..
     iii. MICHAEL KEEBLE.
     iv. RODNEY KEEBLE.
     v.   SANDRA KEEBLE.

219. FLOYD[6] KEEBLE *(JOHN H.[5], TAYLOR S.[4], JAMES H.[3], THOMAS[2], WILLIAM[1])* He married SELINE SMITH.

Children of FLOYD KEEBLE and SELINE SMITH are:
     i.   FLOYD[7] KEEBLE, JR., m. ANN WARNOCK.
     ii. LINDA KEEBLE, m. PETE TRUST.

220. JAMES TAYLOR[6] KEEBLE *(JOHN H.[5], TAYLOR S.[4], JAMES H.[3], THOMAS[2], WILLIAM[1])* was born April 17, 1903, and died July 25, 1974. He married RUBY DELL HODGES November 08, 1928, daughter of THOMAS HODGES and MATTIE PINKARD. She was born July 04, 1903, and died August 04, 1971.

Children of JAMES KEEBLE and RUBY HODGES are:
          i.   JOHN THOMAS[7] KEEBLE, b. September 19, 1921; m. (1) DORIS EMBRY; m. (2) ELIZABETH HUNTER, 1946; m. (3) BEVERLY GABLE, March 24, 1990.
351.   ii. JOE KEEBLE, b. December 22, 1923.
352.   iii. ALLIE JEAN KEEBLE.
353.   iv. MARTHA DAPHNE KEEBLE, b. December 27.
354.   v.   TROY KEEBLE.
355.   vi. ROGER KEEBLE.
356.   vii. ANN KEEBLE, b. May 13, 1938.
357.   viii. PEARL ADELL KEEBLE, b. October 31, 1940.

221. ANNIE RAE[6] KEEBLE *(JOHN H.[5], TAYLOR S.[4], JAMES H.[3], THOMAS[2], WILLIAM[1])* She married (1) GLOVER HICKS. She married (2) MONROE SUNDHEIMER.

Children of ANNIE KEEBLE and GLOVER HICKS are:
     i.   BETTY[7] HICKS.
     ii. EDITH HICKS.
     iii. CLINE HICKS.
     iv. BUD HICKS.
     v.   DEAN HICKS.

222. LURLEEN[6] KEEBLE *(JOHN H.[5], TAYLOR S.[4], JAMES H.[3], THOMAS[2], WILLIAM[1])* She married CARL DUKES.

Children of LURLEEN KEEBLE and CARL DUKES are:
     i.   HIRAM[7] DUKES.
     ii. JUANITA DUKES.
     iii. ANNIE DUKES.

223. INEZ[6] KEEBLE *(JOHN H.[5], TAYLOR S.[4], JAMES H.[3], THOMAS[2], WILLIAM[1])* She married VESTA TAYLOR.

Children of INEZ KEEBLE and VESTA TAYLOR are:
     i.   MARGUERITE[7] TAYLOR.
     ii. IMOGENE TAYLOR.
     iii. FAYE TAYLOR.

    iv.   PEARL TAYLOR.

224. MELBA[6] KEEBLE *(JOHN H.[5], TAYLOR S.[4], JAMES H.[3], THOMAS[2], WILLIAM[1])* She married (1) CLARENCE DAY. She married (2) DILL HOWARD.

Child of MELBA KEEBLE and CLARENCE DAY is:
    i.   DONALD[7] DAY.

Child of MELBA KEEBLE and DILL HOWARD is:
    ii.   DIANE[7] HOWARD.

225. MARY LOU[6] KEEBLE *(JERRY MACK[5], TAYLOR S.[4], JAMES H.[3], THOMAS[2], WILLIAM[1])* was born December 16, 1906. She married (1) TAYLOR SMITH April 13, 1928. She married (2) JOE BONNER March 08, 1959.

Child of MARY KEEBLE and TAYLOR SMITH is:
    i.   JAMES FRANK[7] SMITH, m. SALLY JONES.

226. WILLIAM TAYLOR[6] KEEBLE *(JERRY MACK[5], TAYLOR S.[4], JAMES H.[3], THOMAS[2], WILLIAM[1])* was born June 09, 1911, and died 1977. He married MARY HARRISON August 23, 1930.

Children of WILLIAM KEEBLE and MARY HARRISON are:
    i.   BETTY SUE[7] KEEBLE.
    ii.   JAMES ANDREW KEEBLE.

227. JERRY LILES[6] KEEBLE *(JERRY MACK[5], TAYLOR S.[4], JAMES H.[3], THOMAS[2], WILLIAM[1])* was born October 14, 1916. He married LERA MAE WILLIAMSON July 19, 1937, daughter of ROBIN WILLIAMSON and ETHEL GIBSON. She was born September 19, 1917.

Children of JERRY KEEBLE and LERA WILLIAMSON are:
358.   i.   BARBARA REGINA[7] KEEBLE, b. October 12, 1939.
359.   ii.   GERALDINE KEEBLE, b. January 24, 1943.

228. TRESFORD[6] KEEBLE *(ANDREW DAVIS[5], TAYLOR S.[4], JAMES H.[3], THOMAS[2], WILLIAM[1])* was born June 18, 1913, and died October 18, 1988. He married CLARA ISABELLE DENNLEY September 16, 1933. She was born February 22, 1912.

Child of TRESFORD KEEBLE and CLARA DENNLEY is:
360.   i.   JERRY DION[7] KEEBLE, b. December 19, 1936.

229. (ANDREW DAVIS KEEBLE[6] (A.D.) *(ANDREW DAVIS[5] KEEBLE, TAYLOR S.[4], JAMES H.[3], THOMAS[2], WILLIAM[1])* was born September 26, 1916. He married (1) MARY SIMPLE FRANKS. He married (2) FLORENCE LOUISE MYERS January 15, 1947. She was born March 12, 1924.

Children of (ANDREW (A.D.) and MARY FRANKS are:
361.   i.   DIONA JEAN[7] KEEBLE, b. August 31, 1940.
362.   ii.   JIMMY JOYCE KEEBLE, b. July 24, 1942.

230. VERNA LaMERLE[6] KEEBLE *(BYRD[5], TAYLOR S.[4], JAMES H.[3], THOMAS[2], WILLIAM[1])* was born February 28, 1911. She married GORDON DOUGLAS COOK December 05, 1928.

Children of VERNA KEEBLE and GORDON COOK are:

    i. GORDON DOUGLAS[7] COOK, b. November 02, 1930.
   ii. RODNEY EUGENE COOK, b. September 13, 1935.

231. CURTIS TAYLOR[6] KEEBLE *(BYRD[5], TAYLOR S.[4], JAMES H.[3], THOMAS[2], WILLIAM[1])* was born October 02, 1912. He married AGNES HOUZE.

Child of CURTIS KEEBLE and AGNES HOUZE is:
    i. JENNIFER[7] KEEBLE.

232. EARL CORTEZ[6] KEEBLE *(BYRD[5], TAYLOR S.[4], JAMES H.[3], THOMAS[2], WILLIAM[1])* was born November 05, 1914. He married LUCY NELL BARTLETT.

Children of EARL KEEBLE and LUCY BARTLETT are:
363.   i. GARY EARL[7] KEEBLE.SR., b. September 20, 1936.
364.   ii. JAMES WALLACE KEEBLE, b. February 14, 1938.
365.   iii. DENNIS MORGAN KEEBLE, b. February 05, 1946.
    iv. VIRGINIA BARTLETT KEEBLE, b. August 18, 1961; m. KEVIN JOHN BITTINGER, November 05, 1988.

233. LUCY WILLENE[6] KEEBLE *(ROBERT PATE[5], TAYLOR S.[4], JAMES H.[3], THOMAS[2], WILLIAM[1])* was born May 25, 1915. She married (1) SWANSON WIER in Randolph County, Alabama. She married (2) JESS SCHRIMSHIRE July 20, 1975 in Muscogee County, Georgia.

Children of LUCY KEEBLE and SWANSON WIER are:
    i. ROBERT SWANSON[7] WIER, b. October 13, 1944; m. PATRICIA KENT.
   ii. RONALD ERIC WIER, b. March 15, 1948.

234. MAZELLE[6] KEEBLE *(ROBERT PATE[5], TAYLOR S.[4], JAMES H.[3], THOMAS[2], WILLIAM[1])* was born May 21, 1918. She married ELIJAH LEE PARRIS,JR. December 24, 1958.

Child of MAZELLE KEEBLE and ELIJAH PARRIS is:
    i. WYNENA LYNN[7] PARRIS, m. KENNETH WILLIAMS.

235. JESSE EDWIN[6] KEEBLE *(ROBERT PATE[5], TAYLOR S.[4], JAMES H.[3], THOMAS[2], WILLIAM[1])* was born January 04, 1924. He married BONNELL BOWEN December 20, 1947.

Children of JESSE KEEBLE and BONNELL BOWEN are:
    i. DONALD WAYNE[7] KEEBLE, b. February 09, 1949; m. KATHERINE BROWNLEE.
   ii. SHARON EDWINA KEEBLE, b. February 08, 1951; m. WILLIAM WHITEHEAD.
   iii. ROBERT DINSON KEEBLE, b. September 15, 1954; m. JANET PAYNE.
   iv. JEFFREY ALAN KEEBLE.

236. ROBERT FRANK[6] KEEBLE *(ROBERT PATE[5], TAYLOR S.[4], JAMES H.[3], THOMAS[2], WILLIAM[1])* was born September 21, 1926. He married (1) CHRISTINE CHAPMAN. He married (2) JEANETTE GOLDEN.

Children of ROBERT KEEBLE and CHRISTINE CHAPMAN are:
    i. ALLEN[7] KEEBLE.
   ii. DENNIS ARNOLD KEEBLE, b. November 10, 1948; m. NANCY BABB, July 07, 1979.

Children of ROBERT KEEBLE and JEANETTE GOLDEN are:
   iii. EUGENE[7] KEEBLE.
   iv. DEBRA LYNN KEEBLE.
   v. SUSAN KAY KEEBLE.

237. JULIA MAE[6] KEEBLE *(ROBERT PATE[5], TAYLOR S.[4], JAMES H.[3], THOMAS[2], WILLIAM[1])* was born May 19, 1929. She married HUBERT PARRISH February 02, 1947. He was born June 26, 1926, and died October 01, 1963.

Children of JULIA KEEBLE and HUBERT PARRISH are:

    i.   DELORES[7] PARRISH, b. January 01, 1950; m. (1) FRED JOHNSON; m. (2) BILL FENCHER.
    ii. MELISSA ANN PARRISH, b. July 18, 1953; m. (1) MILTON WAYNE NIX; m. (2) FRED WINDSOR.
    iii. BARBETTE PARRISH, b. August 01, 1957; m. LARRY DRIVER.

238. THOMAS EARNEST[6] KEEBLE *(PIERCE MACK[5], TAYLOR S.[4], JAMES H.[3], THOMAS[2], WILLIAM[1])* was born September 16, 1917. He married MAGGIE IRENE BASSETT August 18, 1936.

Children of THOMAS KEEBLE and MAGGIE BASSETT are:

366.   i.   JIMMY THOMAS[7] KEEBLE, b. March 08, 1938; d. January 15, 1992.
367.   ii. BOBBY GENE KEEBLE, b. August 10, 1939.
368.   iii. JACKIE EUGENE KEEBLE, b. June 18, 1943.
369.   iv. HARRIETT ELAINE KEEBLE, b. June 16, 1950.
370.   v. CHARLES DAVID KEEBLE, b. September 26, 1953.

239. PIERCE MACK[6] KEEBLE,JR. *(PIERCE MACK[5], TAYLOR S.[4], JAMES H.[3], THOMAS[2], WILLIAM[1])* was born August 13, 1921, and died June 30, 1995. He married IDA FRANCES SMITH September 07, 1945 in Randolph County,Alabama, daughter of NEEDHAM SMITH and LUCY HESTER. She was born June 03, 1927, and died July 25, 1998.

Children of PIERCE KEEBLE and IDA SMITH are:

371.   i.   CAROL JACQUELINE[7] KEEBLE, b. October 18, 1946.
372.   ii. PATSY JEANETTE KEEBLE, b. October 04, 1952.

240. HENRY WILLIAM ERASTUS[6] KEEBLE *(WILLIAM EMMETT[5], WILLIAM THOMAS[4], JAMES H.[3], THOMAS[2], WILLIAM[1])* was born April 05, 1903, and died February 09, 1981. He married (1) DOROTHY VIRGINIA. He married (2) MYRA. He married (3) GERTRUDE WILSON September 09, 1922 in Troupe County,Georgia, daughter of WILLIAM KEEBLE and SARAH SMITH. She was born September 28, 1903, and died December 03, 1941.

Child of HENRY KEEBLE and MYRA is:

    i.   SON[7] KEEBLE.

Children of HENRY KEEBLE and GERTRUDE WILSON are:

373.   ii. DOROTHY VIRGINIA[7] KEEBLE, b. August 23, 1923.
374.   iii. SARAH KATE KEEBLE, b. October 28, 1925.
375.   iv. EDNA RAY KEEBLE.
376.   v. JOAN DELORIS KEEBLE.
        vi. CHARLOTTEJEAN KEEBLE, b. July 12, 1938; d. July 12, 1938.
377.   vii. SHIRLEY DEAN KEEBLE, b. July 12, 1938.

241. GLOVER GREEN[6] KEEBLE *(WILLIAM EMMETT[5], WILLIAM THOMAS[4], JAMES H.[3], THOMAS[2], WILLIAM[1])* was born February 20, 1905. He married (1) ANNIE OLA WOOD. He married (2) EDDIE MAUDE BRUCE. He married (3) MAUDIE LEE HOWINGTON.

Child of GLOVER KEEBLE and ANNIE WOOD is:

378.   i.   GERALDINE[7] KEEBLE, b. September 13, 1925.

242. MATTIE BELLE⁶ KEEBLE *(WILLIAM EMMETT⁵, WILLIAM THOMAS⁴, JAMES H.³, THOMAS², WILLIAM¹)* was born November 10, 1907. She married FRED SHARPE.

Child of MATTIE KEEBLE and FRED SHARPE is:
      i.   ELLA MARIE⁷ SHARPE.

243. ESTA RAE⁶ KEEBLE *(WILLIAM EMMETT⁵, WILLIAM THOMAS⁴, JAMES H.³, THOMAS², WILLIAM¹)* was born October 10, 1909. She married REUBEN SMITH.

Children of ESTA KEEBLE and REUBEN SMITH are:
      i.   WAYNOR RUTH⁷ SMITH.
      ii.   JOSEPH WILL SMITH.
      iii.   MARY BETH SMITH.
      iv.   BARBARA ANN SMITH.

244. DORIS⁶ KEEBLE *(WILLIAM EMMETT⁵, WILLIAM THOMAS⁴, JAMES H.³, THOMAS², WILLIAM¹)* was born October 04, 1918. She married HUBERT LIVINGSTON.

Children of DORIS KEEBLE and HUBERT LIVINGSTON are:
      i.   JUDY⁷ LIVINGSTON.
      ii.   NANCY LIVINGSTON.
      iii.   SANDRA LIVINGSTON.

245. LEROY⁶ KEEBLE *(WILLIAM EMMETT⁵, WILLIAM THOMAS⁴, JAMES H.³, THOMAS², WILLIAM¹)* was born July 10, 1919, and died 1996. He married GRACE GARRETT.

Child of LEROY KEEBLE and GRACE GARRETT is:
      i.   ESTA LOUISE⁷ KEEBLE.

246. KATIE MAE⁶ KEEBLE *(WILLIAM EMMETT⁵, WILLIAM THOMAS⁴, JAMES H.³, THOMAS², WILLIAM¹)* was born January 12, 1921. She married (1) ALBERT PERRY. She married (2) CHARLES HENDRICKS June 09, 1946. He was born August 26, 1920, and died January 19, 1995.

Child of KATIE KEEBLE and ALBERT PERRY is:
      i.   JOSEPH⁷ PERRY.

Children of KATIE KEEBLE and CHARLES HENDRICKS are:
      ii.   JOE PERRY⁷ HENDRICKS.
      iii.   ROBERT KEEBLE HENDRICKS, b. January 09, 1948.
      iv.   JON TIMOTHY HENDRICKS, b. June 27, 1953.

247. WILLIAM ALLEN WILSON⁶ KEEBLE *(WILLIAM EMMETT⁵, WILLIAM THOMAS⁴, JAMES H.³, THOMAS², WILLIAM¹)* He married SARAH SMITH.

Child of WILLIAM KEEBLE and SARAH SMITH is:
379.   i.   GERTRUDE⁷ WILSON, b. September 28, 1903; d. December 03, 1941.

248. VACHEL LEE⁶ KEEBLE *(GLOVER TRENT⁵, WILLIAM THOMAS⁴, JAMES H.³, THOMAS², WILLIAM¹)* was born December 26, 1909, and died June 13, 1985. He married MERTIE RUTH SHARMAN December 24, 1932 in Randolph County, Alabama, daughter of EUDORUSBOHANNON SHARMAN and FLORIDA JONES. She was born November 18, 1907, and died August 11, 1991.

Children of VACHEL KEEBLE and MERTIE SHARMAN are:
380.   i.   VACHEL LEE[7] KEEBLE, JR., b. November 08, 1934.
381.   ii.   BENIAN SHARMAN KEEBLE,SR., b. January 31, 1936.
382.   iii. MARY RUTH KEEBLE, b. January 02, 1949.

249. WILLIAM ARTHUR[6] KEEBLE *(GLOVER TRENT[5], WILLIAM THOMAS[4], JAMES H.[3], THOMAS[2], WILLIAM[1])* was born May 03, 1912. He married MARY CHARLES HUDSON.

Child of WILLIAM KEEBLE and MARY HUDSON is:
383.   i.   GAILE THOMAS[7] KEEBLE, b. April 1936.

250. CORA LEE[6] KEEBLE *(TRESSVANT THOMAS[5], WILLIAM THOMAS[4], JAMES H.[3], THOMAS[2], WILLIAM[1])* was born May 22, 1915. She married WELDON EUGENE ROTENBERRY May 20, 1936 in Hopkins County Texas, son of WALTER ROTENBERRY and FLORENCE MIDDLETON. He was born June 29, 1916, and died April 02, 1996.

Child of CORA KEEBLE and WELDON ROTENBERRY is:
        i.   PATRICIA ANN[7] ROTENBERRY, b. March 15, 1939; m. KENNETH LINDSEY.

251. KATHERINE[6] KEEBLE *(TRESSVANT THOMAS[5], WILLIAM THOMAS[4], JAMES H.[3], THOMAS[2], WILLIAM[1])* was born October 01, 1921. She married CECIL TAYLOR WILCOX February 12, 1940. He was born January 02, 1916.

Child of KATHERINE KEEBLE and CECIL WILCOX is:
        i.   RICHARD CECIL[7] WILCOX, b. August 05, 1959.

252. WILLIAM THOMAS[6] KEEBLE *(TRESSVANT THOMAS[5], WILLIAM THOMAS[4], JAMES H.[3], THOMAS[2], WILLIAM[1])* was born October 10, 1926. He married (1) PAULINE RENA BUCHANAN June 01, 1947 in Houston,Texas, daughter of WILLIE BUCHANAN and RENA (UNKNOWN). She was born April 13, 1925, and died August 31, 1971. He married (2) WILLIE MAE EVANS November 03, 1972, daughter of WILLIAM ZACHARY and GEORGIA MILLER. She was born September 01, 1930.

Children of WILLIAM KEEBLE and PAULINE BUCHANAN are:
384.   i.   THOMAS RAY[7] KEEBLE, b. December 14, 1948.
        ii.   GARY LEE KEEBLE, b. May 28, 1954; m. (1) CATHY WAGONEER, March 17, 1979, Harris County,Texas; m. (2) LORETTA PACHECO, July 31, 1981, Harris County,Texas; m. (3) SEMANTHA VIRGINIA ORGERON, December 31, 1994, Harris County,Texas.
385.   iii. JOHN PAUL KEEBLE, b. January 17, 1956.
386.   iv.   TERRY JOE KEEBLE, b. October 24, 1959.

253. MAX RAY[6] KEEBLE,SR. *(TRESSVANT THOMAS[5], WILLIAM THOMAS[4], JAMES H.[3], THOMAS[2], WILLIAM[1])* was born November 22, 1937, and died May 27, 1997. He married CAROL LAVERNE HARLOW December 06, 1958 in Harris County Texas.

Children of MAX KEEBLE and CAROL HARLOW are:
387.   i.   MAX RAY[7] KEEBLE,JR., b. February 03, 1960.
388.   ii.   KAREN ELIZABETH KEEBLE, b. September 10, 1962.
389.   iii. KIMBERLY KATHLEEN KEEBLE, b. July 15, 1966.
        iv.   KASEY KAROL KEEBLE, b. May 04, 1982.

254. MARY REBECCA[6] KEEBLE *(S.T.[5], JOE MORRIS[4], JAMES H.[3], THOMAS[2], WILLIAM[1])* She married ERNEST ROY HALL.

Child of MARY KEEBLE and ERNEST HALL is:
        i.   MARY ERNESTINE[7] HALL, b. June 15, 1931; m. TROY KEEBLE.

255. HoraceChristine[6] Keeble *(Horace Franklin[5], Joe Morris[4], James H.[3], Thomas[2], William[1])* was born July 17, 1917. She married Charles Cecil Edwards March 11, 1939.

Child of HoraceChristine Keeble and Charles Edwards is:
    i.   Charles Ronald[7] Edwards, b. October 07, 1947.

256. James Harold[6] Keeble,Sr. *(Horace Franklin[5], Joe Morris[4], James H.[3], Thomas[2], William[1])* was born 1929. He married Sybil Painter March 29, 1950.

Children of James Keeble and Sybil Painter are:
    i.   James Harold[7] Keeble,Jr., b. January 23, 1958.
    ii.   William Horace Keeble, b. April 15, 1959; m. Ruth Romierez.
    iii.   Sybil Ann Keeble, b. August 13, 1960; m. Gary Potts.

257. Viola[6] Keeble *(William Dockery[5], John[4], William McCutchin[3], Thomas[2], William[1])* was born February 24, 1895. She married Fred Jenkins March 18, 1922 in Sevier County,Tennessee, son of William Jenkins and Nancy Baker. He was born November 16, 1894.

Child of Viola Keeble and Fred Jenkins is:
    i.   Billy Herbert[7] Jenkins, b. March 25, 1930; m. Zita Marie Cates.

258. John Decater[6] Keeble *(William Dockery[5], John[4], William McCutchin[3], Thomas[2], William[1])* was born January 09, 1897, and died September 28, 1964. He married Belva Ruth Rule July 13, 1917 in Sevier County,Tennessee, daughter of Robert Rule and Lututia Burnette. She was born April 28, 1900, and died June 04, 1950.

Children of John Keeble and Belva Rule are:
390.   i.   Willie Velma[7] Keeble, b. July 07, 1919.
        ii.   Kenneth Rule Keeble, b. July 14, 1927; d. February 09, 1928.
391.   iii.   Marie Kathryn Keeble, b. October 19, 1929.

259. Verna Louise[6] Keeble *(Melvin[5], Caleb LaVerne[4], William McCutchin[3], Thomas[2], William[1])* was born June 21, 1918, and died February 21, 1987. She married Vernon Ross Grimes. He was born April 04, 1915, and died April 1985.

Children of Verna Keeble and Vernon Grimes are:
    i.   Stanley Eugene[7] Grimes, b. April 13, 1940; m. Lena Mae Trahan.
    ii.   Gary Ross Grimes, b. April 19, 1945.
    iii.   Jerry Wayne Grimes, b. November 30, 1947; m. Patricia.
    iv.   Gillie Anne Grimes, b. November 07, 1949; m. Frank Willoughby.

260. Burton Chastine[6] Keeble *(Melvin[5], Caleb LaVerne[4], William McCutchin[3], Thomas[2], William[1])* was born September 24, 1919. He married Doris Virginia Jones August 09, 1939 in Grant County,Oklahoma. She was born July 14, 1921.

Child of Burton Keeble and Doris Jones is:
392.   i.   Doris Lerene[7] Keeble, b. February 25, 1940.

261. Dorothy Kathleen[6] Whitehead *(Sarah Alice[5] Keeble, Laban[4], William McCutchin[3], Thomas[2], William[1])* was born May 15, 1923 in Blount County Tennessee, and died September 30, 1982 in Alcoa,Blount County,Tennessee. She married Albert Warren Dockter September 13, 1945 in 1st Methodist

Church,Maryville,Tennessee, son of ALBERT DOCKTER and ELSA MIKSCH. He was born July 12, 1921 in Rochester.Pennsylvania.

Notes for DOROTHY KATHLEEN WHITEHEAD:
Dorothy Kathleen Whitehead was a child of this couple. Jennie Mae Keeble was a half sister to Sarah Alice Keeble and after age 18, Dorothy was legally adopted by William Leonard Gredig and Jennie Mae Keeble.

Children of DOROTHY WHITEHEAD and ALBERT DOCKTER are:
- i. ALBERT WARREN[7] DOCKTER, b. March 07, 1948; d. March 07, 1948.
- ii. HELENE ELAINE DOCKTER, b. September 28, 1949, Maryville,Blount County, Tennessee; m. (1) JOSEPH WILLIAM BAKER,JR., May 30, 1970, Maryville Blount County,Tennessee; b. April 12, 1947, Louisville ,Jefferson Countty,Kentucky; m. (2) JESS LLOYD STANDRIDGE, JR., May 02, 1997, Blount County, Tennessee; b. May 16, 1946, Knoxville,,Knox County,Tennessee.
- 393. iii. KATHRYN DIANE DOCKTER, b. September 26, 1950, Maryville,Blount County, Tennessee.
- 394. iv. ALBERT WILLIAM DOCKTER, b. June 20, 1954, Maryville,Blount County, Tennessee.

262. WILLIAM KENNETH[6] KEEBLE,JR. *(WILLIAM KENNETH[5], LABAN[4], WILLIAM MCCUTCHIN[3], THOMAS[2], WILLIAM[1])* was born January 22, 1934. He married MAXINE IRENE TALLENT April 30, 1954 in Blount County, Tennessee, daughter of HOMER TALLENT and RUBY LEE. She was born May 15, 1934, and died April 05, 2002 in Blount County,Tenn..

More About MAXINE IRENE TALLENT:
Burial: Grandview Cemetery,Maryville,Blount County,Tenn.

Children of WILLIAM KEEBLE and MAXINE TALLENT are:
- 395. i. WILLIAM KENNETH[7] KEEBLE III, b. September 27, 1954.
- ii. CHARLES WESLEY KEEBLE, b. July 09, 1959.
- 396. iii. ELIZABETH LEE KEEBLE, b. October 22, 1961.

263. CARL LOREN[6] KEEBLE *(WILLIAM KENNETH[5], LABAN[4], WILLIAM MCCUTCHIN[3], THOMAS[2], WILLIAM[1])* was born October 27, 1936. He married (1) WILLIE MAE HAYNES August 02, 1956 in Blount County,Tennessee, daughter of CHARLES HAYNES and ETHEL STEWART. She was born June 02, 1936. He married (2) JANE JAMES DUNN February 19, 1962 in Lexington,Kentucky, daughter of CECIL JAMES and GENEVA NICELY. She was born August 03, 1938.

Child of CARL KEEBLE and JANE DUNN is:
- i. SAMUEL CARLTON[7] KEEBLE, b. June 07, 1966.

264. HAROLD ANDERSON[6] KEEBLE *(CALEB ANDERSON[5], LABAN[4], WILLIAM MCCUTCHIN[3], THOMAS[2], WILLIAM[1])* was born February 02, 1935. He married MARY JOYCE SAPPINGTON May 10, 1957 in Calhoun County,Texas, daughter of WILLIAM SAPPINGTON and MARY SIMMONS. She was born January 18, 1937.

Children of HAROLD KEEBLE and MARY SAPPINGTON are:
- 397. i. JOY DORENE[7] KEEBLE, b. March 30, 1960.
- ii. LESLIE HAROLD KEEBLE, b. September 07, 1962.
- iii. WILLIAM ANDERSON KEEBLE, b. February 18, 1969.

265. BETTY MARIE[6] KEEBLE *(CALEB ANDERSON[5], LABAN[4], WILLIAM MCCUTCHIN[3], THOMAS[2], WILLIAM[1])* was born June 22, 1936. She married HERMAN JAMES KNODEL September 05, 1959 in Calhoun County,Texas, son of AUGUST KNODEL and LILLIAN BOYD. He was born June 13, 1936.

Children of BETTY KEEBLE and HERMAN KNODEL are:
- i. JEFFREY SCOTT[7] KNODEL, b. September 09, 1960; m. STACY RICHARDSON.
- ii. JANIS KAY KNODEL, b. September 07, 1963; m. WILLIAM SAGERS.

266. MARILYN CORNELIA[6] KEEBLE *(GEORGE LEONARD[5], LABAN[4], WILLIAM MCCUTCHIN[3], THOMAS[2], WILLIAM[1])* was born April 03, 1936. She married REX ROBERT DAVIS May 04, 1957 in Blount Countty, Tennessee, son of WALTER DAVIS and BELLE DAVIS. He was born May 25, 1935.

Child of MARILYN KEEBLE and REX DAVIS is:
  i. ROBERT LYNN[7] DAVIS, b. July 24, 1960; m. SUZANNE MARIE MOCK.

267. TERRY PICKENS[6] KEEBLE *(GEORGE LEONARD[5], LABAN[4], WILLIAM MCCUTCHIN[3], THOMAS[2], WILLIAM[1])* was born January 26, 1939. He married MARTHA LEE MULL June 30, 1962 in Blount County, Tennessee, daughter of VERNON MULL and RUTH FARMER. She was born March 03, 1940.

Children of TERRY KEEBLE and MARTHA MULL are:
398. i. JEFFREY LEE[7] KEEBLE, b. April 15, 1964.
  ii. GREGORY LYNN KEEBLE, b. March 14, 1966.
  iii. TERRI ANN KEEBLE, b. June 05, 1968; m. WILLARD REED KELLY, November 07, 1992, Hamilton County, Tennessee; b. February 16, 1968.
  iv. TINA LOUISE KEEBLE, b. August 08, 1970; d. August 08, 1970.

268. JULIA ELIZABETH[6] KEEBLE *(GEORGE LEONARD[5], LABAN[4], WILLIAM MCCUTCHIN[3], THOMAS[2], WILLIAM[1])* was born June 29, 1944. She married ROBERT HENRY WALLACE July 02, 1965 in Blount County, Tennessee, son of JOHN WALLACE and ORA O'NEAL. He was born May 06, 1943.

Children of JULIA KEEBLE and ROBERT WALLACE are:
  i. DEBORAH ELIZABETH[7] WALLACE, b. November 06, 1969; m. ANTHONY FRANK LOTTI, JR..
  ii. JULIE RENEE WALLACE, b. December 03, 1971; m. JOHN BRADLEY SELF.

269. JANET TERESA[6] KEEBLE *(GEORGE LEONARD[5], LABAN[4], WILLIAM MCCUTCHIN[3], THOMAS[2], WILLIAM[1])* was born December 28, 1950. She married STEVEN RENO BURCE November 27, 1970 in Blount County, Tennessee, son of DOUGLAS BURCE and MARY WEBB. He was born February 20, 1944.

Children of JANET KEEBLE and STEVEN BURCE are:
  i. BETHANY TAMARA[7] BURCE, b. December 05, 1973.
  ii. JASON CLAY BURCE, b. June 06, 1976.

270. MARY KATE[6] KEEBLE *(CLYDE ECKLES[5], LABAN[4], WILLIAM MCCUTCHIN[3], THOMAS[2], WILLIAM[1])* was born December 07, 1938. She married DAVID UDELL O'KAIN June 04, 1966 in Knox County, Tennessee, son of GRADY O'KAIN and LIZZIE MILLER. He was born April 14, 1946.

Children of MARY KEEBLE and DAVID O'KAIN are:
  i. MARK DAVID[7] O'KAIN, b. April 13, 1968.
  ii. LAURA KATE O'KAIN, b. October 22, 1970; m. ERIC PAUL BRONKALA.
  iii. JOHN ARTHUR O'KAIN, b. July 10, 1973.

271. ETTA KAY[6] KEEBLE *(CHARLES HOWARD[5], LABAN[4], WILLIAM MCCUTCHIN[3], THOMAS[2], WILLIAM[1])* was born February 09, 1941. She married RICHARD MAGNESS KIRKPATRICK August 18, 1963 in Rockdale, Texas, son of G.RICHARD KIRKPATRICK and LORENE FORTENBERRY. He was born September 03, 1939.

Children of ETTA KEEBLE and RICHARD KIRKPATRICK are:
  i. RICHARD CHARLES[7] KIRKPATRICK, b. May 06, 1970; m. ANGELA LYNN DEBOOM.
  ii. SEAN SPENCER KIRKPATRICK, b. September 15, 1974.

272. CYNTHIA FAYE[6] KEEBLE *(JOSEPH THOMAS[5], LABAN[4], WILLIAM MCCUTCHIN[3], THOMAS[2], WILLIAM[1])* was born

May 05, 1946. She married MICHAEL LYNN RAWLINGS,SR. June 15, 1968 in Sevier County,Tennessee, son of LYNN RAWLINGS and MARGARET FOX. He was born January 01, 1946.

Children of CYNTHIA KEEBLE and MICHAEL RAWLINGS are:
    i. MICHAEL LYNN[7] RAWLINGS,JR., b. March 27, 1973.
    ii. CHRISTOPHER LEE RAWLINGS, b. August 24, 1975.

273. LINDA DORIS[6] KEEBLE *(JAMES LABAN[5], LABAN[4], WILLIAM McCUTCHIN[3], THOMAS[2], WILLIAM[1])* was born May 11, 1947. She married (1) RICHARD JOHN BAILEY July 19, 1969 in Blount County,Tennessee, son of JACKFURNESS BAILEY and ARLENE LYNN. He was born August 21, 1945. She married (2) JAMES TRUEMAN HARTLEY September 01, 2001, son of WILLIAM HARTLEY and VENETIA BOWEN. He was born October 05, 1952.

Children of LINDA KEEBLE and RICHARD BAILEY are:
    i. MICHAEL JAMES[7] BAILEY, b. April 01, 1975.
    ii. SARAH CATHERINE BAILEY, b. January 11, 1980.

274. KATHRYN ANN[6] KEEBLE *(JAMES LABAN[5], LABAN[4], WILLIAM McCUTCHIN[3], THOMAS[2], WILLIAM[1])* was born January 21, 1954. She married (1) SAMUAL ALAN BURTON July 23, 1983 in Knox County,Tennessee, son of WILLIAM BURTON and RUTH MENDENHALL. He was born May 01, 1944, and died April 12, 2005. She married (2) WILLIAM SNODGRASS September 15, 1973 in Blount County, Tennessee, son of JAMES SNODGRASS and JUANITA CORNELL. He was born June 11, 1953.

Child of KATHRYN KEEBLE and SAMUAL BURTON is:
    i. CYNTHIA KEEBLE[7] BURTON, b. June 07, 1989.

275. JAMES LABAN[6] KEEBLE,JR. *(JAMES LABAN[5], LABAN[4], WILLIAM McCUTCHIN[3], THOMAS[2], WILLIAM[1])* was born July 13, 1958. He married REBECCA PADGETT May 10, 1980 in Atlanta,Georgia, daughter of SAMUEL PADGETT and MILDRED CRUMP. She was born January 30, 1957.

Children of JAMES KEEBLE and REBECCA PADGETT are:
    i. ANTHONY LABAN[7] KEEBLE, b. November 02, 1980.
    ii. JAMES DUSTIN KEEBLE, b. September 22, 1982.

276. MICHAEL ROBERT[6] KEEBLE *(ROBERT GERALD[5], JAMES EDWARD[4], JOHN ANDERSON[3], THOMAS[2], WILLIAM[1])* was born July 30, 1961. He married YOLANDA JASSO April 21, 1988 in Las Vagas ,Nevada, daughter of JASSO and SYLVIA GONZOLES. She was born July 22, 1954.

Children of MICHAEL KEEBLE and YOLANDA JASSO are:
    i. MICHAEL STEVEN[7] KEEBLE, b. June 27, 1989.
    ii. SARAH ELIZABETH KEEBLE, b. July 10, 1990.

277. CAROL DIANE[6] KEEBLE *(ROBERT GERALD[5], JAMES EDWARD[4], JOHN ANDERSON[3], THOMAS[2], WILLIAM[1])* was born October 17, 1965. She married RUBEN TREVINO May 27, 1989 in Bexar County,Texas, son of JUAN TREVINO and HERLINDA REYEN.

Children of CAROL KEEBLE and RUBEN TREVINO are:
    i. ALEX MATTHEW[7] TREVINO, b. September 09, 1992.
    ii. LINDSEY NICOLE TREVINO, b. December 30, 1994.

278. MARY SUE[6] KEEBLE *(PAUL E.[5], JOHN ROBERT[4], ALFRED HENRY[3], THOMAS[2], WILLIAM[1])* was born April 01, 1930. She married DR. CHARLES M. HYDER, son of LEROY HYDER.

Child of MARY KEEBLE and DR. HYDER is:
   i.   KIRK LEROY[7] HYDER, b. March 10, 1955.

279. PATRICIA ANN[6] KEEBLE *(PAUL E.[5], JOHN ROBERT[4], ALFRED HENRY[3], THOMAS[2], WILLIAM[1])* was born July 21, 1931. She married WILLIAM DON RANDOLPH March 05, 1954 in Blount Countty, Tennessee, son of HOWARD RANDOLPH and DAHLIA ALLISON. He was born August 03, 1931.

Child of PATRICIA KEEBLE and WILLIAM RANDOLPH is:
   i.   WILLIAM HOWARD[7] RANDOLPH, b. November 25, 1954.

280. SANDRA ROSALENA[6] KEEBLE *(LEONARD[5], CHARLES GARFIELD[4], ALFRED HENRY[3], THOMAS[2], WILLIAM[1])* was born January 18, 1963. She married (1) FRED RAY SUNDERLAND, JR. June 20, 1981 in Blount Countty, Tennessee, son of FRED SUNDERLAND and LORENE LEE. He was born May 20, 1962. She married (2) MARTY ALLEN SKINNER September 22, 1995 in Blount Countty, Tennessee, son of CLAUDE SKINNER and STELLA FRANKS. He was born March 19, 1961.

Children of SANDRA KEEBLE and FRED SUNDERLAND are:
   i.   TABITHA ROSE[7] SUNDERLAND, b. October 18, 1983.
   ii. HOLLY RAYNAE SUNDERLAND, b. October 30, 1985.

281. ERIC GARFIELD[6] KEEBLE *(LEONARD[5], CHARLES GARFIELD[4], ALFRED HENRY[3], THOMAS[2], WILLIAM[1])* was born February 01, 1978. He married TONI TEMILLEDODARO in Blount Countty, Tennessee.

Children of ERIC KEEBLE and TONI TEMILLEDODARO are:
   i.   ERIC ANTHONY[7] KEEBLE.
   ii. DEANNA NICOLE KEEBLE, b. October 27, 1997.

282. WILLIAM GARFIELD[6] KEEBLE *(WILLIAM ALFRED[5], CHARLES GARFIELD[4], ALFRED HENRY[3], THOMAS[2], WILLIAM[1])* was born December 29, 1940. He married BEVERLY SMITH.

Children of WILLIAM KEEBLE and BEVERLY SMITH are:
   i.   JEANNIE[7] KEEBLE.
   ii. JANETT KEEBLE.

283. DONALD EDWARD[6] KEEBLE *(WILLIAM ALFRED[5], CHARLES GARFIELD[4], ALFRED HENRY[3], THOMAS[2], WILLIAM[1])* died April 11, 1998. He married SHARIE MORROW.

Children of DONALD KEEBLE and SHARIE MORROW are:
   i.   SHANE E.[7] KEEBLE.
   ii. CASSITY T. KEEBLE.
   iii. THOMAS KEEBLE.

284. JAMES STEVEN[6] KEEBLE, SR. *(JAMES ANDERSON[5], CHARLES GARFIELD[4], ALFRED HENRY[3], THOMAS[2], WILLIAM[1])* was born April 14, 1946, and died June 03, 1976. He married SHARON E. BYRD February 03, 1967 in San Diego County, Californis. She was born August 09, 1948.

Child of JAMES KEEBLE and SHARON BYRD is:
   i.   JAMES STEVEN[7] KEEBLE, JR., b. February 21, 1968.

285. TERRY ALLAN[6] KEEBLE *(JAMES ANDERSON[5], CHARLES GARFIELD[4], ALFRED HENRY[3], THOMAS[2], WILLIAM[1])* was born October 12, 1949. He married LYDIA ANN HERNANDEZ CASTRO February 14, 1992 in Blount Countty, Tennessee, daughter of ANTONIO HERNANDEZ and HORTENSIA UNKNOWN. She was born October 24,

1955.

Children of TERRY KEEBLE and LYDIA CASTRO are:
    i.   MONICA ANN[7] KEEBLE, b. July 24, 1983.
    ii. TESSIE MARIE KEEBLE, b. March 06, 1991.

286. VALERIE ANN[6] KEEBLE *(JAMES ANDERSON[5], CHARLES GARFIELD[4], ALFRED HENRY[3], THOMAS[2], WILLIAM[1])* was born November 16, 1950. She married LARRY G. HAMON January 19, 1968 in San Diego County, Californis.

Children of VALERIE KEEBLE and LARRY HAMON are:
    i.   BRENDA LEE[7] HAMON, b. August 24, 1968; d. May 27, 1978.
    ii. KERI LYNN HAMON, b. August 14, 1973.

287. MARY ANN KEEBLE WAS BORN A[6] THOMPSON *(JAMES ANDERSON[5] KEEBLE, CHARLES GARFIELD[4], ALFRED HENRY[3], THOMAS[2], WILLIAM[1])* was born February 01, 1954. She married JAMES C. HAMON April 15, 1972 in San Diego Co.,California.

More About MARY ANN KEEBLE WAS BORN A THOMPSON:
Adoption: Mary Ann adopted by J.A.Keeble;

Children of MARY THOMPSON and JAMES HAMON are:
    i.   BRANDON JAMES[7] HAMON, b. October 16, 1972.
    ii. JASON CARL HAMON, b. October 28, 1973.
    iii. JESSICA ANNE HAMON, b. February 09, 1978.

288. ALLISON HILDRED[6] KEEBLE,JR. *(ALLISON HILDRED[5], DOCIE DON[4], ALFRED HENRY[3], THOMAS[2], WILLIAM[1])* was born September 14, 1939. He married (1) SANDRA SUE HANNAH December 09, 1966 in Bryson City,North Carolina, daughter of JAMES HANNAH and HELEN MATTOX. She was born October 29, 1944, and died August 16, 1994. He married (2) MARION DOCKTER November 27, 1991 in Nashville Davidson County,Tennessee, daughter of ARNO MEINERT and ELIZABETH DOCKTER. She was born May 28, 1946.

Children of ALLISON KEEBLE and SANDRA HANNAH are:
    i.   ALLISON HILDRED[7] KEEBLE III, b. August 08, 1969; m. MELISSA MCGINNESS, May 15, 1993, Nashville Davidson County,Tennessee; b. July 13, 1968.
    ii. PADRAIC BRION KEEBLE, b. October 23, 1970.

289. VIVIAN JANE[6] KEEBLE *(HAROLD VINCENT[5], DOCIE DON[4], ALFRED HENRY[3], THOMAS[2], WILLIAM[1])* was born November 15, 1946. She married EDWIN RAY MARTIN January 23, 1970 in Savannah,Chatham County,Georgia, son of WILLIAM MARTIN and MYRTLE NELLUMS. He was born April 07, 1947.

Child of VIVIAN KEEBLE and EDWIN MARTIN is:
    i.   BRENT KEEBLE[7] MARTIN, b. June 27, 1973; m. CATHY PHILLIPS.

290. JOHNCURTIS[6] KEEBLE,JR. *(JOHN CURTIS[5], DOCIE DON[4], ALFRED HENRY[3], THOMAS[2], WILLIAM[1])* was born January 29, 1953. He married DOROTHY ROGERS, daughter of LEE ROGERS and MARION. She was born February 04, 1951.

Child of JOHNCURTIS KEEBLE and DOROTHY ROGERS is:
    i.   CODY LEE[7] KEEBLE, b. December 01, 1990.

291. MARK MAULDIN[6] KEEBLE *(JOHN CURTIS[5], DOCIE DON[4], ALFRED HENRY[3], THOMAS[2], WILLIAM[1])* was born May 21, 1958. He married ELLY VOLPERT.

Children of MARK KEEBLE and ELLY VOLPERT are:
    i.   AMY[7] KEEBLE, b. June 11, 1980.
    ii. PAMELA MICHELE KEEBLE, b. July 04, 1981; m. JOSHUA DUKE.
    iii. DAVID JONATHAN KEEBLE, b. June 17, 1989.

292. NATHAN WILSON[6] KEEBLE *(JOHN CURTIS[5], DOCIE DON[4], ALFRED HENRY[3], THOMAS[2], WILLIAM[1])* was born November 01, 1962. He married VIKI WALTERS, daughter of EUGENE WALTERS and ANN PARK. She was born September 01, 1962.

Child of NATHAN KEEBLE and VIKI WALTERS is:
    i.   WILLIAM CHRISTOPHER[7] KEEBLE, b. September 22, 1986.

293. MYRTIS[6] KEEBLE *(CHARLES EGBERT[5], NANCY ANN[4], SAMUEL[3], MANLY[2], WILLIAM[1])* was born January 28, 1917, and died 1999. She married WILLIAN OWNBY December 21, 1935 in Blount Countty, Tennessee, son of P. OWNBY and MARTHA KING. He was born September 29, 1915, and died April 15, 1975.

Children of MYRTIS KEEBLE and WILLIAN OWNBY are:
    i.   AUGUSTA JUNE[7] OWNBY, b. July 23, 1941.
    ii. BILLY LAMON OWNBY, b. March 06, 1943.
    iii. CHARLES ERWIN OWNBY, b. September 29, 1947.

294. MARGARETTE[6] KEEBLE *(CHARLES EGBERT[5], NANCY ANN[4], SAMUEL[3], MANLY[2], WILLIAM[1])* was born August 30, 1920, and died September 24, 1994. She married CLAUDE LEE BREWER October 12, 1940 in Blount Countty, Tennessee, son of JOHN BREWER and MARTHA HAWN. He was born June 13, 1919, and died January 12, 1976.

Children of MARGARETTE KEEBLE and CLAUDE BREWER are:
    i.   PHYLLIS ANN[7] BREWER, b. July 27, 1941; m. BOBBY COMPTON.
    ii. BARBARA B. BREWER, b. March 25, 1943; m. (1) GORDON JONES; m. (2) CLAUDE HICKS, March 16, 1951.

295. EDNA[6] KEEBLE *(EDGAR LAWSON[5], PLEASANT[4], SAMUEL[3], MANLY[2], WILLIAM[1])* She married EDWARD LAMBERT.

Children of EDNA KEEBLE and EDWARD LAMBERT are:
    i.   CARLETTA[7] LAMBERT.
    ii. EDWARD LAMBERT.

296. MARIE[6] KEEBLE *(EDGAR LAWSON[5], PLEASANT[4], SAMUEL[3], MANLY[2], WILLIAM[1])* She married THOMAS ADKINS.

Children of MARIE KEEBLE and THOMAS ADKINS are:
    i.   NORMAN RAY[7] ADKINS.
    ii. EDWARD ADKINS.
    iii. WANDA ADKINS.

297. CHARLOTTE[6] KEEBLE *(EDGAR LAWSON[5], PLEASANT[4], SAMUEL[3], MANLY[2], WILLIAM[1])* She married (1) CARL M. PRYOR. She married (2) JAMES HOUSER.

Child of CHARLOTTE KEEBLE and CARL PRYOR is:
    i.   SHIRLEY ANN[7] PRYOR.

Child of CHARLOTTE KEEBLE and JAMES HOUSER is:
    ii. JOSEPH[7] HOUSER.

298. HELEN[6] KEEBLE *(EDGAR LAWSON[5], PLEASANT[4], SAMUEL[3], MANLY[2], WILLIAM[1])* She married GEORGE WILSON.

Children of HELEN KEEBLE and GEORGE WILSON are:
    i. GEORGE[7] WILSON.
    ii. CONNIE SUE WILSON.
    iii. DEBBIE WILSON.

299. CHARLES EDGAR[6] KEEBLE *(ANDY RICHARD[5], PLEASANT[4], SAMUEL[3], MANLY[2], WILLIAM[1])* was born October 17, 1918. He married LELA FRANCES GRAHAM October 28, 1939 in Blount Countty, Tennessee, daughter of WILLIAM GRAHAM and SARAH LEE. She was born March 19, 1920.

Children of CHARLES KEEBLE and LELA GRAHAM are:
399.   i. KENNETH RICHARD[7] KEEBLE, b. May 26, 1940.
400.   ii. HAROLD DAVID KEEBLE, b. July 21, 1942.
401.   iii. ROBERT LEE KEEBLE, b. August 29, 1947.
402.   iv. KATHY LYNN KEEBLE, b. May 30, 1958.

300. JAMES ELMER[6] KEEBLE *(ANDY RICHARD[5], PLEASANT[4], SAMUEL[3], MANLY[2], WILLIAM[1])* was born April 26, 1921, and died March 21, 1984. He married FRANCES WOODY June 06, 1939 in Monroe County, Tennessee, daughter of GROVER WOODY and ETHEL LILLARD. She was born May 26, 1922.

Child of JAMES KEEBLE and FRANCES WOODY is:
403.   i. JAMES RONALD[7] KEEBLE, b. June 22, 1943.

301. RUBY[6] KEEBLE *(ANDY RICHARD[5], PLEASANT[4], SAMUEL[3], MANLY[2], WILLIAM[1])* was born April 19, 1924, and died 1984. She married ANDREW McBATH May 12, 1941 in Loudon County, Tennessee, son of ANDREW McBATH and VISTA SMITH. He was born February 19, 1924.

Children of RUBY KEEBLE and ANDREW McBATH are:
    i. TOMMY GENE[7] McBATH, b. August 10, 1942.
    ii. FLORA JUANITA McBATH, b. June 27, 1946.
    iii. PATRICIA ANN McBATH, b. October 02, 1947.

302. DOROTHY LAVERNE[6] KEEBLE *(ANDY RICHARD[5], PLEASANT[4], SAMUEL[3], MANLY[2], WILLIAM[1])* was born November 12, 1926, and died October 13, 2004. She married (1) JAMES ROBERT HARMON March 15, 1945, son of LUTHER HARMON and NORA ARCHER. He was born March 29, 1927. She married (2) PAUL ARTHUR CAMPBELL September 15, 1959 in Sevier County, Tennessee. He was born May 18, 1924, and died March 15, 2003.

Children of DOROTHY KEEBLE and JAMES HARMON are:
    i. JAMES MELVIN[7] HARMON, b. March 16, 1946; m. MELBA J. BRANTLEY.
    ii. MICHAEL LYNN HARMON, b. August 23, 1951; m. DEBBIE L. TIPTON.

Child of DOROTHY KEEBLE and PAUL CAMPBELL is:
    iii. VICKY DIANE[7] CAMPBELL, b. September 28, 1960; m. GARY LYNN McNALLY.

303. JOHNNIE[6] KEEBLE *(ANDY RICHARD[5], PLEASANT[4], SAMUEL[3], MANLY[2], WILLIAM[1])* was born June 09, 1929. She married GLEN PICKLESIMER, son of BRUCE PICKLESIMER and BERTHA COLLINS.

Child of JOHNNIE KEEBLE and GLEN PICKLESIMER is:
    i. DONALD STENLEY[7] PICKLESIMER, b. August 1955.

304. WINIFRED OLIN[6] KEEBLE *(BURL ROBERT[5], JOHN RICHARD[4], SAMUEL[3], MANLY[2], WILLIAM[1])* was born August 16, 1931, and died November 06, 1983. He married DELSSIE MARIE CARVER December 31, 1952 in Blount County, Tennessee, daughter of ARTIE CARVER.

Child of WINIFRED KEEBLE and DELSSIE CARVER is:
    i. CYNTHIA ANN[7] KEEBLE, b. January 1959.

305. WILMA INEZ[6] KEEBLE *(BURL ROBERT[5], JOHN RICHARD[4], SAMUEL[3], MANLY[2], WILLIAM[1])* was born April 01, 1933, and died February 10, 1990. She married CHARLES DOUGLAS STALEY December 19, 1952 in Blount County, Tennessee, son of WILLIAM STALEY and ZETTA KEE. He was born February 03, 1933.

Children of WILMA KEEBLE and CHARLES STALEY are:
    i. SHARON LORRAINE[7] STALEY, b. September 27, 1954; m. HUNT.
    ii. MARY CATHERINE STALEY, b. October 01, 1956; m. JAMES HARRIS.
    iii. BRENDA GAIL STALEY, b. July 11, 1960; m. IVAN PRITCHARD.

306. LOIS MARIE[6] KEEBLE *(BURL ROBERT[5], JOHN RICHARD[4], SAMUEL[3], MANLY[2], WILLIAM[1])* was born April 13, 1935. She married (1) CARL STARCHER in Cleveland, Ohio. She married (2) CLEVELAND.

Children of LOIS KEEBLE and CARL STARCHER are:
    i. SANDRA[7] STARCHER.
    ii. MICHAEL STARCHER.

307. JANICE ARLEEN[6] KEEBLE *(BURL ROBERT[5], JOHN RICHARD[4], SAMUEL[3], MANLY[2], WILLIAM[1])* She married (1) WILLIAM STANLEY. She married (2) CARLUCCI. She married (3) LEROY POPLIN March 07, 1966 in Blount Countty, Tennessee.

Child of JANICE KEEBLE and CARLUCCI is:
    i. STEVEN[7] CARLUCCI.

308. EMMA JEAN[6] KEEBLE *(RAY ELIJAH[5], JOHN RICHARD[4], SAMUEL[3], MANLY[2], WILLIAM[1])* was born July 11, 1934. She married EUGENE VANDERGRIFF June 21, 1952 in Blount Countty, Tennessee. He was born October 26, 1932.

Children of EMMA KEEBLE and EUGENE VANDERGRIFF are:
    i. LINDA SUE[7] VANDERGRIFF, b. April 27, 1953; m. WILLIAM AARON LAMBERT.
    ii. MARY LYNN VANDERGRIFF, b. January 08, 1955; m. GARY TIPTON.
    iii. TERRI LEE VANDERGRIFF, b. January 08, 1955; m. HARVEY OWENS.

309. NORMA RAY[6] KEEBLE *(RAY ELIJAH[5], JOHN RICHARD[4], SAMUEL[3], MANLY[2], WILLIAM[1])* was born November 24, 1938. She married (1) JOHN STEVE NOAH October 08, 1958, son of JAMES NOAH and PEARL HART. He was born November 24, 1934. She married (2) ACEY LEWIS JACKSON February 22, 1971 in Blount Countty, Tennessee, son of CLYDE JACKSON and MARY JACKSON. She married (3) WILLIAM HOUSTON HENRY July 09, 1976 in Blount Countty, Tennessee.

Children of NORMA KEEBLE and JOHN NOAH are:
    i. ANTHONY RAY[7] NOAH, b. July 31, 1959; m. REBECCA SANCHEZ.
    ii. STEVEN LEE NOAH, b. November 04, 1960.
    iii. LISA JEAN NOAH, b. June 30, 1962; m. (1) ALBERT BOND; m. (2) JAMES PATRICK KING.

Child of NORMA KEEBLE and ACEY JACKSON is:
    iv.   TRACY LYNN[7] JACKSON, b. April 20, 1972.

310. RUBY LEE[6] KEEBLE *(RAY ELIJAH[5], JOHN RICHARD[4], SAMUEL[3], MANLY[2], WILLIAM[1])* was born January 18, 1941, and died May 31, 1993. She married JAMES ROGER STEWART November 24, 1957 in Chattsworth ,Georgia, son of FRANK STEWART and MONNIE.

Children of RUBY KEEBLE and JAMES STEWART are:
    i.   RAY BOYD[7] STEWART, b. March 04, 1966; m. LUANN LEATHERWOOD.
    ii.   PATRICIA JOY STEWART, b. April 26, 1969; m. (1) DANIEL MCKELVEY; m. (2) JEFF THATCHER.

311. JOYCE ANN[6] KEEBLE *(RAY ELIJAH[5], JOHN RICHARD[4], SAMUEL[3], MANLY[2], WILLIAM[1])* was born April 28, 1948. She married REV.THOMAS WAYNE COMPTON April 13, 1966 in Blount Countty,Tennessee, son of CLAUDE COMPTON and NEVA GRAVES. He was born May 12, 1945.

Children of JOYCE KEEBLE and REV.THOMAS COMPTON are:
    i.   RICHARD RAY[7] COMPTON, b. January 28, 1967; m. CHRISTY GODDARD.
    ii.   THOMAS WAYNE COMPTON, b. March 26, 1970; m. CAROLANN RANKIN.
    iii.   KIMBERLY LEANN COMPTON, b. November 10, 1984.

312. RAY ELIJAH[6] KEEBLE,JR. *(RAY ELIJAH[5], JOHN RICHARD[4], SAMUEL[3], MANLY[2], WILLIAM[1])* was born April 22, 1952. He married BONNIE KATE EVERETT December 25, 1973 in Knox County,Tennessee, daughter of LAWRENCE EVERETT and ROXIE MOSES. She was born December 16, 1951.

Children of RAY KEEBLE and BONNIE EVERETT are:
    i.   MICHELLE RENEE[7] KEEBLE, b. August 22, 1974; m. ANTHONY PAUL RHYNE, June 19, 1993, Blount Countty,Tennessee.
    ii.   MICHAEL RAY KEEBLE, b. August 31, 1977.
    iii.   JOSHUA EVERETT ELIJAH KEEBLE, b. July 07, 1981.
    iv.   JESSICA KATE KEEBLE, b. March 22, 1984.

313. JAMES RICHARD[6] KEEBLE *(RAY ELIJAH[5], JOHN RICHARD[4], SAMUEL[3], MANLY[2], WILLIAM[1])* was born May 01, 1953. He married (1) DONNA LEE WATERS September 15, 1976 in Blount Countty,Tennessee. He married (2) PHYLLIS ROSS February 09, 1995 in Blount Countty,Tennessee.

Children of JAMES KEEBLE and DONNA WATERS are:
    i.   JAMIE LEE[7] KEEBLE, b. April 30, 1977; m. JASON PICKENS, January 29, 2000, Blount Countty,Tennessee.
    ii.   JEREMY RICHARD KEEBLE, b. February 20, 1984.

Child of JAMES KEEBLE and PHYLLIS ROSS is:
    iii.   JAMES RICHARD ROSS[7] KEEBLE, b. February 10, 1995.

314. JACK LEE[6] KEEBLE *(PAUL ANDREWS[5], JOHN RICHARD[4], SAMUEL[3], MANLY[2], WILLIAM[1])* was born January 24, 1937. He married (1) NORMA JEAN CLAMPET July 19, 1956 in Blount Countty,Tennessee, daughter of JOHN CLAMPET and LUCILLE MCAFEE. She was born July 19, 1940. He married (2) SANDRA DARLENE WRIGHT September 20, 1983, daughter of KENNETH VANN and WANDA SHARP. She was born December 06, 1948.

Children of JACK KEEBLE and NORMA CLAMPET are:
404.   i.   JACK LEE[7] KEEBLE,JR., b. March 04, 1957.
405.   ii.   GARY THOMAS KEEBLE, b. February 04, 1958.
        iii.   RANDALL GENE KEEBLE, b. August 04, 1960; d. January 07, 1993; m. JANICE CAROL HILL, April 09, 1979, Blount Countty,Tennessee; b. 1961.
        iv.   KAREN KEEBLE, b. September 04, 1964.

315. BOBBY JEARLD[6] KEEBLE *(PAUL ANDREWS[5], JOHN RICHARD[4], SAMUEL[3], MANLY[2], WILLIAM[1])* was born June 02, 1938, and died February 02, 1989. He married (1) MARLYS MARIE BUMBALOUGH, daughter of HARLEN BUMBALOUGH and DOROTHY GAHIAMER. She was born July 03, 1957. He married (2) ESSIE FAYE DYKE May 30, 1959 in Blount Countty, Tennessee.

Children of BOBBY KEEBLE and ESSIE DYKE are:
    i.   KRISTIN[7] KEEBLE.
   ii.   TAMMY KEEBLE.

316. TRENDLE JAY[6] KEEBLE *(PAUL ANDREWS[5], JOHN RICHARD[4], SAMUEL[3], MANLY[2], WILLIAM[1])* was born October 11, 1942. He married MCGAHA, daughter of GEORGE MCGAHA and TINIA BELL.

Child of TRENDLE KEEBLE and MCGAHA is:
    i.   TINIA[7] KEEBLE, m. TOM KEYEES, August 06, 1983, Blount Countty, Tennessee.

317. DONNA LYNN[6] KEEBLE *(WILLIAM THOMAS[5], SAMUEL WILEY[4], RICHARD HENRY[3], MANLY[2], WILLIAM[1])* was born October 20, 1938. She married CARL E. HALASY September 24, 1964, son of EMERY HALASY and ANNA KLEINHOLZ. He was born October 13, 1927.

Children of DONNA KEEBLE and CARL HALASY are:
    i.   GREG[7] HALASY, b. October 23, 1966.
   ii.   KEITH HALASY, b. December 20, 1969; m. ERIN TRIPP.

318. THOMAS ARTHUR[6] KEEBLE *(WILLIAM THOMAS[5], SAMUEL WILEY[4], RICHARD HENRY[3], MANLY[2], WILLIAM[1])* was born November 26, 1942. He married LINDA GALE MCNEILLY February 25, 1967 in Blount Countty, Tennessee, daughter of BEN MCNIELLY and TROY MCCLANAHAN. She was born December 27, 1945.

Child of THOMAS KEEBLE and LINDA MCNEILLY is:
406.   i.   MISTY MICHELLE[7] KEEBLE, b. September 23, 1973.

319. BETTY SUE[6] KEEBLE *(WILLIAM THOMAS[5], SAMUEL WILEY[4], RICHARD HENRY[3], MANLY[2], WILLIAM[1])* was born November 26, 1942. She married JAMES ELI FIELDS September 21, 1963 in Blount Countty, Tennessee, son of J. FIELDS and UNA RHYNES. He was born October 23, 1943.

Child of BETTY KEEBLE and JAMES FIELDS is:
    i.   JAMA BETH[7] FIELDS, b. September 10, 1967; m. MIKE TARWATER.

320. CHARLOTTE JANE[6] KEEBLE *(EDGAR[5], SAMUEL WILEY[4], RICHARD HENRY[3], MANLY[2], WILLIAM[1])* was born September 05, 1941. She married JOSEPH BURL MCCAMMON June 11, 1961 in Blount Countty, Tennessee, son of JOE MCCAMMON and EUNICE PRYOR. He was born December 28, 1940.

Child of CHARLOTTE KEEBLE and JOSEPH MCCAMMON is:
    i.   VICKIE DENICE[7] MCCAMMON.

321. GLENDA KAY[6] KEEBLE *(EDGAR[5], SAMUEL WILEY[4], RICHARD HENRY[3], MANLY[2], WILLIAM[1])* was born February 21, 1946. She married (1) RALPH DAVID CHRISTENBERRY April 24, 1965 in Blount Countty, Tennessee, son of RALPH CHRISTENBERRY and MARY HENLEY. He was born December 24, 1944. She married (2) JACKIE BRUCE EDMONDSON July 26, 1986 in Blount Countty, Tennessee, son of VIRGIL EDMONDSON and GLADYS SWEET. He was born February 09, 1940.

Children of GLENDA KEEBLE and RALPH CHRISTENBERRY are:
  i.   DAVID EDWARD[7] CHRISTENBERRY, b. June 22, 1967.
  ii. LESLIE HOPE CHRISTENBERRY, b. August 16, 1970.

322. RONALD LYNN[6] KEEBLE *(LLOYD CATLETT[5], SAMUEL WILEY[4], RICHARD HENRY[3], MANLY[2], WILLIAM[1])* was born July 08, 1942. He married NELLIE MAE FIELDS January 16, 1966 in Blount Countty, Tennessee, daughter of BERNIE BOWERS and CHARLOTTE HEADRICK. She was born May 11, 1948.

Children of RONALD KEEBLE and NELLIE FIELDS are:
407.   i.   MARK ANTONY[7] KEEBLE, b. August 16, 1966.
        ii.   TIMOTHY LYNN KEEBLE, b. December 30, 1967; d. April 19, 2004.
408.   iii. ALLEN LLOYD KEEBLE, b. September 26, 1973.

323. JOHN THOMAS[6] KEEBLE, SR. *(LLOYD CATLETT[5], SAMUEL WILEY[4], RICHARD HENRY[3], MANLY[2], WILLIAM[1])* was born October 29, 1944. He married CONSTANCE ANN BOSTIC February 28, 1964 in Alexandria, Virginia, daughter of CLARENCE BOSTIC and GEORGIA WEIKLE. She was born June 14, 1943.

Children of JOHN KEEBLE and CONSTANCE BOSTIC are:
409.   i.   JOHN THOMAS[7] KEEBLE, JR., b. October 02, 1965.
410.   ii.   KARLA SHEA KEEBLE, b. December 10, 1970.

324. DAVID EUGENE[6] KEEBLE *(LLOYD CATLETT[5], SAMUEL WILEY[4], RICHARD HENRY[3], MANLY[2], WILLIAM[1])* was born October 08, 1947. He married DEBORAH JO BRACKETT September 18, 1971 in Blount Countty, Tennessee, daughter of CARR BRACKETT and GOLDIA HOWARD. She was born June 25, 1952.

Children of DAVID KEEBLE and DEBORAH BRACKETT are:
  i.   JASON DAVID[7] KEEBLE, b. April 22, 1975.
  ii. JEFFREY SCOTT KEEBLE, b. August 14, 1979; m. LISA RENEE TOBIAS, July 13, 2002, Davidson County, Tenn.; b. June 15, 1980.

325. GERALDINE[6] KEEBLE *(ROBERT PAUL[5], SAMUEL WILEY[4], RICHARD HENRY[3], MANLY[2], WILLIAM[1])* was born November 10, 1940. She married ROBERT RUSSELL MCKENRY, JR. September 06, 1958 in Blount Countty, Tennessee, son of ROBERT MCKENRY and SARAH BROWN. He was born April 08, 1939.

Children of GERALDINE KEEBLE and ROBERT MCKENRY are:
  i.   ROBIN RENEE[7] MCKENRY, b. July 18, 1960; m. GREGORY DUNCAN ADAMS.
  ii. ROBERT RUSSELL MCKENRY III, b. April 03, 1964; m. LAURA ANN BULTSMA.

326. RANDALL PAUL[6] KEEBLE *(ROBERT PAUL[5], SAMUEL WILEY[4], RICHARD HENRY[3], MANLY[2], WILLIAM[1])* was born October 03, 1942. He married HERTA GUDRUN LEONHARDT April 13, 1963 in Arlington, Virginia, daughter of JAKOB LEONHARDT and AGNES HERWIG. She was born December 25, 1942.

Children of RANDALL KEEBLE and HERTA LEONHARDT are:
        i.   JAMIE SUE[7] KEEBLE, b. November 24, 1964.
411.   ii.   HEIDI LYNN KEEBLE, b. November 10, 1965.

327. SHEILA GAIL[6] KEEBLE *(ROBERT PAUL[5], SAMUEL WILEY[4], RICHARD HENRY[3], MANLY[2], WILLIAM[1])* was born April 04, 1948. She married CHARLES EDWARD MOORE July 25, 1966 in Bryson City, North Carolina, son of WILLIAM MOORE and ROXIE OWNBY. He was born December 16, 1944.

Children of SHEILA KEEBLE and CHARLES MOORE are:
  i.   CHRISTINA GAIL[7] MOORE, b. June 08, 1970; m. JEFFREY MARK WARD.
  ii. JEFFREY CHARLES MOORE, b. December 26, 1973; m. AMANDA PENLEY.

328. DANA HUGH[6] KEEBLE *(ROBERT PAUL[5], SAMUEL WILEY[4], RICHARD HENRY[3], MANLY[2], WILLIAM[1])* was born January 21, 1950. He married (1) CONNIE SUE BROWN June 03, 1972 in Blount Countty, Tennessee, daughter of ROBERT BROWN and BETH MCGILL. He married (2) JACQUELINE M. HICKS August 29, 1983 in Knox County, Tennessee, daughter of NORMAN HICKS and WANDA CUTSHAW. She was born February 28, 1964.

Child of DANA KEEBLE and CONNIE BROWN is:
    i.   SARA BETH[7] KEEBLE.

Children of DANA KEEBLE and JACQUELINE HICKS are:
    ii.   KELLY[7] KEEBLE.
    iii. LEAH KEEBLE.

329. MARTHA ANN[6] KEEBLE *(SAMUEL CARL[5], SAMUEL WILEY[4], RICHARD HENRY[3], MANLY[2], WILLIAM[1])* was born October 02, 1945. She married (1) JIMMY RAY HATCHER August 04, 1966 in Knox County, Tennessee, son of JAMES HATCHER and LYDIA SATTERFIELD. He was born July 08, 1947. She married (2) RONALD O. HUTCHINS October 25, 1986 in Blount Countty, Tennessee, son of OARY HUTCHINS and NELLIE FIFE. He was born June 19, 1942.

Children of MARTHA KEEBLE and JIMMY HATCHER are:
    i.   BRADLEY RAY[7] HATCHER, b. April 06, 1967; m. SANDY SMALL.
    ii.   CARRIE JO HATCHER, b. September 17, 1970; m. DEAN COONS.

330. JOSEPH HOWARD[6] KEEBLE *(SAMUEL CARL[5], SAMUEL WILEY[4], RICHARD HENRY[3], MANLY[2], WILLIAM[1])* was born January 10, 1952. He married ANNA MARIE WILSON, daughter of J. W. WILSON.

Children of JOSEPH KEEBLE and ANNA WILSON are:
    i.   JAMES RUSSELL[7] KEEBLE, b. June 28, 1972.
    ii.   SAMUEL ROBERT KEEBLE, b. November 29, 1976.

331. FLOYD MARION[6] KEEBLE *(JOHN MARION[5], JOHN ELLISON[4], MARION[3], RICHARD PORTER[2], WILLIAM[1])* was born May 14, 1920. He married (1) EDNA MAY NELSON August 25, 1941, daughter of NORMAN NELSON and IVAH MARSH. He married (2) BERNICE MEAD June 27, 1946, daughter of HUDSON MEAD and GLADYS STREIGHT.

Child of FLOYD KEEBLE and EDNA NELSON is:
412.   i.   JERRY A.[7] KEEBLE, b. July 26, 1942.

332. KATHRYN ELIZABETH[6] KEEBLE *(JOHN MARION[5], JOHN ELLISON[4], MARION[3], RICHARD PORTER[2], WILLIAM[1])* was born October 18, 1921. She married (1) RUSSELL M. NELSON August 26, 1939 in Santa Clara, California, son of NORMAN NELSON and IVAH MARSH. He was born Abt. 1920. She married (2) CLIFFORD RALPH JONES, SR. October 02, 1944 in Carson City, Nevada, son of BEN JONES. He was born February 19, 1908, and died March 03, 1959. She married (3) DONALD CHARLES SHAW April 16, 1960. He was born July 09, 1923. She married (4) OLIVER FRANKLIN BENNETT June 06, 1979 in Reno, Nevada. He was born September 11, 1926.

Child of KATHRYN KEEBLE and RUSSELL NELSON is:
    i.   ROBERT FLOYD[7] NELSON, b. December 16, 1940; m. BETTY.

Children of KATHRYN KEEBLE and CLIFFORD JONES are:
    ii.   LINDA MAE[7] JONES, b. September 07, 1947; m. JAMES EDWARD OSHER.
    iii.   CLINTON CHARLES JONES, b. February 17, 1952; m. LORENA L. GIDDINGS.

333. CHARLES RICHARD[6] KEEBLE *(JOHN MARION[5], JOHN ELLISON[4], MARION[3], RICHARD PORTER[2], WILLIAM[1])* was born July 25, 1929, and died November 28, 1998. He married IRENE CECELIA MONTMAN September 20, 1943, daughter of FRED MONTMAN and IDA SCHULZ. She was born Abt. 1924.

Children of CHARLES KEEBLE and IRENE MONTMAN are:
413.   i.   JAYNE ANN[7] KEEBLE, b. March 11, 1945.
414.   ii.   CECELIA JUNE KEEBLE, b. May 05, 1947; d. May 02, 1980.
415.   iii. SHARON ELIZABETH KEEBLE, b. July 20, 1949.

334. EUNICE BONNIE[6] KEEBLE *(EDWARD GEORGE[5], EDWARD GEORGE[4], MARION[3], RICHARD PORTER[2], WILLIAM[1])* was born December 27, 1926, and died February 20, 1998. She married ROY HAYWARD HARRIS November 15, 1945 in Reno Nevada, son of FREDERICK HARRIS and BLANCHE MARRIOTT. He was born January 13, 1918, and died December 28, 1980.

Children of EUNICE KEEBLE and ROY HARRIS are:
        i.   EDWARD FREDERICK[7] HARRIS, b. October 02, 1948; m. KAREN JEANETTE MORSE.
        ii.   GLORIA LOUISE HARRIS, b. July 01, 1949; m. (1) WENDELL LANCE SOUSA; m. (2) MURRY FRANK FUDIM.
        iii. MELANIE ANNE HARRIS, b. August 20, 1951; m. DAVID MICHAEL CULLEN.
        iv.   CARL WILLIAM HARRIS, b. May 21, 1956; m. KATHLEEN SINWELL CARRIGG.
        v.   RODERICK ROY HARRIS, b. December 04, 1958; m. CAROL ANN INMAN.

335. LAURENCE CECIL[6] KEEBLE,SR. *(CECIL[5], STEPHEN[4], NANCY[3], WALTER HARRISON[2], WILLIAM[1])* was born December 19, 1940. He married LINDA JOYCE DIXON June 15, 1963 in Putnam County,Tennessee, daughter of CHARLIE DIXON and FRONNIE WELCH. She was born February 23, 1944.

Children of LAURENCE KEEBLE and LINDA DIXON are:
        i.   LAURENCE CECIL[7] KEEBLE,JR., b. July 14, 1966.
        ii.   STEVEN CHARLES KEEBLE, b. June 29, 1969.

336. KENNETH VANCE[6] KEEBLE *(CECIL[5], STEPHEN[4], NANCY[3], WALTER HARRISON[2], WILLIAM[1])* was born July 21, 1942. He married BONNIE KATHRYN ELLERBEE June 05, 1964 in Blount Countty,Tennessee, daughter of ERNEST ELLERBEE and VIRGINIA EDWARDS. She was born October 25, 1946.

Children of KENNETH KEEBLE and BONNIE ELLERBEE are:
        i.   TINA LYNN[7] KEEBLE, b. January 1968.
        ii.   KENNETH GLENN KEEBLE, b. September 1971.
        iii. LISA MARIE KEEBLE, b. May 1978; d. 1978.

337. DALLAS LEON[6] KEEBLE *(CECIL[5], STEPHEN[4], NANCY[3], WALTER HARRISON[2], WILLIAM[1])* was born August 07, 1945. He married DORINE JANICE BROWN July 12, 1970 in Los Angeles,California, daughter of LEONARD BROWN and MILDRED KIEBORZ. She was born April 04, 1947.

Children of DALLAS KEEBLE and DORINE BROWN are:
        i.   DONNA JANICE[7] KEEBLE, b. July 18, 1976; m. DAVID NORMAN RHEA,JR., October 28, 1995, Blount County,Tennessee; b. August 15, 1975.
        ii.   DERRICK LEON KEEBLE, b. May 13, 1979.

338. JUDITH FAYE[6] KEEBLE *(CARA LONNIE[5], STEPHEN[4], NANCY[3], WALTER HARRISON[2], WILLIAM[1])* was born April 25, 1948. She married FRED ROY BEATY November 01, 1974 in Monroe County,Tennessee, son of NEWTON BEATY and MARY M.DAUGHERTY. He was born August 10, 1924.

Children of JUDITH KEEBLE and FRED BEATY are:

i.   RENEE ANNETTE[7] BEATY, b. September 26, 1966; m. RANDY DEWAINE WHITE.
ii. JONATHAN KEEBLE BEATY, b. July 13, 1980.

More About JONATHAN KEEBLE BEATY:
Adoption: July 13, 1980

339. WYVETTA DELORES[6] KEEBLE *(ROY VIRGIL[5], STEPHEN[4], NANCY[3], WALTER HARRISON[2], WILLIAM[1])* was born August 24, 1943. She married EARL SAMUEL ALEXANDER October 1960 in Blount County, Tennessee, son of WALDEN ALEXANDER.

Children of WYVETTA KEEBLE and EARL ALEXANDER are:
i.   RICKY LYNN[7] ALEXANDER, b. August 08, 1961; d. February 17, 1979.
ii. DONNA SUE ALEXANDER, b. June 27, 1963; m. LEWIS TRUSTY.
iii. HAZEL RENEE ALEXANDER, b. September 26, 1966.
iv. CHRISTI ANN ALEXANDER, b. 1973.

340. VERNON DEWAYNE[6] KEEBLE *(ROY VIRGIL[5], STEPHEN[4], NANCY[3], WALTER HARRISON[2], WILLIAM[1])* was born December 17, 1945. He married EDNA JUNE BURCHFIELD June 18, 1966 in Blount County, Tennessee, daughter of JAMES BURCHFIELD and ELLEN ROBINSON. She was born July 07, 1947.

Child of VERNON KEEBLE and EDNA BURCHFIELD is:
416.   i.   SONDRA ANN[7] KEEBLE, b. March 23, 1967.

341. WANDA SUE[6] KEEBLE *(ROY VIRGIL[5], STEPHEN[4], NANCY[3], WALTER HARRISON[2], WILLIAM[1])* was born December 19, 1946. She married (1) LOY JAMES DOCKERY. She married (2) FRENNY POSEY, JR. November 12, 1983.

Children of WANDA KEEBLE and LOY DOCKERY are:
i.   TREINA LOUISE[7] DOCKERY, m. STEVE HETTERLY.
ii. LOY JAMES DOCKERY II, b. November 02, 1965; m. TAMARA.

342. LARRY STEPHEN[6] KEEBLE *(ROY VIRGIL[5], STEPHEN[4], NANCY[3], WALTER HARRISON[2], WILLIAM[1])* was born August 28, 1949. He married JO ANN SUTTON.

Child of LARRY KEEBLE and JO SUTTON is:
i.   STEPHEN HOYAL[7] KEEBLE, b. August 24, 1977.

Generation No. 7

343. BOBBY LEE[7] KEEBLE *(HOMER PRESTON[6], WILLIAM LAFAYETTE[5], JOHN HOUSTON[4], JAMES H.[3], THOMAS[2], WILLIAM[1])* was born November 04, 1940. He married RONDA MARCHANT.

Child of BOBBY KEEBLE and RONDA MARCHANT is:
i.   RONNIE LEE[8] KEEBLE.

344. JOE WAYNE[7] KEEBLE *(JOSEPH[6], WILLIAM LAFAYETTE[5], JOHN HOUSTON[4], JAMES H.[3], THOMAS[2], WILLIAM[1])* was born August 31, 1927. He married (1) LOIS RENEE RANDAL 1946 in Dallas, Texas. She was born November 22, 1928. He married (2) WANDA HICKS 1965.

Child of JOE KEEBLE and LOIS RANDAL is:
417.   i.   JOANN[8] KEEBLE, b. June 15, 1952.

345. PATSY RUTH[7] KEEBLE *(JOSEPH[6], WILLIAM LAFAYETTE[5], JOHN HOUSTON[4], JAMES H.[3], THOMAS[2], WILLIAM[1])* was born November 23, 1930, and died May 1991. She married (1) ROBERT ALLEN FORDYCE June 29, 1946. She married (2) JOHN WILL NOBLE December 26, 1953 in Dallas, Texas, son of RALPH NOBLE and BERTHA EDDY. He was born July 17, 1929.

Child of PATSY KEEBLE and ROBERT FORDYCE is:
      i.   RICHARD STEVEN[8] FORDYCE, b. February 18, 1952; m. LIZABETH ANN RUDLOFF.

Child of PATSY KEEBLE and JOHN NOBLE is:
      ii.   RICHARD STEVEN[8] NOBLE(ADOPTED), b. February 28, 1952; m. LIZABETH ANN RUDLOFF.

346. DORIS JEANNENE[7] KEEBLE *(JOSEPH[6], WILLIAM LAFAYETTE[5], JOHN HOUSTON[4], JAMES H.[3], THOMAS[2], WILLIAM[1])* was born September 05, 1933. She married (1) R. D. BAILEY. She married (2) TOMMY EARL CARTWRIGHT February 08, 1970.

Child of DORIS KEEBLE and R. BAILEY is:
      i.   RONALD DAVID[8] BAILEY, b. November 20, 1951.

347. KENNETH JERRY[7] KEEBLE *(JOSEPH[6], WILLIAM LAFAYETTE[5], JOHN HOUSTON[4], JAMES H.[3], THOMAS[2], WILLIAM[1])* was born June 26, 1937. He married (1) MARY SNOW. He married (2) GRACE ROSEMARY BURTON ZINKE March 06, 1965.

Child of KENNETH KEEBLE and GRACE ZINKE is:
      i.   LORI KENDRA[8] KEEBLE, b. August 31, 1966.

348. MYRA DELORA[7] KEEBLE *(WILLIAM GLOVER[6], SAMUEL E.[5], TAYLOR S.[4], JAMES H.[3], THOMAS[2], WILLIAM[1])* was born February 03, 1940. She married (1) TRUMAN RAY FRENCH June 07, 1958 in Randolph County, Alabama, son of LARKIN FRENCH and RUBY PARKER. He was born January 24, 1937, and died March 09, 1988. She married (2) WALLACE LEDFORD WILLIAMSON September 10, 1992 in Randolph County, Alabama, son of WILLIAM WILLIAMSON and OLETHA CHAFFIN. He was born November 12, 1942.

Children of MYRA KEEBLE and TRUMAN FRENCH are:
      i.   MICHELLE RAE[8] FRENCH, b. June 10, 1960; m. PATRICK MARTIN SMITH.
      ii.   ELIZABETH JANE FRENCH, b. December 19, 1961; m. WARREN COLEMAN POWELL.
      iii.   RICHARD DEWAYNE FRENCH, b. January 24, 1965.

349. ALLEN BARBER[7] KEEBLE *(ALLEN TAYLOR[6], SAMUEL E.[5], TAYLOR S.[4], JAMES H.[3], THOMAS[2], WILLIAM[1])* was born June 11, 1941. He married MARGARET ELIZABETH HOEHNE August 25, 1968 in Muscogee County, Georgia, daughter of HARRY HOEHNE and FLORA BAXLEY. She was born January 27, 1947.

Children of ALLEN KEEBLE and MARGARET HOEHNE are:
      i.   SCOTT ALLEN[8] KEEBLE, b. September 10, 1971.
      ii.   ADAM TAYLOR KEEBLE, b. December 17, 1974.

350. DAVID MICHAEL[7] KEEBLE *(ALLEN TAYLOR[6], SAMUEL E.[5], TAYLOR S.[4], JAMES H.[3], THOMAS[2], WILLIAM[1])* was born December 20, 1957. He married PHYLISS SMITH April 10, 1981.

Child of DAVID KEEBLE and PHYLISS SMITH is:
      i.   DAVID TAYLOR[8] KEEBLE, b. December 15, 1983.

351. JOE[7] KEEBLE *(JAMES TAYLOR[6], JOHN H.[5], TAYLOR S.[4], JAMES H.[3], THOMAS[2], WILLIAM[1])* was born December 22, 1923. He married DELL CUNNINGHAM.

Children of JOE KEEBLE and DELL CUNNINGHAM are:

418. i. JAMES JOSEPH[8] KEEBLE, b. October 25, 1944.
      ii. MARY J. KEEBLE, b. September 1959.

352. ALLIE JEAN[7] KEEBLE *(JAMES TAYLOR[6], JOHN H.[5], TAYLOR S.[4], JAMES H.[3], THOMAS[2], WILLIAM[1])* She married FRED RICHARDSON.

Children of ALLIE KEEBLE and FRED RICHARDSON are:
      i.   FREDDIE[8] RICHARDSON.
      ii. WAYNE RICHARDSON.
      iii. MARTHA DELL RICHARDSON.
      iv. DEBBIE RICHARDSON.
      v.   CINDY RICHARDSON.

353. MARTHA DAPHNE[7] KEEBLE *(JAMES TAYLOR[6], JOHN H.[5], TAYLOR S.[4], JAMES H.[3], THOMAS[2], WILLIAM[1])* was born December 27. She married SNYDER GODFREY.

Children of MARTHA KEEBLE and SNYDER GODFREY are:
      i.   CLAIRE[8] GODFREY.
      ii. ROBERT GODFREY.
      iii. THOMAS GODFREY.
      iv. JANE GODFREY.
      v.   SNYDER GODFREY.
      vi. JOHN GODFREY.

354. TROY[7] KEEBLE *(JAMES TAYLOR[6], JOHN H.[5], TAYLOR S.[4], JAMES H.[3], THOMAS[2], WILLIAM[1])* He married ERNESTINE HALL.

Children of TROY KEEBLE and ERNESTINE HALL are:
      i.   MICHAEL[8] KEEBLE.
      ii. DAVID KEEBLE.
      iii. AMY KEEBLE.
      iv. STEVE KEEBLE.
      v.   MARY KEEBLE.

355. ROGER[7] KEEBLE *(JAMES TAYLOR[6], JOHN H.[5], TAYLOR S.[4], JAMES H.[3], THOMAS[2], WILLIAM[1])* He married JUNE BONNER.

Children of ROGER KEEBLE and JUNE BONNER are:
      i.   STEVEN[8] KEEBLE.
      ii. LYNN KEEBLE, m. ALEX SHERRER.

356. ANN[7] KEEBLE *(JAMES TAYLOR[6], JOHN H.[5], TAYLOR S.[4], JAMES H.[3], THOMAS[2], WILLIAM[1])* was born May 13, 1938. She married ROBERT F. CARTER.

Children of ANN KEEBLE and ROBERT CARTER are:
      i.   KIRKLAND LEE[8] CARTER.
      ii. LEILANI MARIE CARTER.

357. PEARL ADELL[7] KEEBLE *(JAMES TAYLOR[6], JOHN H.[5], TAYLOR S.[4], JAMES H.[3], THOMAS[2], WILLIAM[1])* was born October 31, 1940. She married (1) NEWTON W. ANDERSON, JR. June 1958. She married (2) WILLIAM EARL LESTER October 15, 1982.

Children of PEARL KEEBLE and NEWTON ANDERSON are:

    i.   KATHRYN LYNN[8] ANDERSON, b. May 15, 1959.
    ii. RICHARD GLEN ANDERSON, b. May 02, 1961; m. NANCY COLE.
    iii. BERRY EUGENE ANDERSON, b. July 02, 1966; m. (1) KRISTIE LONGSHORE; m. (2) CATHY HAY.
    iv. TIMOTHY LANE ANDERSON, b. November 26, 1970.

358. BARBARA REGINA[7] KEEBLE *(JERRY LILES[6], JERRY MACK[5], TAYLOR S.[4], JAMES H.[3], THOMAS[2], WILLIAM[1])* was born October 12, 1939. She married VICTOR ROBBINS 1959.

Children of BARBARA KEEBLE and VICTOR ROBBINS are:

    i.   DEBORAH[8] ROBBINS, b. 1961.
    ii. STEPHANIE ROBBINS, b. 1965.
    iii. VICTOR ROBBINS,JR., b. 1968.

359. GERALDINE[7] KEEBLE *(JERRY LILES[6], JERRY MACK[5], TAYLOR S.[4], JAMES H.[3], THOMAS[2], WILLIAM[1])* was born January 24, 1943. She married JOHN THOMAS SMITH 1960.

Children of GERALDINE KEEBLE and JOHN SMITH are:

    i.   TAMARA[8] SMITH.
    ii. ROBERT SMITH.
    iii. MARK SMITH.

360. JERRY DION[7] KEEBLE *(TRESFORD[6], ANDREW DAVIS[5], TAYLOR S.[4], JAMES H.[3], THOMAS[2], WILLIAM[1])* was born December 19, 1936. He married THETA FAE ROMANS November 03, 1956. She was born March 03, 1938.

Children of JERRY KEEBLE and THETA ROMANS are:

419.   i.   TONY DION[8] KEEBLE, b. July 08, 1960.
          ii. JUDY KAY KEEBLE, b. January 04, 1963.
          iii. ANDREW ERIC KEEBLE, b. July 02, 1965; m. LEANNE MARIE EVANS, August 22, 1992.

361. DIONA JEAN[7] KEEBLE *((ANDREW DAVIS KEEBLE[6] (A.D.), ANDREW DAVIS[5] KEEBLE, TAYLOR S.[4], JAMES H.[3], THOMAS[2], WILLIAM[1])* was born August 31, 1940. She married (1) JOE HENDERSON May 06, 1956. She married (2) LEWIS PAFFORD March 02, 1958.

Child of DIONA KEEBLE and JOE HENDERSON is:

    i.   DEBRA[8] HENDERSON, b. February 21, 1957.

Children of DIONA KEEBLE and LEWIS PAFFORD are:

    ii. TAMMY[8] PAFFORD, b. December 27, 1958.
    iii. HOWARD LYNN PAFFORD, b. October 28, 1960.

362. JIMMY JOYCE[7] KEEBLE *((ANDREW DAVIS KEEBLE[6] (A.D.), ANDREW DAVIS[5] KEEBLE, TAYLOR S.[4], JAMES H.[3], THOMAS[2], WILLIAM[1])* was born July 24, 1942. He married BOBBIE NICHOLS September 02, 1957. She was born September 14, 1936.

Children of JIMMY KEEBLE and BOBBIE NICHOLS are:

    i.   ARANDO SUE[8] KEEBLE, b. June 19, 1958.
    ii. TINA RENEE KEEBLE, b. May 06, 1960.

363. GARY EARL[7] KEEBLE.SR. *(EARL CORTEZ[6] KEEBLE, BYRD[5], TAYLOR S.[4], JAMES H.[3], THOMAS[2], WILLIAM[1])* was born September 20, 1936. He married SANDRA.

Children of GARY KEEBLE.SR. and SANDRA are:
    i.   GARY EARL[8] KEEBLE,JR..
    ii. LEE KEEBLE.

364. JAMES WALLACE[7] KEEBLE *(EARL CORTEZ[6], BYRD[5], TAYLOR S.[4], JAMES H.[3], THOMAS[2], WILLIAM[1])* was born February 14, 1938. He married FRANCES FINNEY.

Children of JAMES KEEBLE and FRANCES FINNEY are:
    i.   BLAKE[8] KEEBLE.
    ii. WALLACE KEEBLE.

365. DENNIS MORGAN[7] KEEBLE *(EARL CORTEZ[6], BYRD[5], TAYLOR S.[4], JAMES H.[3], THOMAS[2], WILLIAM[1])* was born February 05, 1946. He married CAROLYN ELAINE NEWBY February 18, 1966. She was born June 09, 1945.

Child of DENNIS KEEBLE and CAROLYN NEWBY is:
    i.   ALLEN NEWBY[8] KEEBLE, b. April 27, 1967.

366. JIMMY THOMAS[7] KEEBLE *(THOMAS EARNEST[6], PIERCE MACK[5], TAYLOR S.[4], JAMES H.[3], THOMAS[2], WILLIAM[1])* was born March 08, 1938, and died January 15, 1992. He married BETTY JANE WEST October 29, 1960. She was born August 24, 1937.

Children of JIMMY KEEBLE and BETTY WEST are:
           i.   DEBBIE WEST[8] KEEBLE, b. December 21, 1952; m. DANIEL MOSS.
420.   ii. WADE WEST KEEBLE, b. February 19, 1954.
421.   iii. CHERISE LaRUE KEEBLE, b. August 20, 1963.
          iv. TINA MICHELLE KEEBLE, b. August 10, 1966.

367. BOBBY GENE[7] KEEBLE *(THOMAS EARNEST[6], PIERCE MACK[5], TAYLOR S.[4], JAMES H.[3], THOMAS[2], WILLIAM[1])* was born August 10, 1939. He married EULA BELLE MATTHEW 1961.

Children of BOBBY KEEBLE and EULA MATTHEW are:
422.   i.   KIMBLYN KAYE[8] KEEBLE, b. October 06, 1962.
423.   ii. BETTY LYN ANN KEEBLE, b. September 11, 1964.
          iii. REBECCA ANN KEEBLE, b. April 30, 1969; m. TIMOTHY HINES, February 02, 1991.

368. JACKIE EUGENE[7] KEEBLE *(THOMAS EARNEST[6], PIERCE MACK[5], TAYLOR S.[4], JAMES H.[3], THOMAS[2], WILLIAM[1])* was born June 18, 1943. He married DUSTY LEIGH KENNEDY July 06, 1963.

Child of JACKIE KEEBLE and DUSTY KENNEDY is:
    i.   CHRISTOPHER WAYNE[8] KEEBLE, b. August 22, 1967.

369. HARRIETT ELAINE[7] KEEBLE *(THOMAS EARNEST[6], PIERCE MACK[5], TAYLOR S.[4], JAMES H.[3], THOMAS[2], WILLIAM[1])* was born June 16, 1950. She married DON JOHNSON November 28, 1967.

Children of HARRIETT KEEBLE and DON JOHNSON are:
    i.   ALISA RENEE[8] JOHNSON, b. March 09, 1971.
    ii. JAIMEY JOHNSON, b. May 05, 1973.

370. CHARLES DAVID[7] KEEBLE *(THOMAS EARNEST[6], PIERCE MACK[5], TAYLOR S.[4], JAMES H.[3], THOMAS[2], WILLIAM[1])* was born September 26, 1953. He married (1) MARY COTNEY. He married (2) CINDI STARLIN 1986.

Child of CHARLES KEEBLE and MARY COTNEY is:
    i.   DEAN COLEMAN[8] KEEBLE, b. July 05, 1974.

Children of CHARLES KEEBLE and CINDI STARLIN are:
    ii.   SAVANNAH[8] KEEBLE, b. September 29, 1987.
    iii.   JENNA KEEBLE, b. March 24, 1989.
    iv.   JORDAN KEEBLE, b. March 13, 1991.

371. CAROL JACQUELINE[7] KEEBLE (*PIERCE MACK[6], PIERCE MACK[5], TAYLOR S.[4], JAMES H.[3], THOMAS[2], WILLIAM[1]*) was born October 18, 1946. She married (1) JAMES THROWER December 25, 1964 in Randolph County, Alabama, son of HOMER THROWER and ALMA SEYMOUR. He was born September 05, 1946, and died September 13, 1967. She married (2) ALVIN MCCORMACK March 19, 1973 in Randolph County, Alabama, son of ROSS MCCORMACK and LAURA TARVER. He was born October 14, 1938, and died July 17, 1993.

Children of CAROL KEEBLE and JAMES THROWER are:
    i.   TERESA ANN[8] THROWER, b. December 07, 1965; m. (1) STEVEN ALLEN; m. (2) JAMES DECKER.
    ii.   WILLIAM DEAN THROWER, b. May 07, 1967; m. LACONGA JOHNSON.

372. PATSY JEANETTE[7] KEEBLE (*PIERCE MACK[6], PIERCE MACK[5], TAYLOR S.[4], JAMES H.[3], THOMAS[2], WILLIAM[1]*) was born October 04, 1952. She married (1) JIMMY DELL GREGG January 28, 1970 in Randolph County, Alabama, son of FARLIN GREGG and BESSIE UNKNOWN. He was born December 19, 1948. She married (2) THOMAS WALTER CARVALHO August 07, 1981 in Gwinette County, Georgia, son of EMANUEL JR. and HELENA FRASER. He was born July 16, 1948. She married (3) RONALD LANE LONG July 24, 1996 in Clay County, Alabama, son of BARYON LONG and JEAN JONES. He was born February 18, 1954.

Child of PATSY KEEBLE and THOMAS CARVALHO is:
    i.   JOSHUA THOMAS[8] CARVALHO, b. February 26, 1982.

373. DOROTHY VIRGINIA[7] KEEBLE (*HENRY WILLIAM ERASTUS[6], WILLIAM EMMETT[5], WILLIAM THOMAS[4], JAMES H.[3], THOMAS[2], WILLIAM[1]*) was born August 23, 1923. She married WILLIAM LACY FOWLER May 18, 1941.

Children of DOROTHY KEEBLE and WILLIAM FOWLER are:
    i.   WILLIAM EARL[8] FOWLER, b. March 31, 1943.
    ii.   HENRY WAYNE FOWLER, b. March 19, 1944.
    iii.   ROY LEE FOWLER, b. September 05, 1946.
    iv.   BRENDA JEAN FOWLER, b. August 05, 1948.

374. SARAH KATE[7] KEEBLE (*HENRY WILLIAM ERASTUS[6], WILLIAM EMMETT[5], WILLIAM THOMAS[4], JAMES H.[3], THOMAS[2], WILLIAM[1]*) was born October 28, 1925. She married JOSEPH N. SASSO July 15, 1955.

Children of SARAH KEEBLE and JOSEPH SASSO are:
    i.   JOSEPH WAYNE[8] SASSO, b. May 06, 1959.
    ii.   TENVA MARIA SASSO, b. March 04, 1960; m. RAYMOND C. HUSTON.

375. EDNA RAY[7] KEEBLE (*HENRY WILLIAM ERASTUS[6], WILLIAM EMMETT[5], WILLIAM THOMAS[4], JAMES H.[3], THOMAS[2], WILLIAM[1]*) She married GORDON LEE DOBBS, SR..

Children of EDNA KEEBLE and GORDON DOBBS are:
    i.   PATRICIA JANE[8] DOBBS.
    ii.   CHARLOTTE DEAN DOBBS.
    iii.   GORDON LEE DOBBS, JR..

376. JOAN DELORIS[7] KEEBLE *(HENRY WILLIAM ERASTUS[6], WILLIAM EMMETT[5], WILLIAM THOMAS[4], JAMES H.[3], THOMAS[2], WILLIAM[1])* She married (1) JAMES ARTHUR JOHNSON. She married (2) WILLIE DOUGLAS WHITNER. She married (3) ALVIN J. BENNER. She married (4) GARLAND FRANKLIN GRICE.

Children of JOAN KEEBLE and JAMES JOHNSON are:
    i.   KATHIE MARIE[8] JOHNSON, b. December 24, 1952.
    ii. ARTHUR RAY JOHNSON, d. 1979.
    iii. DANNY JOE JOHNSON.

Child of JOAN KEEBLE and WILLIE WHITNER is:
    iv. JAKE DOUGLAS[8] WHITNER, d. 1991.

377. SHIRLEY DEAN[7] KEEBLE *(HENRY WILLIAM ERASTUS[6], WILLIAM EMMETT[5], WILLIAM THOMAS[4], JAMES H.[3], THOMAS[2], WILLIAM[1])* was born July 12, 1938. She married (1) T. G. BOYD. She married (2) DONALD L. KREBS.

Children of SHIRLEY KEEBLE and T. BOYD are:
    i.   BELINDA[8] BOYD.
    ii. TERRY BOYD.
    iii. DONNA BOYD.
    iv. RICKY BOYD.
    v.   DEANNA BOYD.
    vi. RANDY BOYD.

378. GERALDINE[7] KEEBLE *(GLOVER GREEN[6], WILLIAM EMMETT[5], WILLIAM THOMAS[4], JAMES H.[3], THOMAS[2], WILLIAM[1])* was born September 13, 1925. She married (1) HOWARD RAY STRENGTH July 02, 1942. He was born October 07, 1922, and died October 17, 1970. She married (2) EDWARD EARL STRENGTH October 04, 1976. He was born December 06, 1924, and died November 22, 1977. She married (3) CHARLES WATKINS June 24, 1981. He was born September 11, 1924.

Children of GERALDINE KEEBLE and HOWARD STRENGTH are:
    i.   MICHAEL RAY[8] STRENGTH, b. May 30, 1943.
    ii. KENNETH WAYNE STRENGTH, b. June 23, 1947.
    iii. PAMELA ANNE STRENGTH, b. November 23, 1957.
    iv. TAMERA FRAN STRENGTH, b. November 23, 1957.

379. GERTRUDE[7] WILSON *(WILLIAM ALLEN WILSON[6] KEEBLE, WILLIAM EMMETT[5], WILLIAM THOMAS[4], JAMES H.[3], THOMAS[2], WILLIAM[1])* was born September 28, 1903, and died December 03, 1941. She married HENRY WILLIAM ERASTUS KEEBLE September 09, 1922 in Troupe County, Georgia, son of WILLIAM KEEBLE and KATIE OWENS. He was born April 05, 1903, and died February 09, 1981.

Children are listed above under (240) Henry William Erastus Keeble.

380. VACHEL LEE[7] KEEBLE, JR. *(VACHEL LEE[6], GLOVER TRENT[5], WILLIAM THOMAS[4], JAMES H.[3], THOMAS[2], WILLIAM[1])* was born November 08, 1934. He married CLARA ANNE HORTON July 18, 1958 in Fulton County, Georgia, daughter of HAROLD HORTON and MARGARET GLEAGUE. She was born April 12, 1935.

Children of VACHEL KEEBLE and CLARA HORTON are:
424.   i.   VACHEL LEE[8] KEEBLE III, b. January 28, 1964.
425.   ii. ALICE RUTH KEEBLE, b. February 09, 1966.

381. BENIAN SHARMAN[7] KEEBLE, SR. *(VACHEL LEE[6], GLOVER TRENT[5], WILLIAM THOMAS[4], JAMES H.[3], THOMAS[2], WILLIAM[1])* was born January 31, 1936. He married (1) JESSIE GRACE POWELL October 29, 1954 in Meridan, Mississippi, daughter of JESSE POWELL and ENOLA SALTER. She was born May 11, 1937, and died February 20, 1976. He married (2) CHRISTINE PRICE June 28, 1963 in Elmore County, Alabama, daughter of

LEONARD PRICE and ANNIE MANN. She was born April 08, 1938.

Children of BENIAN KEEBLE and JESSIE POWELL are:
426.   i.   LINDA DIANE⁸ KEEBLE, b. October 15, 1955.
427.   ii.   TERESA LYNN KEEBLE, b. November 16, 1956.
428.   iii.   BENIAN SHARMAN KEEBLE,JR., b. April 02, 1958.
429.   iv.   TIMOTHY STEVEN KEEBLE, b. April 30, 1962.

382. MARY RUTH⁷ KEEBLE *(VACHEL LEE⁶, GLOVER TRENT⁵, WILLIAM THOMAS⁴, JAMES H.³, THOMAS², WILLIAM¹)* was born January 02, 1949. She married (1) JOHN DAVID FORD June 03, 1972 in Elmore County,Alabama, son of WILLIAM FORD and SADIE CALLAHAN. He was born March 21, 1946. She married (2) JOHN FOREST RUDD July 28, 1990 in Elmore County,Ala., son of VICTOR RUDD and NANNIE EASLEY. He was born May 09, 1945.

Child of MARY KEEBLE and JOHN FORD is:
    i.   FARAH SHARMAN⁸ FORD, b. January 16, 1977; m. DAVID BRANDON ISBEL, September 18, 1999.

383. GAILE THOMAS⁷ KEEBLE *(WILLIAM ARTHUR⁶, GLOVER TRENT⁵, WILLIAM THOMAS⁴, JAMES H.³, THOMAS², WILLIAM¹)* was born April 1936. He married BARBARA (UNKNOWN).

Children of GAILE KEEBLE and BARBARA (UNKNOWN) are:
    i.   GERRY⁸ KEEBLE.
    ii.   REBECCA KEEBLE.
    iii.   WOODROW KEEBLE.

384. THOMAS RAY⁷ KEEBLE *(WILLIAM THOMAS⁶, TRESSVANT THOMAS⁵, WILLIAM THOMAS⁴, JAMES H.³, THOMAS², WILLIAM¹)* was born December 14, 1948. He married MARY KATHLEEN ATKINSON February 21, 1968 in Harris County,Texas, daughter of CARL ATKINSON and JOY ARCHER. She was born September 18, 1950.

Child of THOMAS KEEBLE and MARY ATKINSON is:
430.   i.   GREGORY WAYNE⁸ KEEBLE, b. October 04, 1968.

385. JOHN PAUL⁷ KEEBLE *(WILLIAM THOMAS⁶, TRESSVANT THOMAS⁵, WILLIAM THOMAS⁴, JAMES H.³, THOMAS², WILLIAM¹)* was born January 17, 1956. He married DEBBIE LYNN SIMMONS June 27, 1986 in Hopkins County Texas, daughter of JOHN SIMMONS and CLARA DEE. She was born July 08, 1968.

Children of JOHN KEEBLE and DEBBIE SIMMONS are:
    i.   SHAYLA NICOLE⁸ KEEBLE, b. November 08, 1987.
    ii.   JONATHAN SCOT KEEBLE, b. May 19, 1989.

386. TERRY JOE⁷ KEEBLE *(WILLIAM THOMAS⁶, TRESSVANT THOMAS⁵, WILLIAM THOMAS⁴, JAMES H.³, THOMAS², WILLIAM¹)* was born October 24, 1959. He married MELINDA KAY WALKER May 22, 1981 in Harris County Texas, daughter of GLENN WALKER. She was born July 29, 1959.

Child of TERRY KEEBLE and MELINDA WALKER is:
    i.   HEATHER LYNN⁸ KEEBLE, b. January 29, 1990.

387. MAX RAY⁷ KEEBLE,JR. *(MAX RAY⁶, TRESSVANT THOMAS⁵, WILLIAM THOMAS⁴, JAMES H.³, THOMAS², WILLIAM¹)* was born February 03, 1960. He married TAMMI HALLOWICK December 19, 1986.

Children of MAX KEEBLE and TAMMI HALLOWICK are:
    i.   JUSTIN CHASE⁸ KEEBLE, b. January 15, 1988.
    ii.   CAMERON RAY KEEBLE, b. July 27, 1992.

388. KAREN ELIZABETH[7] KEEBLE *(MAX RAY[6], TRESSVANT THOMAS[5], WILLIAM THOMAS[4], JAMES H.[3], THOMAS[2], WILLIAM[1])* was born September 10, 1962. She married GARY STEVEN BREITSCHOPE September 03, 1983 in Gonzoles, Texas.

Children of KAREN KEEBLE and GARY BREITSCHOPE are:
  i. AMBER NICOLE[8] BREITSCHOPE, b. July 22, 1984.
  ii. AMANDA ELIZABETH BREITSCHOPE, b. July 16, 1986.

389. KIMBERLY KATHLEEN[7] KEEBLE *(MAX RAY[6], TRESSVANT THOMAS[5], WILLIAM THOMAS[4], JAMES H.[3], THOMAS[2], WILLIAM[1])* was born July 15, 1966. She married MARVIN WAYNE GIBSON December 06, 1986.

Children of KIMBERLY KEEBLE and MARVIN GIBSON are:
  i. KIMBERLY KRISTINE[8] GIBSON, b. May 26, 1989.
  ii. TRAVIS WAYNE GIBSON, b. July 03, 1991.

390. WILLIE VELMA[7] KEEBLE *(JOHN DECATER[6], WILLIAM DOCKERY[5], JOHN[4], WILLIAM MCCUTCHIN[3], THOMAS[2], WILLIAM[1])* was born July 07, 1919. She married SAMUEL LONE MOORE December 21, 1935 in Sevier County, Tennessee, son of HARRISON MOORE and SARAH HATCHER. He was born March 04, 1915.

Children of WILLIE KEEBLE and SAMUEL MOORE are:
  i. PRISCILLA J.[8] MOORE, b. May 03, 1939.
  ii. JUDITH ANN MOORE, b. March 29, 1944.
  iii. RONNIE EDWARD MOORE, b. March 10, 1949.

391. MARIE KATHRYN[7] KEEBLE *(JOHN DECATER[6], WILLIAM DOCKERY[5], JOHN[4], WILLIAM MCCUTCHIN[3], THOMAS[2], WILLIAM[1])* was born October 19, 1929. She married JACKSON CARNES FOX August 09, 1957 in Sevier County, Tennessee, son of LAVATOR FOX and EDNA CARNES. He was born April 17, 1925.

Child of MARIE KEEBLE and JACKSON FOX is:
  i. GINA[8] FOX, b. December 04, 1958.

392. DORIS LERENE[7] KEEBLE *(BURTON CHASTINE[6], MELVIN[5], CALEB LAVERNE[4], WILLIAM MCCUTCHIN[3], THOMAS[2], WILLIAM[1])* was born February 25, 1940. She married CLIFFORD PAUL SCHORNICK, son of CLIFFORD SCHORNICK and PAULINE RIMBEY. He was born March 18, 1940.

Children of DORIS KEEBLE and CLIFFORD SCHORNICK are:
  i. DEBORAH ELAINE[8] SCHORNICK, b. September 30, 1960; m. GEORGE ROBERT NOBLE.
  ii. SUZANNE MARIE SCHORNICK, b. July 17, 1967; m. BRETT SMITH.
  iii. SANDRA LYNN SCHORNICK, b. February 26, 1971; m. BILLY RAY SEARS.

393. KATHRYN DIANE[7] DOCKTER *(DOROTHY KATHLEEN[6] WHITEHEAD, SARAH ALICE[5] KEEBLE, LABAN[4], WILLIAM MCCUTCHIN[3], THOMAS[2], WILLIAM[1])* was born September 26, 1950 in Maryville, Blount County, Tennessee. She married LARRY KETNER WEST October 07, 1967 in Dalton, Georgia, son of WINFRED WEST and ZELPHA REAGAN. He was born November 20, 1947 in Maryville , Blount County, Tennessee.

Child of KATHRYN DOCKTER and LARRY WEST is:
431. i. WILLIAM THOMAS KETNER[8] WEST, b. April 30, 1968, Knoxville,,Knox County, Tennessee.

394. ALBERT WILLIAM[7] DOCKTER *(DOROTHY KATHLEEN[6] WHITEHEAD, SARAH ALICE[5] KEEBLE, LABAN[4], WILLIAM MCCUTCHIN[3], THOMAS[2], WILLIAM[1])* was born June 20, 1954 in Maryville, Blount County, Tennessee. He married (1) BARBARA GRAYCE MCCURRY June 17, 1978 in Maryville ,Blount County, Tennessee, daughter of ERSKINE MCCURRY and MARGARET BAILEY. She was born March 20, 1954 in Maryville, Blount County, Tennessee. He married (2) TERESA ANN GEORGE March 15, 1986 in Alcoa Blount County,Tennessee, daughter of ROBERT GEORGE and BARBARA LARUE. She was born March 19, 1960 in Knoxville,Knox County,Tennessee, and died January 03, 2001 in Knoxville,Knox County,Tennessee. He married (3) DOROTHY DARLENE GASAWAY June 01, 2001 in Las Vagas,Nevada, daughter of HORACE CAMP and JANUITA GASAWAY. She was born June 28, 1957 in Chattanooga,Hamilton County,Tennessee.

Child of ALBERT DOCKTER and BARBARA MCCURRY is:
    i. ALBERT WARREN⁸ DOCKTER, b. March 03, 1982.

Children of ALBERT DOCKTER and TERESA GEORGE are:
    ii. KELLI NICOLE⁸ DOCKTER, b. March 21, 1989, Maryville,Blount County, Tennessee.
    iii. NATALIE DIANE DOCKTER, b. July 29, 1993, Maryville,Blount County, Tennessee.
    iv. MADELYN LEIGH DOCKTER, b. January 08, 1997, Maryville,Blount County, Tennessee.
    v. BENJAMIN WILLIAM DOCKTER, b. December 28, 2000, Maryville,Blount County, Tennessee.

395. WILLIAM KENNETH⁷ KEEBLE III *(WILLIAM KENNETH⁶, WILLIAM KENNETH⁵, LABAN⁴, WILLIAM MCCUTCHIN³, THOMAS², WILLIAM¹)* was born September 27, 1954. He married DEBRA LYNN HAMMONTREE March 19, 1976 in Blount County,Tennessee, daughter of GEORGE HAMMONTREE and BETTY FELTY. She was born March 03, 1958.

Child of WILLIAM KEEBLE and DEBRA HAMMONTREE is:
    i. HEATHER MICHELLE⁸ KEEBLE, b. February 27, 1977; m. MARVIN JAWAN GOINS, November 2002, Blount Countty,Tennessee; b. 1976.

396. ELIZABETH LEE⁷ KEEBLE *(WILLIAM KENNETH⁶, WILLIAM KENNETH⁵, LABAN⁴, WILLIAM MCCUTCHIN³, THOMAS², WILLIAM¹)* was born October 22, 1961. She married ROGER DALE FRENCH, son of WALTER FRENCH and BARBARA ROGERS. He was born July 03, 1962.

Child of ELIZABETH KEEBLE and ROGER FRENCH is:
    i. TANNER LEE⁸ FRENCH, b. August 25, 1992.

397. JOY DORENE⁷ KEEBLE *(HAROLD ANDERSON⁶, CALEB ANDERSON⁵, LABAN⁴, WILLIAM MCCUTCHIN³, THOMAS², WILLIAM¹)* was born March 30, 1960. She married JOE W. RUTHERFORD,JR. July 21, 1984 in Calhoun County,Texas, son of JOE RUTHERFORD and MARY WILLIAMS. He was born January 21, 1959.

Children of JOY KEEBLE and JOE RUTHERFORD are:
    i. SHANNA ELAINE⁸ RUTHERFORD, b. May 22, 1989.
    ii. CODY CALEB RUTHERFORD, b. August 01, 1991.
    iii. MASON COLE RUTHERFORD, b. June 11, 1996.

398. JEFFREY LEE⁷ KEEBLE *(TERRY PICKENS⁶, GEORGE LEONARD⁵, LABAN⁴, WILLIAM MCCUTCHIN³, THOMAS², WILLIAM¹)* was born April 15, 1964. He married LINDA LEE WILKEY March 08, 1986 in Hamilton County,Tennessee, daughter of GEORGE WILKEY and NANCY COPPINGER. She was born July 06, 1963.

Children of JEFFREY KEEBLE and LINDA WILKEY are:
    i. KRISTINA ABAGAIL⁸ KEEBLE, b. December 06, 1991.
    ii. ALEXANDRA NICOLE KEEBLE, b. May 16, 1994.

399. KENNETH RICHARD⁷ KEEBLE *(CHARLES EDGAR⁶, ANDY RICHARD⁵, PLEASANT⁴, SAMUEL³, MANLY², WILLIAM¹)* was born May 26, 1940. He married DELORES ANN CRAIG August 22, 1961 in Cincinatti,Ohio, daughter of ALBERT CRAIG and MARY.

Children of KENNETH KEEBLE and DELORES CRAIG are:
    i. CHARLES ALBERT⁸ KEEBLE, b. March 21, 1962.

    ii.   KENNETH DAVID KEEBLE, b. October 24, 1965.
    iii. GLENDA FAYE KEEBLE.

400. HAROLD DAVID[7] KEEBLE *(CHARLES EDGAR[6], ANDY RICHARD[5], PLEASANT[4], SAMUEL[3], MANLY[2], WILLIAM[1])* was born July 21, 1942. He married LOLA BOND in Norwood Ohio.

Children of HAROLD KEEBLE and LOLA BOND are:
    i.   DAVID EDWARD[8] KEEBLE, b. April 03, 1968.
    ii. STEPHANIE MARIE KEEBLE, b. April 23, 1971.
432.   iii. ROBERT LEE KEEBLE, b. August 29, 1947.

401. ROBERT LEE[7] KEEBLE *(CHARLES EDGAR[6], ANDY RICHARD[5], PLEASANT[4], SAMUEL[3], MANLY[2], WILLIAM[1])* was born August 29, 1947. He married BRENDA KAY TRETT July 02, 1966 in Lawrenceburg,Ind., daughter of EGBERT TRETT and BEULAH CARR.

Children of ROBERT KEEBLE and BRENDA TRETT are:
    i.   BRIDGET KAY[8] KEEBLE, b. October 24, 1975.
    ii. JESSE KEEBLE, b. May 06, 1978.
    iii. LESLIE RENAY KEEBLE, b. April 01, 1980.

402. KATHY LYNN[7] KEEBLE *(CHARLES EDGAR[6], ANDY RICHARD[5], PLEASANT[4], SAMUEL[3], MANLY[2], WILLIAM[1])* was born May 30, 1958. She married ROBERT OLSON November 27, 1982 in Loveland,Ohio, son of LEROY OLSON. and ELLEN SAMS. He was born December 18, 1960.

Children of KATHY KEEBLE and ROBERT OLSON are:
    i.   DANIEL[8] OLSON, b. January 31, 1986.
    ii. BRIAN OLSON, b. January 15, 1990.

403. JAMES RONALD[7] KEEBLE *(JAMES ELMER[6], ANDY RICHARD[5], PLEASANT[4], SAMUEL[3], MANLY[2], WILLIAM[1])* was born June 22, 1943. He married DOROTHY MAUDE CLARK August 01, 1962 in Blount Countty,Tennessee, daughter of BRONCE CLARK and MAMIE TILLEY. She was born June 09, 1945.

Children of JAMES KEEBLE and DOROTHY CLARK are:
    i.   LISA ANETTE[8] KEEBLE, b. October 24, 1963; m. KENNETH DALE GREENE, July 17, 1982, Blount Countty,Tennessee; b. June 17, 1963.
    ii. JAMES MICHAEL KEEBLE, b. March 12, 1967.

404. JACK LEE[7] KEEBLE,JR. *(JACK LEE[6], PAUL ANDREWS[5], JOHN RICHARD[4], SAMUEL[3], MANLY[2], WILLIAM[1])* was born March 04, 1957. He married MARLYS MARIE BUMBALOUGH June 26, 1976 in Blount Countty,Tennessee, daughter of HARLEN BUMBALOUGH and DOROTHY GAHIAMER. She was born July 03, 1957.

Children of JACK KEEBLE and MARLYS BUMBALOUGH are:
    i.   JACK LEE[8] KEEBLE III, b. August 14, 1977; m. MISTY SUE RUSSELL, May 22, 1999, Blount Countty,Tennessee; b. April 19, 1977.
    ii. ANGELA MARIE KEEBLE, b. February 27, 1979.
    iii. TELENA RENEE KEEBLE, b. July 07, 1986.

405. GARY THOMAS[7] KEEBLE *(JACK LEE[6], PAUL ANDREWS[5], JOHN RICHARD[4], SAMUEL[3], MANLY[2], WILLIAM[1])* was born February 04, 1958. He married (1) LISA HENRY February 1977 in Knox County,Tennessee, daughter of CLYDE HAENRY,JR. and JESSIE HYATT. She was born January 16, 1961. He married (2) KIMBERLEY KAY ATCHLEY November 18, 1983 in Blount Countty,Tennessee, daughter of GEORGE ATCHLEY and SHIRLEY HARVESTON. She was born September 04, 1962.

Child of GARY KEEBLE and LISA HENRY is:
    i.   MARINDA JEAN[8] KEEBLE, b. March 14, 1979.

Children of GARY KEEBLE and KIMBERLEY ATCHLEY are:
    ii. TIFFANY ANN[8] KEEBLE, b. January 18, 1987.
    iii. THOMAS EDWARD KEEBLE, b. June 10, 1990.

406. MISTY MICHELLE[7] KEEBLE *(THOMAS ARTHUR[6], WILLIAM THOMAS[5], SAMUEL WILEY[4], RICHARD HENRY[3], MANLY[2], WILLIAM[1])* was born September 23, 1973. She married (1) DAVID LYNNE COOPER June 28, 1997 in Blount Countty, Tennessee, son of CHARLES COOPER and ANNA GATLIN. He was born January 27, 1975. She married (2) H. PAUL PERRY March 2002 in Blount Countty, Tennessee, son of ROBERT PERRY and NANCY.

Child of MISTY KEEBLE and DAVID COOPER is:
    i.   EMILY[8] COOPER, b. June 11, 1999.

407. MARK ANTONY[7] KEEBLE *(RONALD LYNN[6], LLOYD CATLETT[5], SAMUEL WILEY[4], RICHARD HENRY[3], MANLY[2], WILLIAM[1])* was born August 16, 1966. He married TERRIE LYNN KNAPPEN August 03, 1985 in Blount Countty, Tennessee, daughter of WILLIAM KNAPPEN and RUTH INTRONE. She was born October 14, 1965.

Child of MARK KEEBLE and TERRIE KNAPPEN is:
    i.   NATHAAN DAKOTA[8] KEEBLE, b. January 06, 1998.

408. ALLEN LLOYD[7] KEEBLE *(RONALD LYNN[6], LLOYD CATLETT[5], SAMUEL WILEY[4], RICHARD HENRY[3], MANLY[2], WILLIAM[1])* was born September 26, 1973. He married KEONA MARIE LILLY April 07, 2001 in Ocala. Florida, daughter of MARK LILLY and KAREN.

Child of ALLEN KEEBLE and KEONA LILLY is:
    i.   SIMON TYLER[8] KEEBLE, b. March 26, 2002.

409. JOHN THOMAS[7] KEEBLE, JR. *(JOHN THOMAS[6], LLOYD CATLETT[5], SAMUEL WILEY[4], RICHARD HENRY[3], MANLY[2], WILLIAM[1])* was born October 02, 1965. He married AMY ELIZABETH BROYLES May 06, 1989 in Blount Countty, Tennessee, daughter of JOHN BROYLES and SONJA MORTON. She was born January 15, 1965.

Children of JOHN KEEBLE and AMY BROYLES are:
    i.   HOLLY ELIZABETH[8] KEEBLE, b. January 26, 1992.
    ii. SY THOMAS KEEBLE, b. January 14, 1995.

410. KARLA SHEA[7] KEEBLE *(JOHN THOMAS[6], LLOYD CATLETT[5], SAMUEL WILEY[4], RICHARD HENRY[3], MANLY[2], WILLIAM[1])* was born December 10, 1970. She married TONY CHARLES BERRY June 05, 1993 in Blount Countty, Tennessee, son of KENNETH BERRY and DOROTHY BYRD. He was born October 03, 1966.

Child of KARLA KEEBLE and TONY BERRY is:
    i.   ANTHONY BATESON[8] BERRY, b. March 10, 1995.

411. HEIDI LYNN[7] KEEBLE *(RANDALL PAUL[6], ROBERT PAUL[5], SAMUEL WILEY[4], RICHARD HENRY[3], MANLY[2], WILLIAM[1])* was born November 10, 1965. She married (1) MARK DOUGLAS. She married (2) BIE GIE LEE April 25, 1998 in Centerville, Virginia, son of MAN LEE and MEE NGAI. He was born June 13, 1972.

Child of HEIDI KEEBLE and MARK DOUGLAS is:
    i.   KYLE[8] DOUGLAS, b. September 18, 1988.

Children of HEIDI KEEBLE and BIE LEE are:
- ii. ELIZABETH[8] LEE, b. January 20, 2000.
- iii. OLIVIA GRACE LEE, b. September 25, 2001.

412. JERRY A.[7] KEEBLE *(FLOYD MARION[6], JOHN MARION[5], JOHN ELLISON[4], MARION[3], RICHARD PORTER[2], WILLIAM[1])* was born July 26, 1942. He married (1) BARBARA MAY COOPER September 07, 1960. She was born May 16, 1945, and died January 06, 1980.

Children of JERRY KEEBLE and BARBARA COOPER are:
- 433.　i. YVONNE MARIE[8] KEEBLE, b. June 25, 1961.
- ii. DIANE LENETTE KEEBLE, b. March 29, 1964.
- iii. BRENDA LEE KEEBLE, b. December 27, 1965.
- iv. JOHN MARION KEEBLE, b. December 18, 1970.

Child of JERRY A. KEEBLE is:
- v. JANNET SUE[8] KEEBLE, b. October 08, 1981.

413. JAYNE ANN[7] KEEBLE *(CHARLES RICHARD[6], JOHN MARION[5], JOHN ELLISON[4], MARION[3], RICHARD PORTER[2], WILLIAM[1])* was born March 11, 1945. She married (1) ZACHARY TAYLOR RICE IV October 27, 1963. He was born October 21, 1943. She married (2) GARY CURTIS June 08, 1975. He was born Abt. 1945.

Children of JAYNE KEEBLE and ZACHARY RICE are:
- i. ELIZABETH ANN[8] RICE, b. August 23, 1964.
- ii. ZACHARY TAYLOR RICE V, b. April 19, 1968.
- iii. VICTORIA LEE RICE, b. May 03, 1969; d. August 17, 1974.

414. CECELIA JUNE[7] KEEBLE *(CHARLES RICHARD[6], JOHN MARION[5], JOHN ELLISON[4], MARION[3], RICHARD PORTER[2], WILLIAM[1])* was born May 05, 1947, and died May 02, 1980.

Children of CECELIA JUNE KEEBLE are:
- i. JUSTIN LATIMER[8] KEEBLE, b. October 27, 1972.
- ii. KIMBERLIE DAWN KEEBLE, b. October 28, 1972.

415. SHARON ELIZABETH[7] KEEBLE *(CHARLES RICHARD[6], JOHN MARION[5], JOHN ELLISON[4], MARION[3], RICHARD PORTER[2], WILLIAM[1])* was born July 20, 1949. She married DAVID ARTHUR TANNER August 01, 1970. He was born May 26, 1949.

Child of SHARON KEEBLE and DAVID TANNER is:
- i. FELICIA ANASTASIA SATINA[8] TANNER, b. November 07, 1971.

416. SONDRA ANN[7] KEEBLE *(VERNON DEWAYNE[6], ROY VIRGIL[5], STEPHEN[4], NANCY[3], WALTER HARRISON[2], WILLIAM[1])* was born March 23, 1967. She married DANNY MUSSER September 07, 1986.

Child of SONDRA KEEBLE and DANNY MUSSER is:
- i. JOSHUA DEWAYNE[8] MUSSER, b. May 14, 1989.

Generation No. 8

417. JOANN[8] KEEBLE *(JOE WAYNE[7], JOSEPH[6], WILLIAM LAFAYETTE[5], JOHN HOUSTON[4], JAMES H.[3], THOMAS[2], WILLIAM[1])* was born June 15, 1952. She married KENNETH EARL CONNELLY January 22, 1969.

Children of JOANN KEEBLE and KENNETH CONNELLY are:
  i.   DAVID HEWES[9] CONNELLY, b. July 21, 1969.
  ii. KENNETH EARL CONNELLY, b. June 09, 1971.
  iii. RICKY DWAYNE CONNELLY, b. June 09, 1971.

418. JAMES JOSEPH[8] KEEBLE *(JOE[7], JAMES TAYLOR[6], JOHN H.[5], TAYLOR S.[4], JAMES H.[3], THOMAS[2], WILLIAM[1])* was born October 25, 1944. He married VERA BROWN.

Children of JAMES KEEBLE and VERA BROWN are:
  i.   PAUL[9] KEEBLE, b. 1971.
  ii. KATHERINE KEEBLE, b. 1976.

419. TONY DION[8] KEEBLE *(JERRY DION[7], TRESFORD[6], ANDREW DAVIS[5], TAYLOR S.[4], JAMES H.[3], THOMAS[2], WILLIAM[1])* was born July 08, 1960. He married ROBIN ANN RIDDLE June 12, 1982.

Children of TONY KEEBLE and ROBIN RIDDLE are:
  i.   IAN DION[9] KEEBLE, b. August 31, 1987.
  ii. GEDDY MARK KEEBLE, b. February 22, 1993.

420. WADE WEST[8] KEEBLE *(JIMMY THOMAS[7], THOMAS EARNEST[6], PIERCE MACK[5], TAYLOR S.[4], JAMES H.[3], THOMAS[2], WILLIAM[1])* was born February 19, 1954. He married LYNDA.

Child of WADE KEEBLE and LYNDA is:
  i.   JEREMY[9] KEEBLE, b. September 16, 1979.

421. CHERISE LARUE[8] KEEBLE *(JIMMY THOMAS[7], THOMAS EARNEST[6], PIERCE MACK[5], TAYLOR S.[4], JAMES H.[3], THOMAS[2], WILLIAM[1])* was born August 20, 1963. She married CHARLES E. WASSBORN December 22, 1981.

Child of CHERISE KEEBLE and CHARLES WASSBORN is:
  i.   CHARLES T.[9] WASSBORN, b. July 23, 1982.

422. KIMBLYN KAYE[8] KEEBLE *(BOBBY GENE[7], THOMAS EARNEST[6], PIERCE MACK[5], TAYLOR S.[4], JAMES H.[3], THOMAS[2], WILLIAM[1])* was born October 06, 1962. She married TOBY MURRAY June 07, 1986.

Child of KIMBLYN KEEBLE and TOBY MURRAY is:
  i.   MATTHEW[9] MURRAY, b. August 26, 1980.

423. BETTY LYN ANN[8] KEEBLE *(BOBBY GENE[7], THOMAS EARNEST[6], PIERCE MACK[5], TAYLOR S.[4], JAMES H.[3], THOMAS[2], WILLIAM[1])* was born September 11, 1964. She married BALES 1982.

Child of BETTY KEEBLE and BALES is:
  i.   JUSTIN[9] BALES, b. May 24, 1983.

424. VACHEL LEE[8] KEEBLE III *(VACHEL LEE[7], VACHEL LEE[6], GLOVER TRENT[5], WILLIAM THOMAS[4], JAMES H.[3], THOMAS[2], WILLIAM[1])* was born January 28, 1964. He married ROBIN ELIZABETH ODOM July 18, 1987 in Jefferson County, Alabama, daughter of ELWOOD ODOM and SANDRA SMITH. She was born June 22, 1963.

Children of VACHEL KEEBLE and ROBIN ODOM are:
  i.   HEATHER MICHELLE[9] KEEBLE, b. June 05, 1985.
  ii. SANDRA CLARA KEEBLE, b. May 11, 1988.
  iii. TREYCE ROBIN KEEBLE, b. April 17, 1991.
  iv. VACHEL LEE KEEBLE IV, b. March 16, 1993.

425. ALICE RUTH[8] KEEBLE *(VACHEL LEE[7], VACHEL LEE[6], GLOVER TRENT[5], WILLIAM THOMAS[4], JAMES H.[3], THOMAS[2], WILLIAM[1])* was born February 09, 1966. She married JAMES WYATT FREEMAN III February 17, 1990 in Jefferson County, Alabama, son of JAMES FREEMAN and BARBARA BARKER. He was born May 08, 1965.

Children of ALICE KEEBLE and JAMES FREEMAN are:
- i.   JAMES WYATT[9] FREEMAN IV, b. August 30, 1993.
- ii. CLAYTON ALEXANDER FREEMAN, b. November 08, 1995.

426. LINDA DIANE[8] KEEBLE *(BENIAN SHARMAN[7], VACHEL LEE[6], GLOVER TRENT[5], WILLIAM THOMAS[4], JAMES H.[3], THOMAS[2], WILLIAM[1])* was born October 15, 1955. She married DONALD MARK SMART March 05, 1976 in Elmore County, Alabama. He was born May 24, 1955.

Children of LINDA KEEBLE and DONALD SMART are:
- i.   BRADLEY MARK[9] SMART, b. July 09, 1978.
- ii.   STEVEN LEE SMART, b. January 21, 1981.
- iii. JEREMY TAYLOR SMART, b. February 04, 1984.

427. TERESA LYNN[8] KEEBLE *(BENIAN SHARMAN[7], VACHEL LEE[6], GLOVER TRENT[5], WILLIAM THOMAS[4], JAMES H.[3], THOMAS[2], WILLIAM[1])* was born November 16, 1956. She married MICHAEL BOYD COX June 26, 1976 in Elmore County, Alabama, son of BILLY COX and CLAUDIA HOLTON. He was born November 19, 1955.

Children of TERESA KEEBLE and MICHAEL COX are:
- i.   MICHAEL BOYD[9] COX, JR., b. June 29, 1981.
- ii.   JESSICA GRACE COX, b. August 15, 1983.
- iii.   REBECCA ANN COX, b. September 26, 1985.
- iv.   CAROLINE MARIE COX, b. June 09, 1998.
- v.   GRACE ANN MARIE COX, b. June 21, 1990.
- vi.   KATELYN RUTH COX, b. November 23, 1992.
- vii.   SUSAN KAY COX, b. January 31, 1995.

428. BENIAN SHARMAN[8] KEEBLE, JR. *(BENIAN SHARMAN[7], VACHEL LEE[6], GLOVER TRENT[5], WILLIAM THOMAS[4], JAMES H.[3], THOMAS[2], WILLIAM[1])* was born April 02, 1958. He married DEBORA JEAN LESWICK December 29, 1979 in Elmore County, Alabama, daughter of JOHN LESWICK and WOOL KANG. She was born June 26, 1960.

Children of BENIAN KEEBLE and DEBORA LESWICK are:
- i.   JARED BLAKE[9] KEEBLE, b. September 22, 1981.
- ii.   MATTHEW CHASE KEEBLE, b. June 04, 1983.
- iii. JOHN LOGAN KEEBLE, b. November 04, 1991.
- iv.   BENIAN CONNER KEEBLE, b. October 22, 1993.
- v.   ALDEN GRACE KEEBLE, b. September 24, 1997.

429. TIMOTHY STEVEN[8] KEEBLE *(BENIAN SHARMAN[7], VACHEL LEE[6], GLOVER TRENT[5], WILLIAM THOMAS[4], JAMES H.[3], THOMAS[2], WILLIAM[1])* was born April 30, 1962. He married LINDA GAIL NOBLE December 02, 1985 in Montgomery County, Alabama, daughter of OREE NOBLE and BONNIE MCNIELL. She was born February 01, 1962.

Children of TIMOTHY KEEBLE and LINDA NOBLE are:
- i.   TIMOTHY AUSTIN[9] KEEBLE, b. June 20, 1988.
- ii. KELLY GAIL KEEBLE, b. May 31, 1990.

430. GREGORY WAYNE[8] KEEBLE *(THOMAS RAY[7], WILLIAM THOMAS[6], TRESSVANT THOMAS[5], WILLIAM THOMAS[4], JAMES H.[3], THOMAS[2], WILLIAM[1])* was born October 04, 1968. He married SHELLEY TOINI KAPTCHINSKIE

September 04, 1990 in Harris County, Texas, daughter of JOSEPH KAPTCHINSKIE and MAE PATTERSON.

Children of GREGORY KEEBLE and SHELLEY KAPTCHINSKIE are:
    i. ASHLEY RENE[9] KEEBLE, b. September 25, 1991.
    ii. DRAKE THOMAS KEEBLE, b. January 29, 1996.

431. WILLIAM THOMAS KETNER[8] WEST *(KATHRYN DIANE[7] DOCKTER, DOROTHY KATHLEEN[6] WHITEHEAD, SARAH ALICE[5] KEEBLE, LABAN[4], WILLIAM MCCUTCHIN[3], THOMAS[2], WILLIAM[1])* was born April 30, 1968 in Knoxville,,Knox County, Tennessee. He married ATHENA LYNN HOUVOURAS February 19, 1994 in Knoxville,Knox County, Tennessee, daughter of JOHN HOUVOURAS and LINDA PARKER. She was born July 02, 1962 in Springfield, Ohio.

Child of WILLIAM WEST and ATHENA HOUVOURAS is:
    i. JESSICA RACHEL[9] WEST, b. January 20, 1995, Knoxville ,Knox County, Tennessee.

432. ROBERT LEE[8] KEEBLE *(HAROLD DAVID[7], CHARLES EDGAR[6], ANDY RICHARD[5], PLEASANT[4], SAMUEL[3], MANLY[2], WILLIAM[1])* was born August 29, 1947. He married BRENDA KAY TRETT July 02, 1966 in Lawrenceburg,Indiana, daughter of EGBERT TRETT and BEULAH CARR.

Children of ROBERT KEEBLE and BRENDA TRETT are:
    i. BRIDGETT KAY[9] KEEBLE, b. October 24, 1975.
    ii. JESSE KEEBLE, b. May 06, 1978.
    iii. LESLIE RENAYE KEEBLE, b. April 01, 1980.

433. YVONNE MARIE[8] KEEBLE *(JERRY A.[7], FLOYD MARION[6], JOHN MARION[5], JOHN ELLISON[4], MARION[3], RICHARD PORTER[2], WILLIAM[1])* was born June 25, 1961.

Child of YVONNE MARIE KEEBLE is:
    i. RASHELL NELDA LYNN[9] KEEBLE, b. June 23, 1980.

Index of Individuals

Ira: 17
Louis Anderson: 17
Lucy: 17
Lydia E.: 15
Manerva: 17
Margaret Ann: 16
Otha: 17
Sadie: 17
Virgil: 17
William: 16
William: 17
William Edward: 17

Barger -
Mary: 22

Barker -
Barbara: 81

Bartlett -
Lucy Nell: 49
Rufus: 9

Bassett -
Maggie Irene: 50

Bates -
Gladys: 43

Baxley -
Flora Mae: 68

Beall -
Peggy: 43

Bean -
Kenneth: 35
Mabel Mathis: 7

Beard -
Ben: 44

Beaty -
Fred Roy: 66
Hazel Renee (name: Hazel Renee Alexander): 67
Jonathan Keeble: 67
Newton Henry: 66
Renee Annette: 67

Beaver -
Thelma: 21

Bedford -
Unnamed: 19

Bell -
Tinia: 63

Benavides -
Consuelo: 32

Benefield -
Lois Elector: 45
William Lemyard: 45

Benner -
Alvin J.: 73

Bennett -
Carl K.: 15
Oliver Franklin: 65
Ray: 20
Susan Mabel: 41

Berdette -
Speer III: 46

Berry -
Anthony Bateson: 78
Kenneth Lee: 78

Tony Charles: 78

Betty -
Unnamed: 65

Birdwell -
Bobbie Jeanne: 43
Mildred Valera: 43
Robert William: 43
Wanda Ruth: 43

Bittinger -
Kevin John: 49

Bivens -
Anna Mae: 20

Blair -
Earl: 33
Margaret: 3
Margaret Ann: 2
Wanda: 33

Blazier -
Carolyn Jean: 40
Charles Walker: 40
Diane Kay: 40
John Elder ,Jr.: 40
John Elder ,Sr.: 40
Lucille: 40

Blevins -
Bess: 17

Bogle -
Charles Edwin: 40
James Black: 40
James Ellis: 40
James Walter: 40

Boling -
Alva: 11
Arthus C.: 5
Cecelia: 11
Charles: 11
Eliza Jane: 5
Ella: 6
Fred: 6
James W.: 5
John: 11
John H.: 5
John Sims: 5
Margaret: 5
Martha: 30
Mary: 11
Nancy C .: 5
Robert: 5
Rutha: 2
Samuel: 11
Samuel: 5
Tennessee: 4
Thomas L.: 5

Bond -
Albert: 61
Lola: 77

Bonner -
Joe: 48
June: 69

Bostic -
Clarence Mson: 64
Constance Ann: 64

Bowen -

Butler -
  David Carter: 34
  Ernest Eugene: 34
  Gary Lynn: 34
  Hazel: 14
  Linda Gail: 34
  Ricky Eugene: 34
Byrd -
  Dorothy: 78
  Sharon E.: 57
C.Miller -
  Samuel: 38
Cagle -
  Angeline Matilda: 6
  George: 6
  George Anderson: 6
  Hobart: 14
  James: 6
  Jesse: 6
  Lucille Rhonda: 6
  Rebecca: 6
  Sarah Ellen: 6
  William Holbert: 6
Callahan -
  Sadie Virginia: 74
Camp -
  Horace Joseph: 76
Campbell -
  Alvin: 43
  Christina: 40
  Jolean: 43
  Paul Arthur: 60
  Vicky Diane: 60
Cannon -
  John: 1
  Nancy Ann: 1, 2
Cappiello -
  Unnamed: 38
Caretto -
  John: 12
Cargal -
  Sadie Sarah: 25
Carlucci -
  Unnamed: 61
  Steven: 61
Carnes -
  Edna: 75
Carr -
  Beulah: 82
  Beulah: 77
  Claude E.: 26
  Oren Dennis: 16
Carrigg -
  Kathleen Sinwell: 66
Carroll -
  Mary Ann: 17
Carter -
  Kirkland Lee: 69
  Leilani Marie: 69
  Nellie: 41
  Robert F.: 69
Cartwright -

Tommy Earl: 68
Carvalho -
  Joshua Thomas: 72
  Thomas Walter: 72
Carver -
  Artie: 61
  Delssie Marie: 61
Case -
  Della Raby: 22
  William: 22
Castro -
  Lydia Ann Hernandez: 57, 58
Cates -
  Zita Marie: 53
Catlett -
  Lucy: 12
Caylor -
  Millard: 17
Chaffin -
  Oletha: 68
Chamberlain -
  W. B.: 15
Chambers -
  Ollie: 30
Chapman -
  Christine: 49
  Claudette: 36
Chappell -
  Velma: 27
Charlotte -
  Unnamed: 22
Charlton -
  James Arthur: 37
Chase -
  Betty: 33
Christenberry -
  David Edward: 64
  Leslie Hope: 64
  Ralph David: 63, 64
  Ralph H.: 63
Christopher -
  LaFayette: 11
Clabough -
  Unnamed: 21
Clampet -
  John: 62
  Norma Jean: 62
Clampett -
  Sally: 5
Clancy -
  Mary: 16
Clark -
  Bronce Lee: 77
  Dorothy Maude: 77
  John: 7
  Lela: 11
  Martha Jane: 7, 8, 13, 14
  Mary Jane: 39
Clay -
  Eloise: 14
Cleveland -
  Unnamed: 61

Cutshaw -
    Sam: 38
    Wanda Sue: 65
    Willa Rhea: 38
Daugherty -
    Unnamed: 29
    Virginia: 29
Davis -
    Anthony: 18
    Belle: 55
    Charlotte: 3
    Dempsey: 9
    Dorothy Kennedy: 18
    Elijah: 3
    James: 6
    James: 3
    James (Hickory Jim): 5
    James Wiley: 18
    Jane: 3
    Joseph: 9
    Lois Elizabeth: 18
    Mary: 6
    Mary: 3
    Millie Jane: 5
    Nancy J.: 2
    R.Jane: 3
    Rebecca: 3
    Rex Robert: 55
    Robert Lynn: 55
    Samuel: 9
    Sarah: 3
    Sarah: 5
    Sarah C.: 13
    Sarah Caroline: 2
    Stephen: 3
    Thomas: 3
    Walter: 3
    Walter Elmer: 55
    William: 5
    William: 3
    William Guss: 18
Day -
    Clarence: 48
    Donald: 48
DeBoom -
    Angela Lynn: 55
Decker -
    James: 72
Dee -
    Clara: 74
Defrien -
    Evan: 45
Demory -
    Irene: 40
Dennis -
    Calvin: 46
    Deborah Ann: 46
    Larry Calvin: 46
Dennley -
    Clara Isabelle: 48
Dickenson -
    Clarence Ovid: 38
Ditto -

    James Ambrose: 29
Dixon -
    Charlie Wade: 66
    Eliza: 13
    Linda Joyce: 66
Dobbs -
    Charlotte Dean: 72
    Gordon Lee ,Jr.: 72
    Gordon Lee ,Sr.: 72
    Patricia Jane: 72
Dobkins -
    Dorcas: 2
Dockery -
    Johnnie: 28
    Loy James: 67
    Loy James II: 67
    Treina Louise: 67
Dockter -
    Albert Warren: 53, 54
    Albert Warren: 54
    Albert Warren: 76
    Albert Wartz: 54
    Albert William: 54, 75, 76
    Benjamin William: 76
    Elizabeth: 58
    Helene Elaine: 54
    Kathryn Diane: 54, 75, 82
    Kelli Nicole: 76
    Madelyn Leigh: 76
    Marion: 58
    Natalie Diane: 76
Dollar -
    C . M.: 25
    Sallie: 25
Donaldson -
    James: 5
    Nancy: 30
    Rachel F.: 5, 6
Doss -
    Virginia: 28
Doudell -
    Raymond: 41
Dougher -
    Unnamed: 37
Douglas -
    Kyle: 78
    Lee: 28
    Mark: 78
Doyle -
    Jacob: 45
Drinnen -
    Margaret: 16
Driver -
    Larry: 50
Duckett -
    Arnold Eugene: 37
    Elmer Lee: 37
    Evelyn Bernice: 37
    Harold Vernon: 37
    Lillian Marie: 37
    Mildred Carolyn: 37
    Robert Christopher: 37
    William Richard Vincent: 37

William Sherman: 37
Duggan -
   Ann: 5
Duke -
   Joshua: 59
Dukes -
   Annie: 47
   Carl: 47
   Hiram: 47
   Juanita: 47
Duncan -
   Donald: 39
Dunlap -
   Adam H: 2
   Adam ,Jr.: 2
   Andrew L.: 17
   Caroline: 17
   Charles: 46
   Charles Anderson: 14
   Dora: 17
   Elijah Andrew: 17
   Elizabeth Caroline: 18
   Hiram P .: 17, 18
   Houston: 14
   Hyrum: 2
   James C.: 2
   Jefferson: 2
   Jennie: 17
   John: 17
   Joseph: 2
   Joseph Anderson: 2
   Judy: 46
   Lorenzo: 2
   Mary: 2
   Maud Estelle: 18
   Polly: 2
   Rhoda: 2
   Robert A.: 17
   Samuel P: 2
Dunn -
   Carl Homer: 20
   Jane James: 54
Durham -
   The Rev.Clarence Gunn: 30
Dyer -
   James: 21
   Loye Annis: 21
Dyke -
   Essie Faye: 63
E.Keeble -
   Paul ,Jr.: 32
Eakins -
   James Andrew: 37
   Oma Lee: 37
Earles -
   Annie Lee: 24
Easley -
   Nannie Lee: 74
Eddy -
   Bertha Demaris: 68
Edmondson -
   Al: 42
   Donald: 42

Jackie Bruce: 63
Stephen Dale: 42
Susan Dean: 42
Virgil O.: 63
Edwards -
   Charles Cecil: 53
   Charles Ronald: 53
   Virginia Kathryn: 66
Eggers -
   John: 32
Elizabeth -
   Unnamed: 3
Ellerbee -
   Bonnie Kathryn: 66
   Ernest Lee: 66
Elliff -
   George Francis: 41
Embry -
   Doris: 47
Endman -
   Glen: 14
Etheleen -
   Unnamed: 14
Evans -
   Leanne Marie: 70
   Matthew: 11
   Willie Mae: 52
Everett -
   Bonnie Kate: 62
   Brena: 15
   Brenda: 34
   Lawrence Frank: 62
   Melissa Diane: 32
   Noah: 13
Everhart -
   Carolyn Jane: 35
   George: 35
   Johnny Conard: 35
   Linda Joyce: 35
   Pamela Marie: 35
Ewig -
   Jack: 35
Fairbetter -
   Mildred: 28
Fancher -
   Martha Alice: 38
Farmer -
   Arthur Alvin: 14
   Benjamin Franklin: 14
   Cora Jane: 13
   Eli: 5, 19, 20
   Elizabeth: 3, 7, 8
   Ella G.: 14
   Elly Grace: 5
   Grace Gertrude: 14
   Houston: 3
   James: 3
   James Robert: 14
   John: 3
   John: 3
   John Martin: 14
   Joseph: 5
   Joseph: 3

Carrie Victoria: 20
John Edward: 20
John Edward: 20
Lennie Lee: 20
Lillie Jane: 20
Malvina Mae: 20
Martha Gertrude: 20
Mary Georgia: 20
Rene Arelle: 20
Samuel Jackson: 20
William Houston: 20

Gardener -
Claude Eugene: 33

Gardner -
Frankie: 14

Garner -
Belle: 35, 36
Callie Versie: 15
Catherine: 13
Eli: 6
Elijah: 6
Francis: 13
Hattie Leore: 15
Herbert Glen: 15
Jane: 6
John Clayton: 32
John Francis: 6
Leon Chester: 15
Levi: 15
Maggie Mae: 15
Margarette Jane: 6
Marshall: 15
Martin: 15
Matthew: 20
Matthew Bogle: 6
Rebecca E.: 6
Samuel: 6
Theodore Virgil: 15
William: 35
Zora: 15

Garrett -
Grace: 51

Gasaway -
Dorothy Darlene: 76
Januita: 76

Gaston -
Elizabeth: 25

Gatlin -
Anna Ruth: 78

George -
Ima: 46, 47
Robert Landis: 76
Teresa Ann: 76

Gibson -
Doyle LaFayette: 28
Ethel: 48
Flora Jane: 28
Geraldine: 34
Hettie: 22
James Callaway: 28
Jane: 4
Jasper: 28
Kimberly Kristine: 75

Marvin Wayne: 75
Mary Hazel: 28
Sam Wiley: 28
Tina Gertrude: 28
Travis Wayne: 75

Giddings -
Lorena L.: 65

Giles -
Gerry: 29

Gleague -
Margaret Alice: 73

Glenn -
Callie: 39

Glover -
Commodore Peery: 23
Joseph Leonard: 23

Goddard -
Christy: 62
James Oliver: 7

Godfrey -
Claire: 69
Jane: 69
John: 69
Robert: 69
Snyder: 69
Snyder: 69
Thomas: 69

Goggin -
Irwin: 33

Goins -
Marvin Jawan: 76

Golden -
Jeanette: 49

Gonzales -
Raymond: 32
Syvia: 32

Gonzoles -
Sylvia: 56

Gordon -
Jack: 33

Gorman -
Georgia Bell: 12
Jake: 12
James Gaston: 12
John Catlett: 12
Joseph McClellan: 12
Martha: 12
Mary Edna: 12
Robert William: 12

Graham -
Alice: 13
George: 13
Lela Frances: 60
William: 60

Granger -
Eula: 14

Graves -
Addie Elizabeth: 37
Martin Edward: 21
Neva: 62
Riley: 20
Riley A.: 20, 21
Sina Edna: 21

Gray -
    James Dwight: 37
Gredig -
    Mary: 17
    William Leonard: 13
Green -
    Anna: 20
    Dennis: 34
Greene -
    Kenneth Dale: 77
Gregg -
    Farlin: 72
    Jimmy Dell: 72
Grice -
    Garland Franklin: 73
Griffin -
    Robert: 42
Grimes -
    Gary Ross: 53
    Gillie Anne: 53
    Jerry Wayne: 53
    Stanley Eugene: 53
    Vernon Ross: 53
Grooms -
    Arnold: 19
Grow -
    Harold: 30
Guess -
    Joseph McCammon: 18
Haenry.Jr. -
    Clyde: 77
Haines -
    Isaac: 36
    Ruth: 36
Halasy -
    Carl E.: 63
    Emery Joseph: 63
    Greg: 63
    Keith: 63
Hale -
    Charles Vincent: 32
    Edward Silas: 32
    Kathryn Denise: 32
    Mollie: 33
    Paul B.: 33
Hall -
    Ernest Roy: 52
    Ernestine: 69
    Hazel Agnes: 37
    James: 37
    Lucinda: 9
    Mary Ernestine: 52
Hallowick -
    Tammi: 74
Hamilton -
    Unnamed: 19
    Paul: 21
    Samuel: 21
Hammer -
    David L.: 33
Hammontree -
    Debra Lynn: 76

    George Edward: 76
Hamon -
    Brandon James: 58
    Brenda Lee: 58
    James C.: 58
    Jason Carl: 58
    Jessica Anne: 58
    Keri Lynn: 58
    Larry G.: 58
Hannah -
    James Francis: 58
    Sandra Sue: 58
Hardy -
    Dallas: 10
Hargis -
    Dave: 32
    Dora Belle: 32
Harlow -
    Carol Laverne: 52
Harmon -
    A .R .: 5
    Jacob H.: 4
    James Melvin: 60
    James Robert: 60
    Luther Vernon: 60
    Michael Lynn: 60
    W. R.: 5
Harrell -
    Joan Ann: 35
Harris -
    Beatrice Jane: 14
    Carl William: 66
    Edward Frederick: 66
    Frederick Henry: 66
    Gloria Louise: 66
    James: 61
    Melanie Anne: 66
    Roderick Roy: 66
    Roy Hayward: 66
Harrison -
    Mary: 48
Hart -
    Pearl: 61
    Rob: 44
Hartley -
    James Trueman: 56
    William Carlton: 56
Harveston -
    Shirley Ann: 77
Haspelman -
    Anna: 38
Hatcher -
    Alex: 20
    Alice: 15
    Bradley Ray: 65
    Callie L.: 15
    Carrie Jo: 65
    Charles: 20
    Edna Gertrude: 20
    Fred Martin: 20
    George: 41
    Harvie Baker: 41
    Homer: 20

Iva: 20
James Ollie: 65
Jimmy Ray: 65
Joseph Walker: 20
Kyle: 41
Lennie: 20
Martha: 20
Martha Ann: 34
Mary Catherine: 20
Mary Jane: 17
Ray: 41
Rose: 20
Sarah Ellen: 75
Vester: 15
Vester: 15
Wade Houston: 20
William Jack: 20

Haun -
Hazel: 17

Hawk -
Ella Marie: 14

Hawn -
Martha Elvira: 59

Hay -
Cathy: 70

Haynes -
Charles T.: 54
Earl: 16
Eli: 16
Henry Boyd: 16
Jordan Andrew: 16
Sarah: 16
Willie Mae: 54

Headfrick -
William Wright: 19

Headrick -
Carolyn Sue: 35
Catherine Jane: 19
Charles Leon: 35
Charlotte A.: 64
Daniel Holston: 12
Donna Jean: 35
Douglas: 12
Harold Robert: 34
James: 20
James Harold: 34
James Robert: 34
Judy Charlene: 35
Letie Mae: 12
Lola Marinda: 12
Lottie Faye: 12
Mabel: 28
Martha Ann: 35
Mattie Victoria: 12
Nancy Ann: 12
Rose Marie: 35
William W.: 12
William Wright: 12

Heath -
Sarah: 29

Heidle -
John Carey: 44
Mary Elizabeth: 44

Helton -
Alexander: 11
Harrison: 11
James Caleb: 11
Jeptha LaFayette: 11
John Houk: 11
Joseph Harrison: 11
Margaret: 11
Thomas Gradon: 11
William Alexander: 11

Henderson -
Debra: 70
Jo Ann: 20
Joe: 70

Hendon -
Della Mae: 10
Lewis: 10
Thomas M: 10
Will: 10
William David: 10

Hendricks -
Charles: 51
Joe Perry: 51
Jon Timothy: 51
Robert Keeble: 51

Hendrix -
Jack: 11

Henley -
Mary Catherine: 63

Henry -
Charlie: 14
Girl: 14
Imodene: 14
James Robert: 14
Lisa: 77, 78
Max: 14
Rev.Pleasant Hugh: 2
Sam: 17
Sarah A.: 3
Stanley: 14
William Houston: 61

Hensley -
Maude: 21
Omer: 21

Hernandez -
Antonio: 57

Herwig -
Agnes: 64

Hester -
Lucy Mae: 50

Hetterly -
Steve: 67

Hicks -
Betty: 47
Bud: 47
Claude: 59
Cline: 47
Dean: 47
Edith: 47
Glover: 47
Jacqueline M.: 65
Melissa: 34
Norman Lee: 65

Donald Wayne: 49
Donna Janice: 66
Donna Lynn: 39, 63
Donnie Eugene: 42
Doris: 26, 51
Doris Jeannene: 44, 68
Doris Lerene: 53, 75
Dorothy: 45
Dorothy Jean: 16, 35
Dorothy LaVerne: 36, 60
Dorothy Mae: 45
Dorothy Nell: 43
Dorothy Virginia: 50, 72
Drake Thomas: 82
Earl Cortez: 25, 49, 70, 71
Earl Elgert: 18, 38
Eddie: 30
Edgar: 19, 39, 63
Edgar Lawson: 16, 36, 59, 60
Edgar Rhea: 7
Edna: 36, 59
Edna: 19, 39, 40
Edna Ray: 50, 72
Edward: 7
Edward George ,Jr.: 20, 41, 66
Edward George ,Sr.: 8, 20, 41, 66
Edytha Ellen: 19
Eleanor Louise: 18
Eli: 6
Eliza: 11, 28, 29
Eliza Jane: 2, 5, 13, 14, 19, 20
Eliza Jane: 6, 15
Elizabeth: 15
Elizabeth J.: 4, 9
Elizabeth Jane: 8, 13, 19
Elizabeth Lee: 54, 76
Ella Marie: 13, 32
Ellen: 6
Ellen Tennessee: 19, 38
Elma: 19
Emily: 6
Emma Jean: 37, 61
Eric Anthony: 57
Eric Garfield: 33, 57
Esta Louise: 51
Esta Rae: 26, 51
Etta Kay: 31, 55
Eugene: 49
Eugene Dauful: 23
Eula Mae: 36
Eunice Bonnie: 41, 66
Eunice Inez: 24, 44
Evaline: 6, 17
Fanny Carolyn: 4, 12
Flora Elizabeth: 19, 39
Florence Josephine: 20, 41
Florence Marie: 19
Floyd: 25, 47
Floyd Marion: 41, 65, 79, 82
Floyd ,Jr.: 47
Frances: 24, 46
Frank O'Neal: 27
Franklin Byron: 22
Fred: 14

Gaile Thomas: 52, 74
Gary Earl ,Jr.: 71
Gary Lee: 52
Gary Thomas: 62, 77, 78
Geddy Mark: 80
George Leonard: 13, 31, 55, 76
George Washington: 22, 43
Georgia Houston: 9, 22
Georgia Mae: 26
Georgia O.: 8
Geraldine: 50, 73
Geraldine: 40, 64
Geraldine: 48, 70
Gerry: 74
Gertrue Estel: 16
Gladys: 14
Glenda Faye: 77
Glenda Kay: 39, 63, 64
Glover Green: 26, 50, 73
Glover Trent: 10, 26, 51, 52, 73, 74, 80, 81
Gordon: 34
Gregory Lynn: 55
Gregory Wayne: 74, 81, 82
Hannah Stamps: 1, 2
Harold: 19
Harold Anderson: 31, 54, 76
Harold David: 60, 77, 82
Harold Vincent: 16, 35, 58
Harriett Elaine: 50, 71
Harriott: 1
Hattie: 10, 25
Hazel: 14
Hazel Beatrice.: 21
Hazel Mae: 15, 33
Hazen: 18, 38
Heather Lynn: 74
Heather Michelle: 76
Heather Michelle: 80
Heidi Lynn: 64, 78, 79
Helen: 36, 60
Helen: 19
Helen Elizabeth: 18
Helen Ruth: 22, 43
Helen Ruth: 16, 35
Helen Ruth: 30
Henry Fitchue: 8
Henry William Erastus: 26, 50, 72, 73
Holly Elizabeth: 78
Homer Preston: 23, 43, 67
Homer T.: 29
Horace Franklin: 11, 27, 53
HoraceChristine: 27, 53
Houston Kelly: 8
Hubert: 12, 29
Hugh Leonard: 6
Hula Virginia: 22, 42
Ian Dion: 80
Ida Lillian: 23
Ida Lou: 24, 46
Inez: 25, 47
Irene: 15
Irene Belle: 26
Isa Mae: 21, 42
Isaac: 4

Isabel Katherine: 26
Izora Maude: 7, 19
J.D.: 9, 24, 44, 45
Jack Lee: 37, 62, 77
Jack Lee III: 77
Jack Lee ,Jr.: 62, 77
Jackie Eugene: 50, 71
James: 29
James Anderson: 15, 34, 57, 58
James Andrew: 25
James Andrew: 48
James Dustin: 56
James Earl: 38
James Edward: 6
James Edward: 5, 14, 32, 56
James Elmer: 36, 60, 77
James H.: 2, 4, 9, 10, 22-27, 43-53, 67-75, 79-81
James Harold ,Jr.: 53
James Harold ,Sr.: 27, 53
James Jerome: 23
James Joseph: 69, 80
James Laban ,Jr.: 32, 56
James Laban ,Sr.: 13, 32, 56
James Michael: 77
James Ray: 22
James Richard: 7
James Richard: 7
James Richard: 37, 62
James Richard Ross: 62
James Ronald: 60, 77
James Russell: 65
James Steven , Jr.: 57
James Steven ,Sr.: 34, 57
James Taylor: 9, 22, 43
James Taylor: 25, 47, 68, 69, 80
James Taylor: 25
James Thomas: 4, 11, 27, 28
James Thomas: 9, 23, 24, 44
James W.: 4, 10
James Wallace: 49, 71
Jamie Lee: 62
Jamie Sue: 64
Jane: 3, 8, 21, 22, 42, 43
Jane: 8
Jane Henry: 1
Janet Teresa: 31, 55
Janett: 57
Janey Irene: 24, 46
Janice Arleen: 37, 61
Jannet Sue: 79
Jared Blake: 81
Jason David: 64
Jayne Ann: 66, 79
Jeannie: 57
Jeffrey Alan: 49
Jeffrey Lee: 55, 76
Jeffrey Scott: 64
Jenna: 72
Jennie Mae: 13
Jennifer: 49
Jeremy: 80
Jeremy Richard: 62
Jerome: 45
Jerry A.: 65, 79, 82

Jerry Dion: 48, 70, 80
Jerry Liles: 25, 48, 70
Jerry Mack: 10, 25, 48, 70
Jesse: 45
Jesse: 82
Jesse: 77
Jesse D.: 45
Jesse Edwin: 25, 49
Jesse Howard: 11, 27
Jessica Kate: 62
Jessie Jewel: 23
Jessie Mae: 22
Jewel: 45
Jimmy: 24
Jimmy Carroll: 43
Jimmy Joyce: 48, 70
Jimmy Rae: 43
Jimmy Thomas: 50, 71, 80
Joan Deloris: 50, 73
JoAnn: 67, 79, 80
Joe: 47, 68, 69, 80
Joe Morris: 4, 10, 11, 26, 27, 52, 53
Joe Wayne: 44, 67, 79
John: 23
John: 1
John: 3, 8, 21
John: 4, 11, 29, 53, 75
John Anderson: 2, 5, 14, 32, 56
John Curtis ,Sr.: 16, 35, 58, 59
John David: 9, 23
John Decater: 29, 53, 75
John Edmund: 7, 18, 38
John Ellison: 8, 19, 40, 65, 66, 79, 82
John H.: 10, 24, 46-48, 68, 69, 80
John Harrison: 3
John Houston: 4, 9, 22, 23, 43, 44, 67, 68, 79
John Jason: 8, 22
John Logan: 81
John Marion: 19, 40, 65, 66, 79, 82
John Marion: 79
John Paul: 52, 74
John Richard: 6, 17, 37, 38, 61-63, 77
John Richard: 37
John Robert: 5, 15, 32, 56, 57
John Taylor: 22
John Thomas: 47
John Thomas ,Jr.: 64, 78
John Thomas ,Sr.: 40, 64, 78
JohnCurtis ,Jr.: 35, 58
Johnnie: 36, 60, 61
Johnny Elmer: 17
Jonathan Scot: 74
Jordan: 72
Joseph: 23, 44, 67, 68, 79
Joseph H.: 2
Joseph Howard: 40, 65
Joseph Samuel: 23
Joseph Thomas: 13, 31, 55
Joshua Everett Elijah: 62
Joy Dorene: 54, 76
Joyce Ann: 37, 62
Judith Faye: 42, 66
Judy Kay: 70
Julia Elizabeth: 31, 55

Mary Rebecca: 27, 52
Mary Rebecca: 2, 6
Mary Ruth: 52, 74
Mary Sue: 32, 56, 57
Matilda Clarinda: 8, 20
Matthew Chase: 81
Matthew Johnson: 35
Mattie Belle: 26, 51
Mattie Vera: 23
Maud: 15, 33
Maude Elaine: 19
Max Ray ,Jr.: 52, 74
Max Ray ,Sr.: 26, 52, 74, 75
Maynelle Carmen: 11, 27
Mazelle: 25, 49
Melba: 25, 48
Melvin: 12, 29, 53, 75
Merle: 27
Michael: 47
Michael: 69
Michael Leonard: 32
Michael Ray: 62
Michael Robert: 32, 56
Michael Steven: 56
Michelle Renee: 62
Mildred: 15, 32
Milford Taylor: 26
Millie Jane: 17, 37
Misty Michelle: 63, 78
Monica Ann: 58
Myra Delora: 45, 68
Myrtis: 36, 59
Myrtle: 14
Myrtle Annie Eller: 17, 38
Nancy: 1
Nancy: 3, 8, 21, 41, 42, 66, 67, 79
Nancy Ann: 8
Nancy Ann: 6, 16, 35, 59
Nancy T.: 11
Nathaan Dakota: 78
Nathan Wilson: 35, 59
Nellie Arizona: 6, 17, 18
Nettie: 27
Nita Jane: 13, 31
Nora Elizabeth: 7, 18
Nora Florence: 19, 38
Norma Ray: 37, 61, 62
Orphelia: 4, 10
Otis Virgil: 16, 36
Owen: 24, 46, 47
Owen , Jr.: 47
Padraic Brion: 58
Pamela Michele: 59
Patricia Ann: 32, 57
Patsy Jeanette: 50, 72
Patsy Ruth (aka: Richard Steven Fordyce): 44, 67, 68
Paul: 80
Paul Andrews: 17, 37, 62, 63, 77
Paul E. ,Sr.: 15, 32, 56, 57
Pauleda: 36
Pearl: 8, 21
Pearl Adell: 47, 69, 70
Peggy Jean: 45
Pete: 45

Phillip Michael: 35
Phillip Ray: 43
Pierce Mack ,Jr.: 26, 50, 72
Pierce Mack ,Sr.: 10, 26, 50, 71, 72, 80
Pleasant: 6, 16, 36, 59, 60, 76, 77, 82
Pleasant Marion: 3, 6, 17, 18, 38
Polly Ann: 15, 34
Preston Bates: 43
Prudance: 4, 12, 13
Randall Gene: 62
Randall Paul: 40, 64, 78
Randy: 33
Rashell Nelda Lynn: 82
Ray Elijah ,Jr.: 37, 62
Ray Elijah ,Sr.: 17, 37, 61, 62
Reba: 12, 29
Reba Sue: 36
Rebecca: 74
Rebecca: 1, 3, 7, 8
Rebecca: 7
Rebecca Ann: 71
Rebecca Jane: 6, 17
Rebecca Jane: 20, 41
Reuben Taylor: 24, 44, 45
Reubin Travis: 45
Richard: 1
Richard: 3, 7, 8
Richard Henry: 3, 7, 18, 19, 38-40, 63-65, 78
Richard Porter: 1, 3, 7, 19-21, 40, 41, 65, 66, 79, 82
Richard Porter: 8
Robert Dinson: 49
Robert Frank: 25, 49
Robert Gerald: 14, 32, 56
Robert Lee: 60, 77
Robert Lee: 77, 82
Robert Marion: 2
Robert Pate: 10, 25, 49, 50
Robert Paul: 19, 40, 64, 65, 78
Rodney: 47
Roger: 47, 69
Ronald Lynn: 40, 64, 78
Ronnie Lee: 67
Rosa Belle: 24, 45
Rosa Lee: 8
Roy Elmer: 16, 36
Roy Lynn: 42
Roy Virgil: 21, 42, 67, 79
Ruby: 36, 60
Ruby Lee: 37, 62
Rudine: 47
Ruth Jane: 36
Ruth Oela: 43
S.T.: 11, 27, 52
Sallie M.: 2
Sally: 1
Sally: 4, 11
Sally Jane: 11, 28
Sally Lou: 24, 44
Sam Houston: 23
Sam Wiley: 6
Sammy: 33
Samuel: 1
Samuel: 3, 6, 16, 17, 35-38, 59-63, 76, 77, 82
Samuel: 3, 8, 21

103

William: 22
Middleton -
    Florence Rebecca: 52
Miksch -
    Elsa Dolly: 54
Miller -
    Alma: 38
    Curtis Greer: 42
    Donavan Lee: 38
    Georgia Mae: 52
    Hazel Marie: 15, 16
    James W.: 38
    John: 13
    John A.: 15
    Katherine: 38
    Lizzie Catherine: 55
    Norma: 38
Milligan -
    Kyle: 42
Mills -
    Jewel: 39
Minor -
    George Alexander: 34
    John Alexander: 34
    Opal Mae: 34
Mitchell -
    Margaret: 14
    Sam: 20
Mize -
    Sarah: 3
Mock -
    Suzanne Marie: 55
Moffett -
    Wade: 20
Monday -
    Clarinda: 18
Monnie -
    Unnamed: 62
Monroe -
    G. D.: 28
Montman -
    Fred Groves: 66
    Irene Cecelia: 66
Moody -
    Roy: 24
Moore -
    Charles Edward: 64
    Christina Gail: 64
    Harrison: 75
    Jeffrey Charles: 64
    Judith Ann: 75
    Lois: 34
    Priscilla J.: 75
    Ronnie Edward: 75
    Samuel Lone: 75
    William: 64
Morgan -
    Bobby: 40
Morrow -
    Sharie: 57
Morse -
    Karen Jeanette: 66

Morton -
    Lucy A.: 9
    Sonja Davis: 78
Moses -
    Roxie Edna: 62
Moss -
    Daniel: 71
Muldrew -
    Caroline Houston: 9
    John D .: 9
    Martha Caroline: 9
    Martha Jane: 9
    Mary Emma: 9
    Sarah Frances: 9
    William Alfred: 9
    Willie Maybell: 9
Mull -
    Martha Lee: 55
    Vernon Lee: 55
Murphy -
    Billy: 44
    Donna: 44
    Harold: 44
    Lonnie: 44
    Sarah Catherine: 27
Murphye -
    Malachi: 2
    Rebecca Jane: 2
Murray -
    Matthew: 80
    Toby: 80
Murrin -
    Andrew Jackson: 3, 4
    Mary: 4
    Robert: 3
Musser -
    Danny: 79
    Joshua DeWayne: 79
Myers -
    Brenda Gail: 34
    Florence Louise: 48
    Larry Glen: 34
    Lee: 34
    Linda Darlene: 34
    Lloyd Alvin: 34
    Michael Lynn: 34
    Roger: 32
    Roger Dale: 34
    Sandra: 34
    Teresa Kay: 34
    Willard Ray: 34
    William Kenneth: 34
Myra -
    Unnamed: 50
Nancy -
    Unnamed: 1
    Unnamed: 78
Nellums -
    Myrtle: 58
Nelson -
    Edna May: 65
    Norman Norris: 65
    Robert Floyd: 65

Russell M.: 65

Neubert -
John: 7

Newby -
Carolyn Elaine: 71

Newcomer -
James: 42

Newman -
Gerald Kenneth: 46
Gladys: 46
Janie Bernice: 46
Ural Rufus: 46
Verbie C.: 46
William LeRoy: 46
William R .: 46

Ngai -
Mee Ying: 78

Nicely -
Geneva: 54

Nichols -
Bobbie: 70
Woodrow: 33

Niman -
Mary: 7

Nipper -
Nancy W.: 7

Nix -
Milton Wayne: 50

Noah -
Anthony Ray: 61
James: 61
John Steve: 61
Lisa Jean: 61
Steven Lee: 61

Noble(Adopted) -
Richard Steven (aka: Richard Steven Noble): 68

Noble -
George Robert: 75
John Will: 68
Linda Gail: 81
Oree: 81
Ralph Edward: 68
Richard Steven (name: Richard Steven Noble(Adopted)): 68

Nobley -
Mzry Jeanette: 46

Noe -
Raleigh: 13

Norred -
Hazel: 46

Norton -
George Cown: 38
Ira: 38
Yvowna: 38

Nuchols -
Mae: 21

Oche -
David: 33

Odom -
Bill: 37
Elwood: 80
Permilia Deleigh: 26

Robin Elizabeth: 80

O'Kain -
David Udell: 55
Grady L.: 55
John Arthur: 55
Laura Kate: 55
Mark David: 55

Oldham -
Mildred: 28

Olson -
Brian: 77
Daniel: 77
Robert: 77

Olson. -
Leroy ,Jr.: 77

O'Neal -
Doris Willene: 10
Howard Eucarey: 10
Hubert Elmer: 10
John W.: 10
Mary Eugenia: 10
Mayzelle: 10
Myrtle Lee: 10
Omar Lamar: 10
Ora Irene: 55
William Hoyt: 10
William Jasper: 10

Orgeron -
Semantha Virginia: 52

Osborne -
Iva (Sweet): 25

Osher -
James Edward: 65

Oster -
Kenneth: 35

Ostrander -
Eucebia: 19

Owens -
Harvey: 61
Katie Belle: 26, 73

Ownby -
Amos: 40
Augusta June: 59
Billy Lamon: 59
Charles Erwin: 59
John: 38
P. M.: 59
Roxie: 64
Sarah Ruth: 40
Willian: 59

Oxley -
Duane Edwin: 31

Pacheco -
Loretta: 52

Packe -
Unnamed: 38

Padgett -
Rebecca: 56
Samuel: 56

Pafford -
Howard Lynn: 70
Lewis: 70
Tammy: 70

Paine -
    Liza: 15
    Liza: 15
Painter -
    Sybil: 53
Parham -
    Larry: 38
Park -
    Ann: 59
Parker -
    Elizabeth: 39
    Essie: 17
    Linda Sue: 82
    Ruby: 68
Parks -
    Joseph: 8
    Nancy A.: 8
Parris -
    Elijah Lee ,Jr.: 49
    Wynena Lynn: 49
Parrish -
    Barbette: 50
    Delores: 50
    Hubert: 50
    Melissa Ann: 50
Parrott -
    Lon: 12
Pass -
    Lucy: 41
Patricia -
    Unnamed: 53
Patterson -
    Elma: 28
    Lillas: 43
    Mae Belle: 82
Patty -
    Arthur: 39
    Carl Elbert: 38
    Don Edmund: 38
    Floyd: 39
    Floyd Lamar: 39
    Isaac Nelson: 38
Payne -
    Deborah: 45
    Donald Lucins: 16
    James: 21
    Janet: 49
    Janice: 39
Payton -
    Doris: 46
Pearl -
    Unnamed: 9
Pedigo -
    Mary Belle: 14
Penley -
    Amanda: 64
Perkins -
    Bobby Jack: 44
    Charles Alvin: 21
    Isaac: 21
    Marion Stanford: 21
    Thomas: 43, 44

    Thomas Keeble: 44
    Warren Stanford: 21
Perry -
    Albert: 51
    Bonnie Jeanette: 41
    H. Paul: 78
    Joseph: 51
    Robert: 78
Phillips -
    Cathy: 58
    Charles W.: 45
Pickens -
    Donna Rayette Vance: 33
    Jason: 62
    Oliver: 31
    Viola: 31
Picklesimer -
    Bruce: 60
    Donald Stenley: 61
    Glen: 60, 61
Pierce -
    Lydia louisa: 28
    Martha Susan: 29
Pike -
    Lothell: 45
Pinkard -
    Mattie Paraquay: 26, 47
Pitner -
    Lovica: 6
Pitts -
    Unnamed: 10
    Fanny: 9
Poe -
    William: 22
Poplin -
    Bobby: 35
    LeRoy: 61
Porter -
    Margaret: 2
Posey -
    Frenny ,Jr.: 67
Potts -
    Gary: 53
    Wyatt Lee: 24
Powell -
    Jesse Archie: 73
    Jessie Grace: 73, 74
    Warren Coleman: 68
Price -
    Christine: 73
    Leonard Shaddix: 74
Priscilla.Farmer -
    Clemmie: 14
Pritchard -
    Ivan: 61
Proctor -
    Gilbert E.: 28
Pryor -
    Carl M .: 59
    Eunice Evelyn: 63
    Shirley Ann: 59
Purkey -

Fred: 51

Shaver -
    Lizzie E.: 8
Shaw -
    Donald Charles: 65
Sheets -
    Gary Lee: 46
    H. U.: 46
    Herman Lamar: 46
    JoAnn Keeble: 46
    Larry: 46
Shelley -
    Rachel: 11
Shelnutt -
    Thomas Sanford: 10
Sheppard -
    Emma: 9
    John: 9
    Lizzie: 9
    Milton: 9
    William: 9
Sherrer -
    Alex: 69
Sherrill -
    Sam R.: 5
Sherwood -
    Mary: 36
Shields -
    William Toye: 21
Shoemaker -
    Rhoda: 6
Shoman -
    Ada: 22
Shular -
    Linnie Poe: 22
Shultz? -
    Martha: 29
Silva -
    Unnamed: 14
Silyers -
    Cordia: 36
Simerly -
    Jessie: 14
    Lucy: 36
    Margaret Tennessee: 37
    Nathaniel Taylor: 14, 36
Simmons -
    Debbie Lynn: 74
    John: 74
    Mary: 54
Simons -
    Edward Lee: 41
    Elmer Ezra: 41
    Harvey Lee: 41
Skinner -
    Claude Nathaniel: 57
    Marty Allen: 57
Slavin -
    Edna Boone: 25
Sloan -
    Genela Malzene: 14
Small -

Sandy: 65

Smart -
    Bradley Mark: 81
    Donald Mark: 81
    Jeremy Taylor: 81
    Steven Lee: 81
Smedley -
    Era: 46
Smith -
    Ann: 37
    Barbara Ann: 51
    Beverly: 57
    Brett: 75
    Carole Diane: 31
    Elizabeth: 1, 2
    Ida Frances: 50
    James Frank: 48
    John Thomas: 70
    Joseph: 1
    Joseph Will: 51
    Louisa Matilda: 22
    Louisa Matilda: 23
    Mark: 70
    Mary Beth: 51
    Needham Ernest: 50
    Patrick Martin: 68
    Phyliss: 68
    Reuben: 51
    Robert: 70
    Sandra: 80
    Sarah: 50, 51
    Seline: 47
    Tamara: 70
    Taylor: 48
    Vista: 60
    Waynor Ruth: 51
Sneed -
    Mary Ann: 4
    Taylor: 4
Snodgrass -
    James: 56
    William: 56
Snow -
    Mary: 68
Sousa -
    Wendell Lance: 66
Spencer -
    Laura Etta: 31
    Melvin Valentine: 31
Spinks -
    Samuel Q.: 23
Spradlin -
    Polly: 46
    Winnie Mae: 44
St John -
    Myra June: 37
Staley -
    Brenda Gail: 61
    Charles Douglas: 61
    Mary Catherine: 61
    Sharon Lorraine: 61
    William Sidney ,Sr.: 61
Stamps -

Hannah: 1
Standridge -
    Jess Lloyd , Jr.: 54
Stanley -
    William: 61
Stansell -
    Audrey Joyce: 42
    Betty Wyl: 42
    Hildrith Clarke: 42
    Linda Lou: 42
    William: 42
Starcher -
    Carl: 61
    Michael: 61
    Sandra: 61
Starlin -
    Cindi: 71, 72
Staton -
    Glenn: 45
Steele -
    Mary Elizabeth: 14, 36
Stempfly -
    Sara Ann: 31
Stephens -
    Margaret Ann: 32
Stephenson -
    Unnamed: 21
Sterling -
    Willie: 17
Stevens -
    Marion Richard: 9
    Rebecca Jane: 20
Stewart -
    Donald H.: 38
    Ethel: 54
    Frank: 62
    James Roger: 62
    Matilda Ann: 10
    Patricia Joy: 62
    Ray Boyd: 62
Still -
    Thelma Elizabeth: 24
Stinnett -
    LeRoy: 39
Stodghill -
    Floy: 35
Stone -
    Joel: 7
    Martha Ellen: 7
Stout -
    Moss: 15
Streight -
    Gladys Ethel: 65
Strength -
    Edward Earl: 73
    Howard Ray: 73
    Kenneth Wayne: 73
    Michael Ray: 73
    Pamela Anne: 73
    Tamera Fran: 73
Stuart -
    Etta Bertha: 31

Suddeth -
    Lilla: 10
Sudduth -
    Cordell: 25
Sullivan -
    Link: 20
Summey -
    Emaline: 3
    George: 21
    Martha Florence: 21
Sunderland -
    Fred Ray ,Jr.: 57
    Fred Ray ,Sr.: 57
    Holly Raynae: 57
    Tabitha Rose: 57
Sundheimer -
    Monroe: 47
Susan -
    Unnamed: 22
Susong -
    Herbert Milton: 41
    Sam: 41
Sutherlin -
    Bessie: 44, 45
Suttles -
    Steve: 40
Sutton -
    Jo Ann: 67
Swan -
    Maud: 42
Swann -
    Arthur: 24
    Gertrude: 24
    Jesse: 24
    John D.: 24
    John William: 24
    Katie: 24
    Myrtie Lee: 24
    Ora M.: 24
    Pearl: 24
    S.T.: 24
    Sadie: 24
Swanson -
    Astrid Victoria: 20
Sweet -
    Gladys Ada: 63
Tallent -
    Homer Charles: 54
    Maxine Irene: 54
Tamara -
    Unnamed: 67
Tanner -
    David Arthur: 79
    Felicia Anastasia Satina: 79
Tarver -
    Laura Eugenia: 72
Tarvin -
    Tillie: 45
Tarwater -
    A.Conley: 17
    Ann M: 28
    H. R.: 28

Mike: 63
Millard Edmond: 12
William: 28

Taylor -
Faye: 47
Imogene: 47
John Houston: 29
Marguerite: 47
Pearl: 48
Vesta: 47

Teague -
Donald: 29
William A.: 39
Willie Mae: 39

Tedford -
William Henry: 10

Teffeteller -
Harrison: 37
Hester Marie: 37

TemilleDodaro -
Toni: 57

Termini -
Unnamed: 19

Terry -
Brenda: 43

Thatcher -
Jeff: 62

Thomas -
Bill Joel ,Sr.: 37
Dee: 28
Ernest H. ,Jr.: 26
Ollie: 33

Thompson -
Herman: 22
James: 22
Mary Ann Keeble was born a: 34, 58
Matilda: 7
Opal Mae Minor: 34

Thrower -
Bobby: 44
Carlton: 44
Earl: 44
H.T.(Hoot): 44
Homer ,Jr.: 72
James: 72
Teresa Ann: 72
Vera: 44
William Dean: 72

Tilley -
Mamie Elizabeth: 77

Tiny -
Unnamed: 5

Tippett -
Helen: 45
Hugh: 45
John: 45
Johnny: 45

Tipton -
Gary: 61
Jess: 14
Margaret: 35
William Marion: 6

Tittsworth -

Opal C.: 39

Tobias -
Lisa Renee: 64

Towler -
John: 9
Martha: 9

Townsend -
Mary: 4

Trahan -
Lena Mae: 53

Tredwell -
Jessie Mae: 24

Treece -
Cleo: 18

Trent -
Isabella: 10
Powhatan Green: 10

Trett -
Brenda Kay: 77
Brenda Kay: 82
Egbert: 82
Egbert: 77

Trevino -
Alex Matthew: 56
Juan A.: 56
Lindsey Nicole: 56
Ruben: 56

Tripp -
Erin: 63

Trottner -
Ora Belle: 8

Trust -
Pete: 47

Trusty -
Lewis: 67

Tuck -
Paul: 18

Tulloch -
Betty: 28

Tunnell -
Franklin: 39

Unknown -
Bessie: 72
Beulah: 34
Hortensia: 57
Pritzie: 34
Sarah: 1

Upchurch -
A. G.: 45

Vance -
Gary: 35

Vandergriff -
Eugene: 61
Linda Sue: 61
Mary Lynn: 61
Terri Lee: 61

Vann -
Kenneth David: 62

Vineyard -
Jordan C.: 18
William Thomas: 18

Virginia -